# THE GOSPEL
# IS NOT WESTERN

*Guboo Ted Thomas and two representatives of the Department of Forestry at an Australian Aboriginal cathedral.*

# THE GOSPEL
# IS NOT WESTERN

## Black Theologies from the Southwest Pacific

*Edited by*
*G. W. TROMPF*

ORBIS BOOKS

**Maryknoll, New York 10545**

The Catholic Foreign Mission Society of America (Maryknoll) recruits and trains people for overseas missionary service. Through Orbis Books Maryknoll aims to foster the international dialogue that is essential to mission. The books published, however, reflect the opinions of their authors and are not meant to represent the official position of the society.

Copyright © 1987 by Garry W. Trompf
Published by Orbis Books, Maryknoll, NY 10545
All rights reserved
Manufactured in the United States of America

Photo credit: p. ii, Guboo Ted Thomas and the Institute of Aboriginal Studies

Manuscript editor: Mary J. Heffron

**Library of Congress Cataloging-in-Publication Data**

The Gospel is not Western.

   "Almost all the papers contained in this book were
first presented at a conference held in the Brisbane
suburb of Coorparo (August 10-14, 1981)"—Acknowledgements.
   Bibliography: p.
   1. Christianity—Melanesia—Congresses.   2. Melanesia
—Religion—Congresses.   3. Black theology—Congresses.
I. Trompf, G. W.
BR1495.M4G67   1986      279.3      86-23539
ISBN 0-88344-269-8 (pbk.)

# Contents

*List of Illustrations*                                                          *vii*

*Acknowledgments*                                                                 *ix*

## Part I
### Introduction

*1. Geographical, Historical, and Intellectual Perspective*
Garry Trompf, Australia and Papua New Guinea                                        3

*2. General Perspective:*
    *A Call for Black Humanity to Be Better Understood*
Aruru Matiabe, Southern Central Highlands, Papua                                   16

## Part II
### Christianity versus Tradition?

*3. Interaction between Indigenous and Christian Traditions*
Polonhou S. Pokawin, Manus Island, New Guinea                                      23

*4. Christianity and Melanesian Cosmos:*
    *The Broken Pearls and a Newborn Shell*
Bernard Narokobi, Sepik, Mainland New Guinea                                       32

*5. Church and Culture: An Aboriginal Perspective*
Rose Kunoth-Monks, Central Australia                                              38

## Part III
### The Impact of Indigenous Tradition on Emergent Black Theologies

*6. From Pagan to Christian Priesthood*
Dave Passi, Torres Strait                                                          45

*7. Melanesian Cult Movements as Traditional Religious and*
    *Ritual Responses to Change*
Willington Jojoga Opeba, Northern Coast, Papua                                     49

*8. The Demolition of Church Buildings by the Ancestors*
Esau Tuza, Choiseul Island, Solomon Islands                                        67

9. *The Land Is Sacred: Renewing the Dreaming in Modern Australia*
   Guboo Ted Thomas, Southeastern Australia      90

10. *Aboriginal and Christian Healing*
    An Interview with Mick Fazeldean, Western Australia      95

**Part IV**
**Theological Horizons and Adjustments**

11. *Spirits in Melanesian Tradition and Spirit in Christianity*
    Simeon Namunu, Eastern Papuan Islands      109

12. *Searching for a Melanesian Way of Worship*
    Michael Maeliau, Malaita, Solomon Islands      119

13. *A Plea for Female Ministries in Melanesia*
    Rose Kara Ninkama, Central New Guinea Highlands      128

14. *In Search of a Melanesian Theology*
    John Kadiba, South Coastal Papua and Northern Australia      139

15. *Thinking Theology Aloud in Fiji*
    Sevati Tuwere, Fiji      148

**Part V**
**Politics, Tradition, and Christianity**

16. *The Christian Vision of a New Society*
    John Momis, North Solomons, New Guinea Islands      157

17. *Thoughts of a Melanesian Christian Socialist*
    An Interview with Utula Samana, Morobe, Mainland
       New Guinea      166

18. *An Appeal for Melanesian Christian Solidarity*
    Trwar Max Ireeuw, West Papua      170

19. *Christians in Politics*
    Walter Lini, Vanuatu      183

20. *Can I Remain a Christian in New Caledonia?*
    Pierre Qaeze, Loyalty Islands, New Caledonia      186

21. *A Theology for Justice and Peace in the Pacific*
    Suliana Siwatibau, Fiji      192

*Notes*      *199*

# List of Illustrations

*Maps*

1. Australia, the Torres Straits, and Melanesia    4
2. The Northern District, Papua    51
3. The Western Solomons    68

*Figure*

1. The Nine Graces    89

# Acknowledgments

Almost all the papers contained in this book were first presented at a conference held in the Brisbane suburb of Coorparoo (August 10–14, 1981). The last part of the book developed through my ongoing contacts over the years, including a time away in Holland. Most of the Melanesian contributors are graduates of the University of Papua New Guinea. Many—Polonhou, Willington, Esau, Michael, Utula, and Pierre—have been (and in some cases still are) my students in some way or another. These outstanding young people formed the nucleus around which the work developed. My deepest thanks go to the (Anglican) Australian Board of Mission as sponsors, and especially to Fr. Fred Wandmaker for accepting the idea of the Coorparoo conference and for organizing the finances and other details. Fr. Patrick Gesch, SVD, first conceived of such a conference; he and Sr. Wendy Flannery of the Melanesian Institute were participants in it, and I appreciated their stimulus and assistance. Dr. John May of the Institute was supportive in assuring Orbis Books that these papers are indeed representative of theologies in the southwest Pacific.

It is clear from the table of contents that each writer represents a significant sector of the whole region. I trust that geography has been properly covered in my selection along with the major substantive issues. The representation here, I believe, makes John May's vision of a theology journal for the region (or for Melanesia in particular) quite feasible.

I add a word of gratitude here to Professor Eric Sharpe, who has been a kind of academic patron to the whole exercise; to Anne Crossley and Wendy Cummings for helping to prepare some of the drafts for publication, chasing footnotes, and proofreading; and to Gabi Boutali and Vagoli Bonaka for the maps and figure.

To those who did all the typing—Margaret Gilet (University of Sydney), Liesbeth Daniels and Wilca Van Putten (State University of Utrecht), Nancy Koriam and Kila Pala (UPNG)—many thanks, *dank u wel, tank yu tu mas,* and *nama vagi*!

# Part I

## Introduction

# 1

# Geographical, Historical, and Intellectual Perspective

## GARRY TROMPF
### Australia and Papua New Guinea

The southwest Pacific has been occupied by black peoples for at least fifty thousand years. Toward the end of the Pleistocene epoch, so it seems, there came the region's original discoverers: the first humans found this habitable continent by crossing a vast and previously unnavigated stretch of ocean. They reached the continental shelf now sometimes called Sahul. That shelf incorporated what is today mainland Australia and many of the islands presently close to its seaboard, most significantly Tasmania to the south and the main island of New Guinea to the north, which were then undetached parts of the continent. In a manner still baffling to archeologists and by waves and natural increases of population difficult to estimate, humans adjusted their daily lives to the many and varied parts of the region. Seafaring groups among these black peoples ventured farther eastward into the Pacific, into the chains and clusters of islands now known as the Solomons, Vanuatu (formerly New Hebrides), New Caledonia, and Fiji. Their long-distance voyaging can be paralleled to that of the discoverers of such faraway islands as Tahiti and Hawai'i.

Though the story is difficult to reconstruct we can isolate some important prehistoric developments in this region. After the separation of zones, accomplished by rising sea levels, two distinctive general patterns of adaptation and modes of existence evolved in what is now known as Australia to the south and Melanesia (the "black islands") to the north and east (see map, p. 4). In both zones populations tended to fall into tribal groupings. The Australian Aborigines generally formed mobile hunter-and-gatherer societies (scattered bands moved and encamped throughout large tracts of land that were rich in game and not conducive to agriculture); the Melanesians typically combined their hunting and foraging with gardening and animal husbandry. In the Melanesian tropics, a greater population density could be maintained because of the availabilities of food: various tubers such as yams and sweet potatoes were

# AUSTRALIA, THE TORRES STRAIT, AND MELANESIA

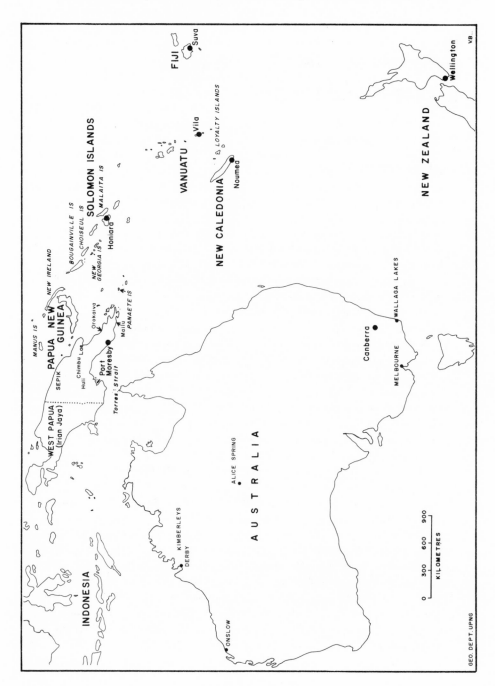

cultivated and pigs were domesticated. Some archeologists have established, indeed, that the so-called agricultural revolution can no longer be said to have been confined to the ancient Near East because of the remarkable achievements of horticulturalists in the New Guinea highlands (9000–7000 B.C.). The Australian saga is no less astounding when one considers that humans survived for millennia in environments that proved so hostile and unpredictable to subsequent European intruders.[1]

The history of the development of consciousness and of the beliefs and thought of the black peoples of the southwest Pacific was an undocumented history, lost in the mists of time, although one might say that rituals, myths, special techniques, and proverbs are storehouses of age-old wisdom, reflecting the labors of the human spirit over many centuries. Whatever the problems of prehistoric reconstruction, though, and whatever we may deduce about the relatively static or changeable nature of primal culturoreligious traditions in the whole area, at least one may affirm that the indigenous peoples there have bequeathed to the world the most complex tapestry of languages and discrete cultures known to humanity. The mythology of the Australian Aborigines is perhaps the richest, most subtle, and impenetrable of any; and from the Kai Islands on the west coast of New Guinea right across to Fiji there subsist over one-fourth of the world's distinct languages and religions. Hundreds of human groupings have been atomized into the landlocked valleys between towering rugged ranges or along scattered island chains.

Over the past two centuries, however, the traditional inhabitants of Australia and Melanesia have fallen subject to outside conquerors, particularly the Europeans, but not forgetting the temporary Japanese rule during the Second World War nor the latter-day neocolonialism of the Java-oriented Indonesians in West Papua (the western half of the New Guinea mainland). As with all tribal peoples or small-scale societies, the first Australians and the indigenous Melanesians have been vulnerable to imperialisms. If the expansion of great powers with higher technologies have always brought with them a mixture of promise and danger, it has transpired too often in the southwest Pacific that the latter has exceeded the former and left indelible scars of oppression.

Many will argue that the intrusions of modern history had to come sooner or later, that the great unknown southland (*terra Australis incognita*) could not remain a European imagining forever, and that the secrets of New Guinea, the interior of which was the globe's last unknown at the end of the nineteenth century, would eventually be laid bare.[2] Many may add that the region's indigenous traditions were far from perfect or had certain undesirable elements that were justly challenged by propagators of the Gospel or bearers of "civilization." Isolated tribes often had the unfortunate habit of avenging each other and of involving virtually everybody in a given society in the pursuit of fierce battle. And a small host of practices—cannibalism, the raping of the women of a rival tribe, brutal methods of punishment, infanticide, "suttee"—most people nowadays would be happy for any culture to relinquish.[3]

Be all these significant points as they may, however, what was offered by the invading latecomers has all too frequently not turned out to be the best alternative. Most of the earliest British settlements in Australia, after all, were penal colonies (from 1788); and this same function Napoleon III assigned to the French acquisition of *Nouvelle Calédonie* (New Caledonia) in 1853. Outcasts from the Old World (some of whom escaped once they reached their new environments) and the officials sent to make the terms of their detention more arduous (and prevent them from escaping) hardly made for the best rapport with the already "restless natives."

But that was just the beginning of things. The whole story of the tragic breakdown of relations has yet to be told in synoptic form: immoral settlers, misinformed missionaries, ruthless officials, paternalistic adminstrators, racist expatriates, and self-interested capitalists. The story runs even further back than Governor Arthur's Drive (1828–31), which led to the virtual extermination of the Tasmanian Aboriginals, and continues right up to the current situation, with the French evasion of *kanak* (native) independence in New Caledonia and the Indonesian army's attempt to suppress the Free Papua Movement (*Organisasi Papua Merdeka*). The path of civilization's coming, then, has been littered with destructive and corrupting influences for the descendants of the archaic Dream Time.[4]

Throughout the whole epic, Christians and their churches played impressive parts. If we try to decide whether their actions and their effects were for better or for worse, we will inevitably make patent value judgments and be led into a tangle of conflicting opinions. One fact stands out above all, however, and must be faced for what it is, quite apart from one's ideological proclivities. It is this: The influence of Christianity on the local peoples of the southwest Pacific has been enormous. Some may question the depth of its reception in this or that particular area; some may point to the extraordinary resilience of Australian aboriginal religions in the face of the high-flown teachings that accompanied the great white flood; and some may admit that Christianity is likely to lose ground in the future because of secularizing tendencies or home-grown pragmatisms. Still its widespread acceptance and the degree of its incorporation into local cultures are truly remarkable. The 1980 census of Papua New Guinea, for instance, showed that 96 percent of the country's inhabitants associated themselves with some Christian denomination or mission. Sheer nominalism taken into account, this betokens an extraordinary social transformation in a country where sizable inland populations were barely touched by the outside world until after the Second World War.

This book contains a lively range of responses to the "great alteration" that has befallen the southwest Pacific over the last two centuries. Almost all the contributions in this book are from black thinkers, as far-flung as Derby (northwestern Australia) and Fiji (the easternmost fringes of Melanesia). All the authors are vitally concerned with the problems of human relationships and well-being in the region and in particular with the plight of their black brothers and sisters. All of these authors, from varying perspectives, address the central issue of values and of how the values are to meet the problems currently facing their peoples. None of them want to turn their backs on their own traditions, but rather to look to them for part of the solution to new predicaments. Virtually all these thinkers welcome Christianity, although it is natural that they want to handle what claims to be Christian with discrimination, and to apply essential Christian orientations on behalf of their compatriots in terms that are valid for black Australasian or Pacific contexts.

The contributors are well aware that Christianity has usually arrived as part of the larger parcel of colonial interventionism, and they know they must uncover the partially obscured truths of the Gospel and avoid being duped. All the thinkers are likely to concur with what one of them, Bernard Narokobi, has expressed elsewhere: that their part of the world

> has been invaded by a huge tidal wave from the West in the form of colonization and Christianization. Like any tidal wave, the West came mercilessly, with all the force and power, toppling over our earth, destroying our treasures, depositing some rich soil, but also leaving behind much rubbish.[5]

In Australia the wave was so enormous that it wreaked destruction on traditional societies and threatened to eliminate the entire Aboriginal population. What could Christianity, borne by so many of the intruders, possibly offer in the unutterable wretchedness of such a storm? The Melanesians too have felt their survival threatened because of "contact": with contagious diseases, the labor trade, and colonial indenturing of plantation workers. In Melanesia distinctions had to be made between "good" and "bad" newcomers, between those who at least tried to help (especially the missionaries) and those who were outright predators. To complicate matters further, Westerners had already attained an extraordinary level of technological achievement. The Melanesians had to disentangle the promise of Christianity from the accompanying "cargo," to discover that the Gospel had first been proclaimed without the aid of steel-hulled vessels or helicopters, wonder drugs and microphones. After the flood of goods then, the question became: How was the good soil to be delivered of its layer of rubbish, and how was the new deposit of good soil going to be mixed with the older layers?[6]

In this book the central problem area and its related questions are handled differently by each contributor, in accordance with each one's special interests, expertise, and location (both geographically and sociologically). Almost all the thinkers attempt theological evaluations, and even those who see themselves as more questioning or more practical than others have not avoided key theological or missiological issues. The book contains a variety of black theologies and integrally related reflections hitherto inaccessible. The collection shows that the growing body of black theological literature from Australia and Melanesia must be considered along with that from Africa and the Americas.

The origins of black theology can be traced to the Bible—perhaps as far back as to the Sudanese eunuch who helped the prophet Jeremiah out of his imprisonment in a well (Jer 38: 7–13), certainly back to the conversion of the Ethiopian eunuch in earliest Christian times (Acts 8: 27–38). From the time of the *Excerpta Latina Barbari* in the sixth century, the Western iconographic tradition identifed the black king Balthasar as one of the (three) wise men or magi (a tradition more consistently preserved in northern European painting than in Southern Europe and in Italy).[7]

By the sixth century there were many black exponents of the Christian faith. In all probability St. Augustine of Hippo, the most influential of all post-biblical theologians, was black; certainly the kingdom of Ethiopia and centers of Nubia (such as Soba) had many black Christian thinkers, even if ideas from the latter area are undocumented.[8] That is not to say that black theology had already been born. In early Christianity the distinction between peoples of different skin pigmentation was barely significant. It would take a "modern" order of imperial oppression—the Western entrance into the African slave trade, above all—to draw out those self-perceptions of negritude and long-sufferance that have so affected black Christian insight and spirituality over the last half-millennium. But the origins do lie a long way back.

With the baptism of slaves into the plantation societies and caste systems of the New World (from the sixteenth century), many more black Africans were absorbed into an expanding Christendom, ironically embracing the faith more fervently and practicing it more authentically than their white overlords.[9] This was the great turning point.

The story of black theological thought and practice in modern history is too complex to be told here. Suffice it to say that because of slavery and the later intensification of Western missionary activity in Africa and elsewhere many phenomena of interest occurred. The first black African bishop—Enrico, son of the Congolese monarch Affonso I—was consecrated in 1518; the preacher Jacobus Capitein of Guinea, however much of an "Uncle Tom" he showed himself to be by denying that slavery was against Christian freedom, was nonetheless the first equatorial African to write a full-scale theological treatise. Other items of interest: The Ethiopic tradition—the looking to Ethiopia, since it was mentioned in the Bible—was a source of inspiration for the christianization of Africans and Africa-originating peoples, some of whom envisaged Ethiopia as their spiritual native land (to take the Rastafarians as a special case); Joseph Mkasa and Charles Lwango, Ugandan martyrs (1885), were canonized in 1964—representatives of twenty-two other sufferers for the faith; Christians increased rapidly in southern and equatorial Africa during this century, when over seven thousand black African independent churches have emerged, perhaps the fastest-growing mass movement of recent times; the black (largely Baptist) congregations in the deep south of the United States have burgeoned and will have a long-term impact on world consciousness—in music, in the challenge to American rhetoric about freedom, in the message of nonviolent action preached by Martin Luther King, Jr., and his courageous followers.[10] And out of the turbulence of the last thirty years black theology has emerged as a self-consciously articulated position or genre, perhaps most skillfully thrust upon the world in the disturbing pages of James Cone, but also crying out from those pockets of the Third World where local theologians struggle to emancipate themselves from systems of thought they deem irrelevant.[11]

Where do Australia and Melanesia fit into all this? They really only entered the story recently. Australasian contact with the outside world has always been limited. It is not impossible that blacks used in human sacrifices in ancient Rome were from western New Guinea. The Moluccas—those famous Spice Islands—border the region, and black slaves may well have been appendages to the spice trade.[12] But these things are hard to prove. As for meeting with the widening horizons of Christendom, Nestorian Christians reached Loyang, the capital of China, by the seventh century, and Francis Xavier baptized the Moluccan Ambonese by 1546, but no version of the Gospel reached farther southeast until the eighteenth or nineteenth century (that is, unless the Macassan traders who established settlements on the north Australian coast—around 1700—were evangelists).[13] Not until mission fields were expanded during the nineteenth century were the seeds of an indigenous Christianity planted.

As background to the emergence of black theological thought in the southwest Pacific we should take into account the role of some of the region's inhabitants themselves in the processes of missionization. Fijian Methodists, for example, were among the first group of Christian missionaries to New Britain (1875); New Guinea Lutheran evangelists, who had been trained in the Kate *lingua franca* on the Huon coast, were assigned to various corners of the central highlands, settling down amid populous fearsome folk whose languages and customs they had to learn (from 1922).[14]

Another important development, especially in Melanesia, was the emergence of unusual local theologies, which were the lifeblood of new religious movements. Most of these movements were in reaction to colonialism, but they were also oriented to explain the astounding phenomenon of "the cargo." Some theologies were framed by cargo cult leaders, and some such cults eventually metamorphosed into independent churches. Famous in this connection is Paliau Maloat of Manus Island, who spun out his special islander version of sacred history (Jesus being acclaimed savior of the blacks and his enemies being depicted as the Australian administration), and who was, although often made out to be a cargoist, founder of the region's first independent church that bears comparison with African models (in 1947). Over fifteen such churches, all with fascinating theological bases, have seen the light of day in Melanesia (the most widely publicized and most African-looking of them all is discussed by Esau Tuza in chapter 8 below). Few of these churches are urban, however, whereas in the inner suburbs of Australian cities one can discover Aboriginal independent churches that have the same disinclination to encourage white participation as do most comparable African churches.[15]

In filling out this background one ought not overlook the earliest point at which the wider tradition of black Christianity and neophyte Melanesian speculations intersect. During the Second World War, black Americans were among the troops of the Pacific campaign, brushing shoulders with their white comrades on apparently equal terms, eating the same food and mastering the same amazing cargo, as well as making an effort to fraternize with "the locals." Some early black liberation theology came out of this. As Ariel Sisili put it in his experimental English (Ariel's contribution was crucial in the framing of the Malaita Declaration of Independence in the Solomons in 1950),

> We never known nor ever did we realize before they came here the true love and friendship mentioned in the Bible and ignorant peoples to become better as one should say, that all men were created equal and that man is a trainity consisting of both spirit soul and body and that from common sense man can distinguish without being educated what was true right and not right, fair and not fair.[16]

A line of descent, however zigzag, runs from these bold (implicity anti-British) sentiments to the more finely wrought formulations in this book.

As for the more immediate background to these chapters, we note that opportunities in higher education, especially over the last twenty years, have resulted in many confidently written theological articulations from black thinkers. Because of the extreme ethnic imbalance of Australia, there are few black students in the (white-built) halls of tertiary learning. When it comes to outstanding leadership in Australia, however, we can hardly pass over other points of spiritual vitality: the poetry of Kath Walker, for instance, or the social work of pastor Doug Nicholls (who, however much he may appear to radicals as a stooge of whites, won the governorship of South Australia, 1976–77).

In the north, there have issued out of Papua New Guinea's seminaries since the 1960s a small chorus of dissentient, theologically conditioned voices (Leo Hannett's attack on the expatriate domination of the churches is the best-known example). The interdenominational Melanesian Institute in the highlands has published most of the serious local attempts at black theology up to now. This book itself discloses the recent unifying effect of religious studies as a discipline pursued within universities, one supplementing and enriching seminary training for various ministries.[17]

Hitherto, however, a representative collection of indigenous theological (and cognate) reflection—from Australia's west to Melanesia's east—has not been made available to the world's reading public. This volume is intended to fill the void and vaporize the cloud of obscurity hanging over lands of great promise and over instructive minds whose thoughts are well worth sharing with the wider community of planet earth. These contributions show that black theology is not uniform in its stances and preoccupations throughout the Christian world and confirm that many expressions of liberation theology are virtually untouched by the rhetoric of Latin America.

Readers may sense a certain ingenuousness, sometimes naivety, in these papers; that special quality is one of their strengths. The conceits of Western intellectualism are refreshingly subdued, and what little is made of them always reduces the abstract in favor of straightforwardness and practicality. There is the quality of search here and little pretense to authoritativeness, an attractive feature probably due to the fact that most contributors belong to a young generation of thinkers, without a longstanding locally contextualized tradition. Those who are beginning to handle the Bible critically, moreover, do not wish to be lost in the minutiae and the ifs-and-buts of Western scholarship. What they take from existing systems of thought and ecclesiastical forms is taken with a healthy disdain for mere aping. One quickly realizes that different schools of biblical interpretation, and even some outlandish departures from Western forms of hermeneutic, should be of less interest to an outsider than the ability of these thinkers to confront dehumanizing tendencies and to forge a new way for their peoples. We must now consider the authors of the articles in this book and attempt to place them in perspective.

*Aruru Matiabe*, a medalist from the University of Papua New Guinea and an academic in quest of a national ideology, is now his country's Minister for Education. He is one of the youngest members of Papua New Guinea's Parliament and comes from the most recently "contacted" culture of those represented in this book. A Huli from the Southern (central) Highlands (on the Papuan side of Papua New Guinea), his tribe in the isolated Koroba area first received government patrols only in 1949. His life's journey has taken him from warrior-oriented tribalism to national politics and international socio-political theory. Christian missionary activity (in his case that of the Church of the Brethren Christian Mission in Many Lands) has been crucial in his personal odyssey and he keenly follows its continuing impact on his people (most recently in the form of a charismatic or Holy Spirit movement). His practical politics was learned in the context of a Huli separatist movement, which questioned the advisability of putting local destinies into the hands of leaders who were as far away as Port Moresby, the capital few Huli have ever seen. Considering the speed with which he and his people have had to cope with the white phenomenon, it is natural that he should consider the most important general perspective of this book to concern mutual understanding among the earth's inhabitants.[18]

In Part II of the book (Christianity versus Tradition?) two New Guineans and a central Australian wrestle with the central problem of missionary impositions on traditional cultures. The newcomers expect Christianity to be duplicated according to culturally preconceived molds; the recipients bear the loss of priceless parts of their own heritages, which might have been creatively grafted on to the new way, and as a result a shallowness and split-level effect appear in missionized communities which have not felt the freedom to develop their own theological initiatives.

*Polonhou Pokawin*, from Manus Island, was chairperson of the Politics Department at the University of Papua New Guinea (UPNG). He is a doctoral candidate researching Paliau Maloat's movement,[19] and is now Premier of the Manus Provincial Government. Pokawin concentrates most of his arresting polemic on the need to replace a copying, subservient mentality with a truly

Melanesianized faith. His denominational background is with the Evangelical (Liebenzell) Mission of Manus.

*Bernard Narokobi*, an Arapesh (or Buki) from the Sepik, former chairperson of New Guinea's Law Reform Commission and member of the Supreme Court, is now in private legal practice and holds an honorary professorship in philosophy at the University of Papua New Guinea. His article is an evocative, almost poetic statement about the tragic loss of traditional spiritual treasures, but it also points to the promises of the future. Through age, experience, and especially the publication of his work *The Melanesian Way*, Bernard Narokobi stands out as Melanesia's leading philosopher.[20] He is a Catholic.

*Rose Kunoth-Monks* grew up within the ambit of the well-known Lutheran Hermannsburg Mission at Alice Springs. Rose is the one Aboriginal woman participant in this symposium. One of the Aranda (Arunta), the best-known and -researched of all the Aboriginal peoples, she played the part of the heroine in the film *Jedda* (1955),[21] and has been more recently the director of the Women's Refuge in Alice Springs. Her paper assesses the ways in which the missions and her own culture have acted on each other.

Part III contains five chapters that illustrate the importance of local beliefs and practices for particular church forms in given areas and for religious movements and theological insights.

*Dave Passi* hails from the Torres Strait Islands, a small island world that straddles Melanesia and Australia. It has greater ethnic affinities with Melanesia, but it falls within the political boundaries of Australia. An Anglican priest with impressive oratorical skills, Dave Passi serves at the cathedral on Thursday Island. His contribution here demonstrates the fascinating continuities between the primal priesthood of his forebears and the Anglican pattern of ministry.

*Willington Jojoga Opeba*, a Jaua (Orokaiva) from the Oro (or Northern) Province on the Papuan side of Papua New Guinea, is also from an Anglican-influenced area, yet he prefers to describe himself as a questioner. He lectures in national history at UPNG and is also a doctoral candidate. His is the most historically oriented of the articles in this book. He takes us back to some of the earliest cult activity documented in Melanesia. In studying the Taro and Baigona cults among the Orokaiva, Opeba discovers that indigenous traditions contain within themselves the capacity to change emphases and direction when new emergencies arise. Opeba was the first to establish (in some of his earlier oral historical studies) that traditional, small-scale religions, far from being static, are highly adaptable and thus mutable. The fact that the central fertility rites or prosperity cults of these religions can alter suggests that the so-called cargo cults of Melanesia are not so much signs that local peoples feel inferior before the overpowering white hegemony as they are indications of the remarkable capacity of pre-Christian religions to survive.[22]

*Esau Tuza*, a Choiseul Islander from the Solomons, is a graduate in religious studies from UPNG and a lecturer there. He has taught at Rarongo Theological Seminary, and is now completing his doctorate at the University of Aberdeen, Scotland. He has written a study that complements Opeba's and is also substantially ethnohistorical in approach. His subject is the theology of Silas Eto (the Holy Mama), which underlies Melanesia's classic example of an independent church: the Christian Fellowship Church founded on New Georgia in 1960. Tuza explores a theme he has taken up before: the Holy Mama's extraordinary integration of traditional Roviana symbology with those Methodist themes of most interest to the islanders.[23]

The two Aboriginal articles in Part III complement each other and add a necessary mainland-Australian dimension to the issue of traditional/ Christianity relationships, a dimension useful for comparative purposes. These contributors draw no hard-and-fast line between their traditions and the Christian outlook—as if Christianity were eternally integral to the Dream Time. This makes psychological and polemical sense, considering the encroachment of white Australia. In contrast to those members of independent nations who can operate more readily and cerebrally using Western theological categories and who are younger thinkers tending to emphasize the gulf between the worst of the pre-Christian past and the best under the new order of existence of the churches, these two Aboriginal participants stand close to their time-honored, never-say-die traditions, and work out their relationship with introduced patterns on a spiritual (more than an intellectual) level.[24]

*Guboo Ted Thomas*, the sole elder of the Yuin tribe (or nation), from Wallaga Lakes, southeastern Australia, is the book's spokesperson for the Aboriginal understanding of land. He has battled with a multinational corporation for the preservation of sacred sites and territory, striven to rebuild his own tribal community, and begun the Renewal of the Dreaming, a movement through which both blacks and whites explore "aboriginal spirituality in its relationship to Christianity."[25]

*Mick Fazeldean*, a man from the central Kimberleys (Western Australia), is a noted, initiated Aboriginal healer, commonly called upon from all corners of the continent. Fazeldean sees no point in belaboring the distinction between traditional and Christian healing. It all originates from the same source. Esau Tuza, from faraway Choiseul, in conversation with Mick Fazeldean arrived at similar conclusions about his own experiences as a healer and had similar insights about the healer's penetration of higher levels of mind. Other Melanesians who conferred with Fazeldean and Guboo Ted Thomas in the making of this collection were impressed that for these two practical spirituality, not mental cut-and-thrust, was what counted. Mick Fazeldean is currently close to the Church of Christ and Guboo Ted Thomas belongs to a charismatic Baptist congregation.

Part IV, Theological Horizons and Adjustments, presents only Melanesian writers, all working at the cutting edge of contextual theology.

*Simeon Namunu*, a Panaeati islander from the chain of islands to the far east of Papua and a United Church minister with experience on New Ireland and Ferguson Island, is well able to explore the relationships between the multiplicity of Melanesian spirits and the one great Spirit of God, whose role becomes clear in the course of the biblical tradition and whose vitalizing effects and gifts are being acclaimed in Melanesian Holy Spirit movements, mostly within existing churches. Simeon Namunu is chaplain at Goroka Teachers College.

*Michael Maeliau*, a Malaitan from the Solomons, formerly lectured at the Christian Leaders' Training College at Banz (Papua New Guinea) and now represents the South Seas Evangelical Church internationally. He also takes stock of the pentecostalist-looking elements, which have been longest known in Melanesia within his own church and which have in some cases accompanied the ministries of his fellow Malaitans to Papua New Guinea. He sees in the spontaneity of these developments the promise of worship expressions truer to the Melanesian soul.

*Rose Ninkama's* article is unique in this collection and is probably the first systematic statement of feminist theology from the region. Rose Ninkama is a Chimbu, belonging to a New Guinea highlands culture characterized by its tribal fighting and strong masculine dominance. The Chimbu were not known to the wider world until the 1930s. Ninkama is a graduate of the Martin Luther Seminary in Lae. She maintains that only a sexist limiting of Christian freedom prevents her from being accepted as a full pastor in the Evangelical Lutheran Church. If liberated from the "savage" past, why should she be shackled afresh by Western-influenced church structures?

*John Kadiba*, a Mailu from coastal Papua, formerly a lecturer in religious studies at UPNG, is now lecturer at Nungalinya (Aboriginal) College, Darwin.

*Sevati Tuwere* is principal of the Pacific Theological College, Suva (Fiji). Their two articles complete Part IV with steadying appeals for theological relevance. Kadiba will put readers in touch with those interdenominational conferences already fostering the concept of a Pacific-wide (or a Pacific islander) theology. Tuwere's article reminds us that some black peoples in the vast, complex region under scrutiny actually border Polynesia and Micronesia and share concerns with the constellations of mini-nations and dependencies scattered over one-third of the earth's watery surface. Kadiba and Tuwere are both ordained, one into the United Church (of Papua New Guinea and the Solomon Islands) and the other into Methodism.

Part V presents articles by political leaders and protagonists for the politically oppressed. In none of these last papers is the main theme about the relations between the traditional and the Christian obscured, yet attention now centers on praxis within the arena of *Realpolitik* rather than on spiritual and theological orientation.

*John Momis*, a Catholic priest from central Bougainville, formerly Minister for Decentralization and Deputy Prime Minister of Papua New Guinea and now leader of the Melanesian Alliance, maps out the kinds of values necessary for a new nation, which cannot afford to sell out its noble traditions of sharing and egalitarianism and its initial welcoming of the Christian message of love and care to the encroachments and enticements of capitalistic greed.[26]

*Utula Samana*, another well-known partisan of the Melanesian Alliance, is the progressive premier of the Morobe Province, Papua New Guinea. Samana's tribe, the Zia, comes from the southeast. A graduate of UPNG,

Samana is a controversial politician and has been an outspoken critic of the national government under Michael Somare. Samana has taken a socialist stance in a new nation that shows few signs of warmth toward leftist sentiments. He grounds his ideology in the values of sharing and community care common to both tradition and Christianity, values by which he judges what he sees as the broken promises and deviousness of the Somare regime and the increasing power of the police.[27]

Next door to Papua New Guinea the most difficult problem for the black peoples of the Pacific has arisen: the recent ethnocidal encroachments of the Indonesian military on Irian Jaya (Indonesia's easternmost province, preferably termed West Papua in honor of its indigenous inhabitants). *Trwar Max Ireeuw,* a staunch opponent of Indonesian neocolonialism, who was forced to flee his native land and who writes in exile from Delft (Holland), puts the case for the Free Papuan Movement.[28] His statement is a complex blend of postwar history and politics, but he does not forget either his ancestors nor the Gospel of liberation (learned from the Dutch Reformed tradition). His position is strikingly similar to one being voiced (among others) in South Africa: the forces of terror and darkness are so great that God will not blame us if we stand up against them with violence.

Moving far to the east of the region, to conclude, different issues are addressed. Anglican priest *Walter Lini* is leader of the successful Vanuaaku Party and the first prime minister of Vanuatu (formerly the Condominium of the New Hebrides), which secured its independence from the French and the British in 1980. Lini recounts the story of independence in his short book *Beyond Pandemonium*. In the article included here he justifies the active role of church leaders in politics (apparently in reaction to disapproving noises made by Vanuatu's first governor general), backing up his arguments by alluding to the sacral roles of traditional chiefs.[29] An outspoken defender of the West Papuan's right to self-determination (as is Utula Samana), Lini is an advocate of speedy independence in New Caledonia.

Two Melanesian brothers plead here the cause of political independence. *Trwar Max Ireeuw* is the first of these; *Pierre Qaeze* of the Loyalty Islands (New Caledonia) is the second. Qaeze is an undergraduate at UPNG (on a scholarship funded by the Uniting Church of Australia Commission for World Mission). He asks the painful question as to whether it is acceptable to call oneself a Christian when so many so-called followers of Jesus do nothing to bring about *kanak* independence from French overlordship.

*Suliana Siwatibau*, the third woman contributor to this collection completes this section and the whole volume. A Fijian, co-author of an antinuclear primer written for the Pacific Council of Churches, Siwatibau now works for the United Nations in Suva. Her article outlines black theology for peace from the country that is closest in the region to nuclear test sites in the Pacific.[30] She reminds us that the most potent threat to all culture and tradition and to God's redemptive work in the world is the senseless intensification of the superpower conflict.

# 2

# General Perspective: A Call for Black Humanity to Be Better Understood

*ARURU MATIABE*
*Southern Central Highlands, Papua*

The subjects grappled with by the authors of this book are immense and the issues often very sensitive. In many parts of the globe at this time, blacks are claiming equality with whites (and with all other types of the human species). Blacks demand the respect and dignity befitting human beings. In short, there is an increasing assertion on the part of blacks for due recognition of their true being and place on this planet. This is only natural, since Caucasians, and, for that matter, those of Asian heritage, have all too consistently misunderstood blacks, often misconceiving them as subhuman or inferior beings.

In religious terms blacks have typically been described as pagan, and in the light of the papers that follow one can see that this is a gross degradation of their true worth. Do not misunderstand me. I do not wish readers to conclude that the seminar that gave rise to the following chapters represented just another opportunity to promote the black cause. The motive behind the papers is not to take revenge on the whites for their past (and often continuing) devaluation of blacks through one-sided broadsides. If the articles serve to promote any cause, it is that of humanity, the humanity in which whites and blacks are equal members.

The contributions represent attempts to remove the debris of ignorance and parochialism that have barred and distorted blacks from being seen in their true light. If concerned social activists and critics, of whatever background, are to make any contribution to the betterment of the human condition, a basic initial step in their labors should be to lay bare the falsities of the mind preventing humanity from seeing itself as it actually is. If one has knowledge of errors yet leaves them unrefuted, one incurs blame. From those who have, much is expected. Marx might add: To leave error unrefuted is to encourage intellectual immorality.[1] It is thus particularly pleasing and gratifying that a seminar was organized to pool the reflections of black Pacific thinkers on the relationship between indigenous traditional beliefs and Christianity. Significantly, the topics addressed by the various authors of this book give long-awaited recognition to the true religious status of blacks, to the power of black men and women to articulate distinctive religious beliefs and values belonging to Australasia (or Sahul) and to present their positions in the complex market of the world's exchange of ideas. If I am right, even if not all the authors take up Christian positions in the book, the volume's existence automatically implies that blacks can no longer be considered "pagan." They can now even claim to be considered "Christian," not just because they might have gone through a christianization process (with the coming of the missionary), but by virtue of their belief in God and their struggle toward a better life in their natural state. Reflected in this book, then, is a profound change of thinking away from the smearing biases of the past and toward a better understanding between branches of humanity. Only with this bettering of understanding can peace be realized and a living harmony between people achieved: whites and blacks must search one another in depth, not with secular superficiality. The issue of religion provides a basic level for mutual understanding because "the surest way to the heart of a people is through their religion."[2]

It would be impossible for any of the papers in this book to have been written without the existence and influence of the Christian Missions in Australia and the southwest Pacific. Yet I would like to submit that the whole missionary approach of introducing the Gospel issued out of an utter misconception of black religion and an appalling willingness to degrade that religion as possessing no status in white Christendom. The religious beliefs and ceremonies of blacks in their natural state imbued life with profound meaning and did allow for true communion with the divine. White Christians could have found much there that was valuable had they looked before so many of them denounced it as totally wrong. Every person is a creature of God, and this God does not belong only to whites. Blacks have a spirit just as whites do; skin color does not matter because, not only are we members of the same species biologically speaking, but also we have the same Spirit within us. (Calling any people pagan, therefore, to my way of thinking seems rather misguided.) It was thus wrong-headed for whites to have expected blacks to renounce their past—in conceptual terms, at any rate, as a totality—and completely accept the ways and the God of the European.

In many parts of the world today anthropologists and theologians are realizing that blacks believe in a Being supreme and unique. Although they believed in the existence of other spirits too, these were considered inferior. Although my own people (the Huli of the Papua New Guinea highlands) possessed wooden carvings, for instance, which they said represented certain spirits, beyond this they believed in the existence of a Supreme Being (Datagali-wabe),[3] as did Australian Aborigines. This Supreme Being, I contend, is the same one whites talk about:

There is evidence from many parts of the world of another, deeper and perhaps older stratum of convictions about the universe in which the figure of a greater God is more or less dimly discerned.[4]

It is my conviction that this is the same Being acknowledged by Christians.

During the visit of the World Council of Churches delegation to investigate the condition of the Aborigines in Australia (June 1981), one of the consultants, Elizabeth Adler, made some remarks in an interview pertinent to this theme. She stated that she "did not know what was meant by the word 'pagan' " when it was applied by some white Christians to the Aborigines. The word *pagani* once referred to unconverted Germans outside the Roman Empire when it was being christianized, but now it seems to be a label for those "people whose culture and life-style we do not necessarily understand." Of aboriginal religion she affirmed that, although so many of its ceremonies were secret, she "had not seen any evidence of anything malicious or destructive in . . . their faith." For her "there is truth in what they say about the need to revere nature," the opportunity to discern God in nature being so neglected by the Europeans.[5]

The way I see it, the conflict between people of different-colored skin who have allegedly divergent beliefs has arisen essentially because of misunderstanding. If you want to know the heart of a people, to repeat, you must understand their religion first, being careful to avoid superficiality and prejudice. Ignorance usually hides reality from the inner eyes of our mind, and even education, organized in a certain way, can keep us from seeing things as they really are. Today, it is clear, humanity stands at the crossroads. In the broadest terms, whether the world comes to an end or we move to a higher level of society depends on what we do now. I believe there is enough knowledge in the world for us to reflect upon and to bring out all the good for the building of a new society.

Martin Luther attacked the corruption in the churches of his day; many saw reality through his efforts and had faith in what he was trying to do. Three centuries passed and another thinker, Karl Marx, was concerned to point out the reality of the human condition. Marx was misinterpreted and people have tried to create a perfect society that he never really discussed. Basically his position was not opposed to what Christians had long been saying about the equality of all human beings in the sight of God. He set himself against hypocrisy, pointing out that the economic order was organized on a master/ servant basis.

Now it is up to us to disclose reality again in a world full of racial tensions. It is up to us to affirm that whether they are red, yellow, black, or white, people are all members of the human species, capable of living in a harmonious society and of understanding each other. I do not hold that we can ever create a perfect society. All we can do is to try to minimize the problems we face while we aim at ideals—at what is right and what is noble—and attempt to achieve the possible.

We are simply striving for the best. We should cooperate, not compete with one another. Not only will we never create a perfect society, but reality itself—in the final analysis—is elusive, even though we are swimming in it all the time. It would be a crime against the human species to give up the struggle for a better understanding between peoples, a more just social order, and a deeper exploration of social realities. It is my hope that this book will confirm that black thinkers of the southwest Pacific are fully engaged in this struggle, and that the humanity they represent needs to be better understood.

# Part II

## Christianity versus Tradition?

# 3

# Interaction between Indigenous and Christian Traditions

## POLONHOU S. POKAWIN
### Manus Island, New Guinea

A misleading assumption has dominated the pulpits of Christian spirituality in Papua New Guinea: that traditional cultures should be separated from Christianity. Traditional cultures have been treated as something merely human—to be easily done away with—but Christianity has been accepted as something from God and not to be questioned. The underlying assumption following European contact was that Christianity must spread into the veins and arteries of the heathens to replace their un-Christian ways, practices, and beliefs and cleanse their souls. Hence evangelization. In simple words, the "Christian culture" was expected to take the place of the traditional cultures.

This article does three things: (1) it discusses this misleading assumption concerning the relationship between the traditional cultures and the Christian culture, arguing that it implies not only Western cultural chauvinism and prejudice but also the Melanesian uncritical acceptance and superficial adherence to Christianity; (2) it introduces Christianity as a tradition that is not so different from indigenous traditions and that is susceptible to continuous changes; and (3) it shows that the indigenous traditional cultures and Christian traditional cultures have constantly affected and influenced each other, a datum which should guide our perception and response to the development of new theologies and innovations now taking place in the churches.

## BACKGROUND

We are discussing relationships; basic to any consideration of these is our notion of the human being. The situation facing humankind results from our perception of ourselves and nature, our relations with others of our kind, the influence of others on us, and our likes and dislikes. No relationship involving human beings exists in a vacuum.

Two groups of human beings are involved in this discussion. First, the indigenous people, the first inhabitants of the islands. Their claim to wherever they are settled is grounded on their first being there or on their acquisition due to conquest. Second, the Europeans and those who entered the Pacific islands during the period of European imperialism.

European contact with the first settlers did not occur in a cultural vacuum. The original inhabitants already possessed the necessary societal machinery to regulate their lives. The Europeans came with their own ways of life, yet they were determined to impose these on the original inhabitants. This determination has been the cause of many situations now being experienced in Papua New Guinea.

Christianity has been part of the process. The spread of Christianity to Papua New Guinea and to this part of the world in general is associated with European colonialism. Christianity was one effective tool of colonization, one way of controlling and taming settlers who were there before the Europeans. The original settlers—the Melanesians—were black or brown; the latecomers were white. This further complicated the relationship between the two groups of human beings, affecting all that has followed. It is within this broad historical canvas that the arguments in this article are developed.

Papua New Guinea is often referred to as a Christian country. The Christian culture and its network of propagation is, however, a recent introduction. It entered the country with European penetration, settlement, and colonization in the late 1800s. It matured hand in hand with other European interests in the economic, political, educational, and cultural areas. The establishment of Christian missions, which involved the building of churches, campaigning for membership, and winning of souls, followed the same pattern as the formation of business interests, which involved the acquisition of land, the recruitment of labor, the laying out of plantations, the creation of dependency on a money economy, the establishment of government stations, and the imposition of authority over the bewildered first settlers, challenging the established traditional leadership to the extent that the local leadership became subservient to the "government."

Thus, in the context of both colonial and post- or neocolonial situations, Christianity was a tool of colonialism. From a cultural point of view, Christianity is part of the white person's way of life. It is part of white tradition. And as the first settlers are urged, forced, and enticed into accepting white culture's money, goods, songs, ways of life, and political systems, so are they expected to adopt Christianity as part and parcel of the European package. The pattern is such that their perception of success and of a worthwhile value system becomes based on the European model. Simply in order to be somebody they must become like the European. This includes adopting the Christian religion. Christianity in both colonial and postcolonial situations, therefore, cannot be separated from whites. This is a basic preconception about Christianity among Papua New Guineans. The situation can be summed up in this way: from the Christian point of view, Christianity used the white settler as its tool to spread itself to the utmost parts of the earth; from the white point of view, Christianity was an effective tool to spread the authority and influence of the white explorer to the newly claimed areas of the world. This is a summary of the black outlook on the new religious order of things during the present, postcolonial period.

## MISLEADING ASSUMPTIONS ABOUT CHRISTIANITY AND ITS EFFECTS

To refer to the indigenous tradition(s) and the Christianity of Papua New Guinea is to represent the country's life story, which is still evolving. The concept of tradition is used both by social scientists and in common day-to-day conversation to refer to the country, its people, and their cultures. It takes into view over seven hundred different language groups, which reflect as many cultural identities. Christianity embodies the ways of the white settlers. Simply put, Christianity came with the white settler to find and win souls, people whose practices and belief systems were different and in need of change from the whites' point of view.[1]

The dichotomy between tradition and Christianity was made so explicit as to suggest that there had to be movement away from the people's former way of life—tradition—to white ways—Christianity—if success, better standards of living, development, and the state of good were to be achieved.

This underlying assumption has for a long time dominated the pulpits of the Christian churches in my country. It derives, of course, from the prevailing political and social thought of the era of Western imperial expansion. The prevailing ideology took any conquered people's way of life to be traditional and human, yet refused to accept Christianity as a tradition. Instead, Christianity was perceived as part and parcel of what was modern and from God. The basic assumption thus has no really mysterious background, yet it is now becoming a fundamental source of conflict within the Christian churches of Papua New Guinea as the people become more conscious of their own precision roots and the ways in which Western Christianity was peddled. The unequal status of tradition as against Christianity is perceived by many thoughtful Melanesians to be due to Western cultural chauvinism and prejudice. This growing (but not yet popular) recognition is highly inflammable.

In many Christian churches, becoming a Christian has involved many dos and don'ts. To be a Christian Papua New Guineans must forgo much of their culture and adopt a new one—the Christian way—which has been virtually identified with the new laws and values brought by the whites. The old ways are often talked about as "dark." The new ways of "light" must be aspired to: the Bible is studied, verses memorized, songs composed and sung, books written and read, films made, and preaching used like propaganda to make Christianity assume the central place in one's thinking and life. This is done so that Melanesians can sift through their traditional and cultural experiences to keep what is acceptably biblical or Christian and remove what is not. Theological schools indoctrinate the people with their special brands of Christian outlook. Traditional cultures are at a disadvantage for lack of a vigorous and structured approach to use in presenting their case to the people. They have been forced into a secondary place in today's structured society and left to their own devices. The Christian tradition or message, by contrast, is presented as the "truth," as if there can be no other "truth."

The rating of PNG as a Christian country indicates the number of its adherents to Christianity. The statement does not compare Christianity and other major religions of the world such as Islam and Buddhism because other major religions are almost completely absent in the country. The statement testifies to the increasing number of Christian churches in existence and their claims to an overall membership that amounts to the majority of the country's population. It goes further and grants credence to the biased ethnocentric idea that before whites and Christianity came to Papua New Guinea's shores, the people and their societies were pagans and heathens. The concept of the "Christian country" therefore suggests the reduction of paganism and heathenism and conveys the "success" story of Christianity. In actual fact, what was branded in culturo-Christian terms as paganism or heathenism was nothing less than the people's way of life, their traditional culture and heritage.

Papua New Guinea, however, lacks in-depth knowledge about Christianity. This lack, coupled with contempt for traditional cultures, has led to uncritical acceptance of Christianity in its Western garb. A culture-bound Western interpretation of the Bible, with its prejudicial application in the villages, contributed greatly to the neglect and ultimate disappearance of many worthy practices among Melanesians and bred a superficial adherence to Christianity. A quick survey in Papua New Guinea would show numerous social, political, and religious ills. One wonders how these can exist in a Christian country. If this is what Christianity is, then it is insufficient. A Christian situation is still to be reached, it may be argued, yet we must lament that Christianity has bred only a superficial adherence. Practices and rituals of Christianity have reflected those of the home countries of the white missionaries, not those of local significance to most of our people.

## CHRISTIANITY AS TRADITION

There are two levels of adherence to the Christian faith. First, there is the basic acceptance of the central theme of Christianity: the recognition of the lordship of the living Jesus Christ. Secondly, there are the observances of certain rituals and habits, such as church services (especially on Sundays) and other practices. These two levels of adherence to the Christian faith over the centuries amount to the Christian tradition. Christianity, apart from the "living Jesus" component is very much a traditional culture comparable to the diverse traditional cultures of our country. This is the central argument of this article: that Christianity in Papua New Guinea must be approached and appreciated in the same way as the people's own traditions. Christianity must be understood in terms of the historical periods in which it originated, developed, matured, and was propagated. It must be grasped as having undergone drastic changes as it adapted itself in history to changing situations.

Christianity represents a tradition of about two thousand years. It is connected with a history that goes back well beyond the birth of its founder, Jesus Christ. Since the time of Jesus, moreover, it has developed and adapted itself to changing situations. If members of the first Christian community were to visit our era, they might well be bewildered at what goes on in churches. They might not even recognize the church they were instrumental in establishing. Their visit to Christian communities, be they churches, villages, or countries, might even produce a negative reaction toward so-called Christian behavior. They might find themselves to be total strangers, in other words, to this period of history. But would this strangeness mean that what goes on in the churches is un-Christian? Or further, that the so-called Christian communities of today are in fact not Christian? It is hard to say that, of course, but the point of this piece of imagination is simply to illustrate that Christianity has become an adaptable tradition over hundreds of years and this long time attests to its survival ability. Even if different people of different ages and places have their own way of maintaining the tradition and expressing the belief, they would continue to keep the essence of the Christian tradition to be able to be associated with the Christian community. Unless Christians in Papua New Guinea realize this and adopt a more discriminatory and critical approach, they may adhere to a superficial Christianity and lose their basic roots. When the chips are down, they are likely to turn their backs on the white religion and go their varied ways.

This raises a basic question. What is the Christian way of living? The answer to the question is essential to maintaining a meaningful and lasting Christian way of life. All communities possess good, bad, and in-between values. Individuals and groups fit into these categories. The categorization is determined by the value system prevailing in the community at any point in time. Many "good" people do not subscribe to the fundamentals of the Christian faith. Yet their ways of life, attitudes, and relations with other people are more outstanding than many of those who profess to be Christian. There are Christian families that have broken up or experienced disharmony over and above the level acceptable within the community. Next to them are Christian families that are happy, kind, and possess other qualities aspired to by Christians. In such situations, what do we say about the families or individuals who profess the Christian faith but do not allow it to govern their lives?

A Christian and a non-Christian may be living side by side. Both possess qualities acceptable to the community, the only difference being that one claims to be a Christian and the other holds no claim to Christianity. Do we say that they are both Christian anyway? Or do we go deeper and suggest that many qualities aspired to by the Christian tradition are also common to other traditions? In both indigenous and Christian traditions common values exist. Furthermore, in both traditions there are people who are good, bad, and inbetween according to the prevailing value system. There are people whose association with Christianity can be known only because they attend church meetings or identify themselves as Christians. But their ways of life do not reflect Christian ways. Then there are non-Christians whose outward behavior meets the ideal of what a Christian should be. Circumstances like these suggest that there must be more to our traditional cultures and to Christianity than has been presented by the messengers of the Christian tradition. This knowledge must ultimately make of Christianity an *in*-thing in life rather than a mere attachment to our names and a threat to our roots.

A more meaningful and harmonious relationship would exist between the Christian culture and the indigenous culture if the two forces were recognized and approached in the same way. Instead of Christianity being seen as God-sent and foreign, it should be approached as a human-influenced tradition that is as subject to change and adaptation as any other tradition. The two traditions ought to be understood at the same level and not considered foreign to each other. In the final analysis, the two traditions deal with how people view their worlds, how they live, relate to each other and nature, and how their belief systems are determined by their experiences. In Papua New Guinea, unlike countries where Christianity began many years earlier and has become a national symbol, the interaction of indigenous and Christian traditions is still affecting and changing both traditions.

## INTERACTION BETWEEN INDIGENOUS
## AND CHRISTIAN TRADITIONS

When missionaries landed on our many shores with their Bibles, prayers, faith, spirit of adventure, culture, and zeal to make Christians out of whomever they found in the new land, our people were going about their businesses and responsibilities. The missionaries and their compatriots, in fact, did not find the people wandering about aimlessly. But following their way of thinking, the missionaries sensed a vacuum. They did not find what they knew and what was familiar to them. To them, Jesus Christ was missing and thus souls needed to be saved. Since then the people's traditions and the Christian tradition have lived side by side, opposed each other, and experienced victory and defeat at the hands of each other. At the fundamentalist level each aimed at completely phasing out, replacing, or annihilating the other, if they could.

There is no doubt that each tradition has greatly influenced and affected the other. Just as Simon Peter would not recognize the form of Christianity in Papua New Guinea today, neither would our ancestors recognize the tradition we live today as the one they left for us to inherit. Many of our traditional medicines have been neglected and forgotten, partly because the ambassadors of the Christian tradition condemned their use and threatened damnation to those who possessed the old healing skills and those who resorted to them. The Bible, they repeated over and over again, did not permit such practices in the new life, and in accepting Christianity such practices were to be forgotten. This has been the fate of many other sides to our culture. In some areas Christianity was opposed initially but later took root. In others, opposition has been more recent and has taken different forms. Such historical, political, and religious phenomena as "cargo cults," new religious movements, new theology, changes in the rituals and practices of the churches, and "Melanesianism" are reactions to conservative, heavy-handed approaches to the propagation of

Christianity that have been couched in Western cultural prejudices.

The churches are experiencing the interactions of these two dynamic forces. Over the past few years, advocacy for changes has increased within the churches—changes in the presentation of Christian belief, the way church services are conducted, and the interpretation of the Bible. The basic idea is to give Papua New Guineans a taste of the practice of Christianity. The idea is also to recognize that aspects of the people's cultures are not opposed to the Christian culture. Thus instead of playing the organ to accompany the singing of hymns, for instance, we play traditional tunes on the kundu and the garamut.

One result of the interactions between the two cultures was the adoption of Christianity by the first settlers (the Melanesians). Christianity as presented has become a dominant force in the country. It is backed by large administrative, organizational, and financial resource bases. It has been instrumental in influencing government decisions and policies. The traditional cultures of the people are merely lived. This situation is more recognizable in the villages, especially in those that had an elaborate system of leadership in the past, or those that are far from the towns (nonetheless even these are undergoing rapidly changing situations). The governments have made statements that both support and condemn aspects of traditional culture. In support of it they keep museums, put on shows for tourists, entertain themselves at public occasions, and teach it to school children. This support, however, enjoys an insignificant financial commitment. The governments oppose traditional culture by spending almost unlimited financial and human resources to promote the culture of modern gadgets.

The traditional cultures have been under intense pressure to change. They have changed. But they have not disappeared to be replaced by the culture of modern gadgets. Elements of traditional cultures continue to survive. The influence of the *wantok* system,[2] the customs of exchange and confirmation of relationships between groups and individuals in the institution of marriage, and the central importance of land show the resilience and adaptation of traditional cultures which in turn have influenced the intruding culture of modern gadgets.

The survival of traditional cultures has also affected the Christian culture. Mention has already been made of new practices in church services, which include the use of traditional instruments and music. There are, however, more fundamental influences.

In the institution of marriage, for instance, couples who are associated with any of the churches have both a church wedding and the traditional exchanges that fulfill traditional obligations. This is not true in every case, but is likely to happen when couples come from the same or neighboring areas, or when they both come from the villages.

A more subtle influence of indigenous cultures on Christian culture has shown itself in the freedom to move between the two cultural spheres. For example, we find that persons who claim to be Christian attend church services, read the Bible, pray and may receive treatment at the hospital, but at the same time they believe that illness or mishaps occur because certain wrongs have been done and must be settled among the family members. They might visit a village *poisen man* (sorcerer/healer) to be treated for illnesses that the hospital is unable to detect, or they explain unusual occurrences in the way that their ancestors did.

Perhaps the most obvious outcome of the relationship is that attending church services and observing church rituals do not necessarily prevent many from becoming involved in practices and behaviors that are considered inappropriate for a Christian. Some of this behavior and practice is "neocultural." Since the majority of Papua New Guineans were young when the missionaries came or were born into a churchgoing family, church attendance has become a habit. This does not prevent people from participating in traditional cultural practices where these continue to be meaningful.

I do not intend to lament over what has happened to our traditional cultures. For many of us they only exist in the mind, not in the heart and in experience. They have become a resource to use when we want to attack what we do not accept about the dominant influences today. Unless traditions result in actions, they will be fantasies, while we move on to become filled with the culture of modern gadgets. This is not to deny, however, that a new culture has been developing, which combines elements of both the indigenous traditional culture and the Christian traditional culture, the latter being associated with the culture of modern gadgets.

The persistent use of the concepts "indigenous traditions," "indigenous cultures," or "traditional cultures" points back to those historical periods that produced the human conglomeration behind the present inhabitants of Melanesia's various island states. It recognizes that the peoples who first inhabited these islands, all of whom were black/brown, have much to contribute to the future of their respective states. It also acknowledges the role of the white way of life.

History has proven wrong the Western prejudicial view that the first inhabitants' way of life would disappear as the influence of the white settler spread. Instead, the people's way of life has affected the newly introduced ways and vice versa. This has led to innovations in government policy, in the education system, capitalist business enterprises, and slowly but surely in the Christian churches. The entire social, religious, economic, and political systems in Papua New Guinea today have been the outcome of interaction between the people's way of life and the new wave of influences of which the Christian culture and tradition are a part. This is what makes black/brown people of the Pacific different from our white compatriots. It also makes our respective states distinctive. Had our ancestors lived only superficial lives, colonialism would have successfully made blacks into Europeans.

## CONCLUSION

In asserting our cultural and national identity in the religious and spiritual context, we must do four things.

First, we must de-emphasize Christian culture as our point of reference or our starting point. Our thinkers and theologians should treat Christianity as a traditional culture—isolating what is essentially Christian from cultural and structural components—and treat our traditional cultures and innovations with respect and seriousness instead of dismissing them as un-Christian. Such treatment should lead the way to establishing Melanesian, Pacific, indigenous theology.

Second, the Bible should not be used as a measuring rod to dismiss or support developing ideas and theologies. Attempts to develop ideas and theologies should be curtailed if the Bible is "overused" to legitimize them, especially when thinkers, theologians, and their critics have been indoctrinated into respective kinds of Christianity. Unless one has been de-indoctrinated, it could actually be preferable not to have the Bible and other theologies so readily accessible!

Third, one way to avoid the problems involved in framing new theologies would be to develop objectivity and a sense of fairness to others' views. An objective approach, influenced by one's real experience, would go a long way toward promoting ideas that would contribute to more meaningful approaches to religion. This, of course, would require enormous de-indoctrination by our national scholars.

And fourth, as new ideas and theologies develop, we should not be too concerned about whether they are practicable. Let time determine the usefulness of an innovation. The approach, however, should be critical and realistic and should stem from interpretation and conceptualization of real-life situations. Our overconcern for the practicality of ideas and theologies only prevents their maturing, breeds conservatism, and quickens the disappearance of indigenous creativity.

These four exercises should result in new ideas and theologies which may not necessarily be in harmony with what was acquired during indoctrination into one or another denomination of Christianity. That is significant. The objective is to develop meaningful ideas from our life experiences, which would ultimately enhance the effectiveness of our beliefs in our day-to-day life. The task is a difficult one, and, as I have already suggested, will take time, but it is not impossible. Moreover, the greatest opposition should be expected to come from among ourselves. Our own security and comfort will be threatened in the process and many will react adversely and oppose change. The opposition could determine either the beginning of a new stage of spiritual and religious development or an end to the aspiration to develop black theology in our part of the world.

In the final analysis, what I am suggesting is not the indigenization of Christianity. Indigenizing Christianity suggests a process of dressing Christianity up with tapa clothes, grass skirts, and malo and supplying it with spears, bows, and arrows. What I am suggesting is an innovation, which will either develop something essentially in tune with prevailing Christian theologies, but distinctly Melanesian, or else something quite different from existing theologies but meaningful to our people.

# 4

# Christianity and Melanesian Cosmos: The Broken Pearls and a Newborn Shell

*BERNARD NAROKOBI*
*Sepik, Mainland New Guinea*

When the carefully formed pearls are broken, there is nothing a living soul can do to put them together. The jealous lover can do no more than lament the lost glory and the would-be treasure. The broken pieces can be gathered and an attempt can be made to make them whole, but it is a fool's task, a lost cause. New treasures must be sought. The old and the broken shall be preserved, not as a broken dream or a wounded wing, but as a source of strength, faith, and hope.

The broken and the rejected shall stand to summon the roaming seagulls, to reach out for greater heights. Birds of the air, fishes of the living waters, and plants and animals of the roaring earth neither read nor write. They neither make robots nor theorize. They live their lives lamenting the cloud that fails to rain and rejoicing in the promise of a new sunrise.

We mortals rejoice in our rational and logical conclusions. We count ourselves supreme among the living. We claim to be gods ourselves. We soar the skies yet we never reach the end. We descend the depths, yet we do not reach the bedrock. We weep, yet we do not exhaust our tears, and we rejoice without burning out our smiles.

Wondering what to say to the great gathering of gods I was to address, I called on my ancestor's gods, Kravari, Womaibonin, Uriongun, and others. I wept before my now dead, but living, mother, and my many ancestors' souls, long departed from the flesh earth, but living in me and dwelling with me in soul life. I consulted the Books of the Living Iruhin. I walked sleepless nights and wooded forests and passed through open sandy beaches.[1]

Toward sunset, I sat down beneath a kalapilum tree, by the Banak beach and looked out into the sea. In front of me were green islands, planted in blue seas and sailing in white clouds. The continuous breaking of the waves gave me music while dolphins performed a dance for me as they jumped out of the sea, one behind another. The birds added to the music and I found myself becoming both the willing audience and the conductor of the entire show.

Happy as I was, my problem was not solved. What am I going to say to my friends across the sea in a land my ancestors never knew to be their home? Just as the sun touched the sea in that gloriously mysterious act in which the end of the earth and the sea open up to receive the dying sun, a voice spoke to me. It was clearly a human voice, but it seemed to come from a bird. The voice was that of a departed ancestor. I looked around, but all I saw was the shadow of the disappearing sun. This is what the voice said:

Listen, my son. I know you are searching for the broken pearl. I also know that you have started cultivating a new pearl shell. There is nothing you can do about the broken pearl. Just as you cannot do much about my departure. I have come to where I had to come. Here there are a lot of pearls. Just keep on cultivating the new pearl shell. But don't forget the broken one. It too is life. Listen, my son, if you lived yesterday, you cannot live again. Yesterday is gone to the tide of eternity. But you can build a new tomorrow from what you remember of yesterday. I must go now, son, for the sake of life.

"Oh, don't go," I replied. "Don't go," I begged. The shadow moved and I followed it in a desperate attempt to hold back my ancestor.

"Listen to me, my ancestor," I said. "I have never heard you speak before. Speak more to me. You seem to be making something important of this broken pearl and of my new shell growing by the reef. Besides, I have as many questions as the grains of sand to ask you. Let me be frank with you, my ancestor. I need advice. People are asking me to talk to them about our Melanesian values and Christianity. I've heard a lot from our people about our gods, spirits, what I may and what I may not do. I've also heard and read a lot about a strange man called Christ and what he did and taught years and years ago."

The shadow stopped moving and responded. For a while I thought I had done something forbidden by talking to my ancestor's shadow. There was total silence. But then the voice came again. It said: "Listen, my son. You don't seem to have much faith in yourself. Look at your body." I looked at myself. "Now, what do you see?"

"Nothing," I replied, "just myself." "What do you see in yourself?" the voice insisted. "Oh, *mi tasol* (just me)," I reaffirmed.

"Look again," the voice insisted, and again I looked at myself.

"Can you see me in you?"

"No," I replied.

"Well, just believe you can," said the voice. "And this is what I want you to do. Listen carefully, my son, because I will not come again."

Fearing I might offend my ancestor and stop the revelation, I remained silent and listened. Again there was silence. The stillness scared me and I started to flee when the voice fixed my feet to the ground.

"Now, listen you man of little faith. Gather the broken pearl. Be sure to collect every element you can find. Now, when you have done that, take it to the reef and place it by the newborn shell. There will be a new pearl."

This surprised me. A new pearl out of the old. "Impossible," I thought.

"No, my ancestor," I broke my silence. "I am sorry to cut in here, but you just told me not to think about my broken pearl. Besides, this newborn shell is not mine at all. It actually belongs to the world-famous Mr. Miki Moto. I am only letting him use my reef to cultivate it, mainly because he has given me some chopsticks."

"Listen, my son," the voice became stern. "If you interrupt again, I will assume you don't need me and I will go."

"I am sorry," I apologized. This comforted my ancestor and he went on.

"Don't worry about the shell being of Japanese origin. The point is, it is growing in your waters and I want to show you how to cultivate it as something that is yours. Now, take the broken pearl and place it against the newborn shell. Each day, say to me: 'Babenomi-babekomi/Pepe tiktik, pepe tiktik/Juke namini iwa/Juke namini iwa.' Now, I must go," the voice spoke, "for your dusk is my dawn, and I must join the rest of your ancestors in a great feast. Don't forget. Come thunder, come lightning, come wet Talio, come dry Rai seasons, believe in yourself and daily utter the sacred words."[2]

The voice disappeared and darkness fell upon me. The sky was light with its unnumbered stars and the moon shone upon the dark sea, throwing forth a powerful beam of light. I stood up, cleaned the sand off myself, and took leave of the beach. As I started walking, a stream of blood beat upon my right arm as if someone had struck me with an arrow. I was happy. I knew it was a happy sign. Then the *sebiten*—the messenger bird—twittered on my right side. I responded immediately:

> Oh, babenomi-babekomi
> Pepe tiktik, pepe tiktik
> Juke namini iwa
> Juke namini iwa.

I felt great peace descend upon me and I moved on. A ring of fireflies came and sat upon my head. That peace which was mine began to flow and I was afraid. I talked to the stars

> Oh, babenomi-babekomi
> Should I go on to the land
>    of the white cloud
> Or are you warning me against going?
>    If it is well for me to go,
>      get up and go!

The stars rose and dispersed. I could hear cricket sounds on my right and I knew all was well. With peace in my heart, I returned and passed the night. The day came and I addressed the great gathering, receiving the total approval of all those assembled.

The message I had received on that open beach was my secret. Each day I uttered the magic words. Winds from different directions blew. Oceans roared. Reefs were broken. But I lost no faith. Days went by and moons went by. The Japanese came and taught me how to culture the pearl, but I never lost the message. One day, a Japanese master came and showed me the future glory— what the pearl from the new shell would be like. I was excited, but I didn't fully appreciate what it was all about. This Japanese man never left me. He came regularly to check upon his pearl shell. But I never forgot my ancestor's words.

One day, this Japanese man became ill and went home. A year went by, two years went by. I harvested the pearl and kept it in my ancestors' *tambaran* house.[3] It became my treasured secret. It was my magic stone with which I won many battles, shot many pigs, and caught many fish. I established myself as a great master and chief among my people and my islands. I learned many new songs and dances and built new houses.

Soon the word spread and many came to see me and learn from me. I built a sacred house and placed the pearl in its center. But I was never happy, because I was afraid the Japanese man might come and ask for his pearl.

The Japanese man came one day when we were having a yam feast. He asked for the pearl and I told him he could not take it. But if he wanted, I could take him to the *tambaran* house and he could see it. I told him the pearl was guarded but that the guards would make way for him if he wanted to see it. I told him too that the new creature was very special and if he took it, we would all die. Being an understanding Japanese, he believed me. He looked at the new pearl and left. He said it was not exactly what the great master Miki Moto had wanted or cultivated. If he took the pearl home, there would be no market for it. No Japanese woman would want it. He qualified this position, however, by saying he thought a Japanese museum could be interested in buying it.

The new pearl became something of a novelty and we ordered our lives around it. Our yam harvests, our funeral, birth, and marriage ceremonies and our initiations centered around this new treasure. We were very happy.

What follows next is an account of some of the things that have happened in my village since the arrival of this new pearl shell. Lots of people realized the aura, power, and the magic in this pearl and began to make their own replicas of the pearl shell. But they did not use pearl shell. Instead, they used the trochar shell. The end-product looked no different from the pearl shell though.

One day I visited a village close to mine. I saw an old man. He had a swollen leg. As I looked on, I saw him heat up a stone over an open fire. He took a coconut shell and placed some leaves and some water in it. He held the replica shell in one hand over the coconut shell, picked up the red-hot stone and immersed it in cold water. As the steam rose, he placed his swollen foot over the steam and spoke to the pearl. He was healed.

I returned to my village and started to talk to my people about life, the new, the old, and the future. There was general agreement that this earth was not a good kingdom and that it would come to an end soon. The rains we'd been having in this normally dry season were evidence of the imminent end of the world.

However, that was not my concern. The national elections were coming and I wanted to talk to them about politics, that I was the right prophet for their hopes and expectations and that my party was the hope of the future. I talked for a long time and liked what I said because when I finished, I thought I had only just started. But a lot of people were shouting "em giaman tasol"—he is not telling the truth.

A councillor came forth. He spoke with deep passion. He said: "We only see the rains. But we do not know where the clouds are made or how they are made. As farmers we know when to plant and when to harvest. If we plant yams or taro in one plot and they do not grow well we can either try again or go to another plot." Referring to me, he said, "I think Narokobi is telling the truth; we should listen to him."

This naturally healed my wounded ego and I smiled with pride. I was ready to go to sleep when an old man scratched my toe and whispered: "Eh, son, do we have any *as*?"

"What do you mean?" I inquired.

"*As*, I mean, you know, the bottom, the basis, the foundation."

I was confused! What was this *longlong* (mad) man talking about? The *longlong* in his wisdom understood my ignorance and explained:

"Well Adam and Eve are our ancestors, Europeans, Asians, and us. Now that was all right until Cain killed his brother, Abel. The Europeans are the children of Abel because they are delivered. Are we, the black people, the children of Cain? You see, we are not yet delivered. Will we be delivered? Who will do it?"

I tried desperately to explain that I didn't think the Melanesian was the descendant of Cain and that the Bible says Christ is the deliverer of all races, black, white, pale, or brown. I told him that God's kingdom was for all races and people.

He was not convinced, or even half-convinced. "Yes, when we die, God will receive us into heaven if we are good. But how is it that Europeans are delivered (*kamap*) and we are not? Do we have any basis?"

I negotiated my way out by saying it's a matter of education, and that not all Europeans had cars and houses and money, if that was what he meant by deliverance. I also explained that some "delivered" people were very hungry for peace and *amamas* (joy).

Now it was my turn to ask a question, I asked the old man: "What do you think of the idea that there are three persons in one God?" He replied: "Yes, you are right: Father, Son and Holy Spirit." That did not answer my question, so I asked again. I reformulated my question:—"Did our ancestors have an idea of one God in three persons?"

He said that was not so. There was only One God of the Above, called the Iruhin, but there are many, many spirits; some do good, some do bad things.

I came back at him. If you say so, then you are not agreeing with the Christian belief that there is God the Father, God the Son, and the Holy Spirit, all in One.

"No! That idea is also true. They are all the same. There is only One God! God is God, Jesus is God's son, and the Holy Spirit is God's Spirit."

I planted another question in the old man: "What do you think Christianity has done for your life and your village?"

"Oh, they brought us schools and hospitals. They also taught us to love one another. They chased away bad spirits. Before the spirits were very close to us. Now, the spirits are gone."

Another man broke in: "With the disappearance of the spirits, the forests and the rivers became empty. There are no animals in the forests now and no fish in the rivers."

Then it was time to go to sleep, so we retired. As we prepared to sleep, a baby cried. It cried and cried. The mother breastfed the child, but the child refused to drink. She washed the child and still it cried. An old woman asked what it was about and the child's parents told her they did not know. The old woman picked a piece of glowing fire, spun it around the child, and drove out the spirits. The child took its mother's breast, fed, and went to sleep.

Another child on another day developed diarrhea. For weeks nothing could stop it. Medical care could not help. A village healer asked to see the child. The healer spoke into a bottle of tap water and the child was bathed in that water. The child was cured within one day.

I find in my life not one but many broken pearls. There are pearls I want to have, but can't have in their fullest glory because they are broken. I lament over their loss, but I keep recalling my ancestor's advice. Do not weep over the broken pearls, cultivate the new pearl shell.

My new pearl shell is really mine. It was brought to me, yes. But I tamed it. I cultivated it. It was not easy to do so. I had to go through many rainstorms to raise it. Now I decorate it with my own masks, sing my own songs, and perform my own dances around it. It is a new creature, but only because I admired and longed for my old, broken pearl.

I am not worried or embarrassed by the coarse and ugly looks of the outer shell. These ugly looks fall by the wayside, for I have found my pearl. If others say my pearl is ugly, I take their word seriously. But inside myself I know I have a treasure many others yearn for but can't have because they no longer see what I see, hear what I hear, feel what I feel, and treasure what I treasure.

The wholeness of the Melanesian cosmos is an unfolding experience. It is a part of the whole humanity in a given locality. Its roots are in the old pearl, but its fullness is its growth, deriving life from the waters and currents of the earth and the sky.

# 5

# Church and Culture: An Aboriginal Perspective

*ROSE KUNOTH-MONKS*
*Central Australia*

Throughout this article,[1] unless the contrary is specifically stated, the word *Aboriginal* refers to people, past and present, who knew or know the most important of Aboriginal traditions, and who have followed or now follow a lifestyle more or less attuned to these traditions. What I write refers only to Central Australia and only to the Aranda and Anmatjera people in that area. My childhood was lived in a closely knit clan, governed strictly by the elders. Our kinship system left us no doubts as to our relationships within the group, which then numbered about a thousand people.

Our traditional life was no bed of roses. Our superstitions made us live in fear. We feared the Kadaitja—who was not a figment of our imagination—invented by our parents to keep us from straying at nights. He was real and we had every reason to be afraid of him. It is important to keep this in mind for the message of Christ spoke most directly to this situation of the Aboriginal people.

Among Aboriginal people, sickness and death were not perceived as being caused by germs or viruses, nor by any of the things to which we now attribute sickness and death. They were caused, so they believed, either by someone manipulating the spirit world, someone who wanted to do them harm, or by someone using *arangutia* (evil spirits), or by their having transgressed some tabu. Hence if you became sick, it was necessary to discover who or what had caused the sickness and also to seek a healer who could manipulate the spirit world to heal you. If it was deemed that a person was behind your sickness, it was important to get back at that person. If someone died, the matter was more serious. The person or persons who had caused the death had to be found and punished.

Ceremonies and practices existed for finding the guilty party and, once this had been established, revenge had to be taken. Often innocent people were blamed and killed. If the guilty party could not be found or caught, any member of the person's extended family would do.

They had to take revenge. This was how "pay back" started—and went on for years, with many lives lost on both sides. People thus lived in fear of the spirit world, in fear of people who might be manipulating the spirit world to do them harm, in fear of being wrongly implicated in someone's death or illness, and therefore in fear of the Kadaitja killing them in the pay back for someone's death.

The missionaries came into all this, and gave the Gospel to the people. The Gospel was truly a God-send. The Gospel of Jesus was readily acceptable to the Aboriginal. However, Aboriginal Christians did not accept all that the missionaries advocated as being part of the Christian faith.

In Central Australia missionaries discouraged Christian men from undergoing initiation, as many missionaries considered this to be a heathen or non-Christian ceremony. But it is clear that the Aboriginal people carried on the initiations and still do so; many Aboriginal Christians do not see this as conflicting with their Christian faith. For them the initiation of boys has a social significance apart from the religious aspects associated with the ceremony. They were not prepared to give this up, and they didn't.

Professor Strehlow writes about the belief of the Aranda and other inland tribes as to the way life emerged at the beginning from a bare and featureless earth. Supernatural beings awoke from eternal sleep and emerged at various places in the plain. The sites of their emergence—caves and water holes—are sacred. The beings had both an animal (or plant) and a human form. All animals and plants are their descendants, as are men and women of each totemic kind. Hence the vital link between human beings, particular animals and plant species, the totemic ancestors, and the landscape forms from which the ancestors came and were transformed into at the end of their period of creative activity. Some remained in the form of *tjurunga* slabs. Even in their present-day sleep the ancestors retain their creative powers and can be induced to exercise them when their human descendants call on them to do so by performing the rites of increase, which they founded and first performed.[2]

Before the missionaries came, the Aboriginals believed that they continued the creative activity of their totemic ancestors and that their food supply—among other things—was dependent on continuing this activity. The Christian faith holds that the God who was revealed in the Christian Scriptures created the world and all that exists and that through the divine past and present activity the needs of God's children are met.

The Aboriginal and Christian beliefs at this point are diametrically opposed, mutually exclusive. The missionaries pointed this out to those who wished to embrace the Christian faith. They had to make a choice. Those who became Christians did give up their traditional belief and practice. Of this there is clear evidence.

The missionaries also advocated that the people give up their *tjurungas*, the slabs of rock or wood that were the representation of the totemic beings, and the songs associated with the wanderings and activities of the totemic ancestors. These, too, were considered incompatible with the Christian faith. This view, however, was not shared by the Aboriginal Christians. For them the *tjurungas* served important social purposes. They therefore kept them for their social purpose and rejected their religious content.

In other words, the Aboriginals distinguished between different functions served by the same object, giving up those that were incompatible with their new faith, but retaining others.

Most Aboriginal Christian men have not performed increase rites for generations. But that they retained their *tjurungas* for special purposes was recently confirmed at Hermannsburg, one of our oldest missions. The mission helped the people to define their traditional land boundaries by using *tjurungas*. When disputes arose in the process of fixing boundaries, these were settled to everyone's satisfaction by using traditional mythology and songs known by Aboriginal Christians.

To sum up, then, it appears that what happened in the religious area was this: The Christian faith was readily accepted because it was seen to address itself to a felt need. However, the Aboriginal Christians discriminated between what they saw as the central tenets of the Christian faith and the Western application of that faith to their specific cultural situation. The latter they did not accept.

Conflict could have arisen at this point. Aboriginal people did not argue about things they felt they could not convince the missionaries of anyway. The Aboriginal way is to listen to what is said, make up one's mind, and then simply do what one has decided. This is what most of my people did in the mission. They were not locked inside an institution. They could come and go at will and were therefore able to limit the influence of the mission to whatever they wished.

I now come to the question many missionaries are asking: What emerges out of the culture contact situation that has relevance for today? Changes in Aboriginal societies are inevitable for the simple reason that the social and physical environment in which Aboriginal people live today must ultimately face change. If we are honest about giving Aboriginals a choice about how or what they wish to change, then suggestions for change (innovation) must be offered in such a way that people actually do have a choice.

This seems to have been the way in which religious innovation was offered at Hermannsburg. People did have a genuine choice, and they chose those aspects they found meaningful and rejected those they could not accommodate in their system. This occurred without conflict simply because choice was actually possible.

If white people, with all the best will in the world, impose change on the Aboriginal people, they must also accept that they will be assuming responsibility for the operation and the final effect of that innovation.

This explains why whites have to service so many programmes and why demands on them continue to escalate. Whites, for example, have made Aboriginal health and living standards their responsibility because of the way in which they have approached these matters. Aboriginals make no request regarding the things they see as belonging to the core and center of their culture and for which they accept responsibility.

In short, innovations that do not offer the possibility of rejection by Aboriginals are destructive to Aboriginal society. I believe that when there has been no real choice, tensions and chaos have resulted. Some blacks (and I use that term to make it explicit that I am not referring to Aboriginals) blame the whites; the whites blame those who stir things up, and in the midst of this the disease that is racism breeds. Of course the Aboriginals are the ones who suffer, like the innocent children in marriage breakups.

The Aboriginal pastors whom I respect make no apology for their faith in Christ and do not have to defend themselves from criticism from people in high places. In closing neither should I, an Aboriginal person, be asked to apologize for my faith in Jesus. Lord, I believe.

# Part III

## The Impact of Indigenous Tradition on Emergent Black Theologies

# 6

# From Pagan to Christian Priesthood

*DAVE PASSI*
*Torres Strait*

My ancestors worshipped a god, Malo,[1] an idol you could see, feel, touch. When the missionaries came to the Torres Strait Islands, my grandfather was a priest of Malo's cult. Yet he was one of the first converts to Christianity.[2] He saw that the Anglican Church was a fulfillment of the old cult; because of his vision I also see the church as fulfillment. It came to fulfill, not to destroy. I see the old cult much as the Old Testament; the New Testament, the church's book, shows the element of grace, which never came into our traditional religion. That element fills to the full extent the traditions of our islands.

The role of priest, as held by my grandfather, was hereditary. It had been held by his father before him. He sat in authority as his fathers had, and those who passed in front of him would have to crawl on their knees and keep their head lower than his head. The priests (*zogoga*) were immensely powerful. A priest possessed special spiritual powers, for example, the gift of sleepwalking (*modu*). By *modu*, the priest could secretly cut the ropes of enemy boats and send them away by the current or he could tighten the ropes of his own people's boats for safety. When his people fished, he would recite the right prayers—the preserved sacred psalms of worship—and these would lead to a good catch or protect those fishing if sharks attacked.

I remember too that my grandfather, when he was very old, foretold the time of his death. "Come here, grandson," he called to my eldest brother. "I have heard what people are saying, so I want you to take me out [to prepare for the funeral]." When my brother told him at night he was ready to do as he was asked, grandfather said: "No, not yet, the rain will not come yet . . . but about this time of night . . . the rain will come." It so happened at the time he died. Before passing away, he promised his son: "Whatever is bad, I will not pass on to you." This was part of the custom of passing down hereditary power. Such things may appear to some as superstitions, but they are not. It would be an insult for the persons who accept these customs to hear them called superstitions. It is sad that these traditions have almost been lost and it is fortunate that some know about them and can pass them on.

My grandfather gave up his old role in the cult to become a Christian. He gave up his authority and all the power that made him who he was, and he became a Christian. I do not really know why, I do not fully understand it, although I see that the power of God was there in his decision to leave everything belonging to him behind and go to work under a Melanesian mission worker.

The London Mission Society (LMS) sent the original missionaries (1871) but they did not impress my grandfather much, even though he did become Christian. Some years later (1915), when the Church of England assumed responsibility for the islands, he accepted the new ways more completely. He saw the Anglican preaching and practice as the fulfillment of the old cult. He asked himself why the LMS had required so many of the old rituals to be discontinued; especially since ritual forms—all the actions he was so used to in the past—had such a great significance for him. As he saw it, the Anglican liturgy and the ritualistic approach of Anglicanism were the fulfillment of the old cult. I do not believe any European influenced him in this; it was his own judgment. He was used to rituals for different times and circumstances, what I would call "opportunistic" worship.

I will give some examples to show why he and others after him made these connections. One simple one has to do with bowing in reverence. My grandfather was used to bowing reverently before Malo. It was a true tradition, for this bowing was to be done before or among the elders, out of respect for people who were civilized. On becoming Christian, my grandfather would bow on entering the church and walk bowed over until he had taken his seat. To explain to missionaries and others who asked him about this, he would reply: "Your God is the true God, yet you do not revere Malo" (that is, the same God who was now worshipped under a different name).

A more complicated example has to do with the initiation of priests in the old cult and the ordination of priests in the Anglican Church. Traditionally, because the office of priest was hereditary, the sons, who were candidates, would lie prostrate, one in a certain category lying on top of one in another, surrounded by warriors, while the sacred drums were played. The belief behind this part of the ceremony was that the god Malo would come when the candidates had "arrived" like this. He would come down and stretch his legs three times over the candidates as they lay there together and fill them with his powers. The god went through and over them. Something like this persists in Anglican ordination. As an ordinand, I had to lie flat. The people in the congregation stood up when they saw me like that, and even though the actual ordination really comes when the bishop says a prayer over the candidate, our people saw the Malo tradition in the prostration and thus a special fulfillment in Anglicanism.

What of God? In Christianity it is hard to pinpoint God; in tradition it was easy. God was there to feel and touch and had a special place in the mountains.

To the islanders the god Malo's nature, existence, and name were quickly perceived. When we think back, our minds could conceive and grasp nothing greater than Malo. Malo was the greatest thing existing on the earth, so reverence and special care with regard to Malo came into traditional life in many and varied ways.

Missionaries and even I myself at this point in time have to hunt for the continuance of this traditional sense of reverence; it can easily be missed since all sorts of other things come into the picture today. Traditional activities connected with the church today, for example, seem to concern money—often an exchange of money (as at a marriage or funeral). We do not find any hint of Malo in the mountains nor do we have any of the special sacred ropes related to his cult. Still I am sure traditional reverence is to be found. It may be hard for an outsider to discover it. One day a person may come across a spiritual place and be stunned into a whisper; yet the next day he or she might just wander through the same place, cutting the bush without any care. Reverence is hard to pin down because it serves a purpose in the head at varying times.

Like the traditional cult, the Anglican liturgy has a definite structure and is an important, constant reminder of reverence. Sometimes the feeling arises that the parts of this liturgy are so robust that they can be handled casually. I believe liturgy is crucial to getting across the idea of awe and reverence, qualities that are disappearing and need to be brought back to life in the Torres Strait.

We should not forget the institutional side of things. The unity of eight different tribes depended on Malo, who was central and whose high priest presided in each of these tribes. What would have happened if there had been no institutions? If there had been no centrality of religion, our society—in a very small world of some five or six miles square—would have lost out to the enemies. Thus the importance of centrality is expressed in my tradition and has directed my own and my people's choice of the Christian model appropriate for us (the Anglican Church government being hierarchical). Mind you, the *zogoga* priests were different from Anglican ones! For the most part, they were not so holy, and in performing ceremonies they were not themselves, not themselves at all, but were taken over by the power of the god (who enabled them to sleepwalk).

Other institutions once existed that do not have an equivalent in the Anglican Church—and ought not to have. I am thinking of sorcery, in which the name of Malo was used and is still evoked today. I am told that people still get a stone and talk to it, saying the magical words "*Malo, omi.*" If they hit an enemy with this stone, he or she surely will die. Sometimes the sorcerer or sorceress and the victim fight with stones and the former usually wins. If after a stone fight the intended victim walks off, the sorcerer or sorceress can still talk to a stone and simply throw it in the air just to make the *noise* of the spell. As soon as victims hear this noise, they forget everything and they know it is time to die. Many people today, of course, will tell you that this is not true, but I have it on my grandfather's authority. We should not have this side to religion in the church, since the church is to preach grace and love.

Other aspects of the old cult may also appear undesirable, but observed in a certain way they are valuable. These concern discipline or law, for there were certain rules, regulations, and wise sayings of Malo that served to hold my people together. For example, it was extremely important—as it is today—that if anything, such as a coconut leaf, falls to the ground, to the earth, it must be left to rot there. I know a place where a large branch has fallen and it remains across the path, about waist high. It is not to be removed and people either go under or jump over it. What is the meaning of all this? It is a reminder about trespassing and theft. Malo (as shown by these falling objects) keeps his own boundaries; so the young learn that we must not walk on other people's land or trespass their boundaries or steal what belongs to other people.

Another example of discipline from the old days: As part of the worship in the high priest's cult the warriors would walk in two lines on the beach near a certain village. This dance-walk was to be performed in such a way that anybody coming after them would think that only two people had walked there, since those following the leaders were to tread exactly where the leaders had trod. The walkers had to be disciplined. So perfectly was this part of the ritual to be followed, in fact, that if a warrior put one foot outside the track, he would be killed straightaway. This was a hard discipline. Now when I think about how my people think, I appreciate that there are certain aspects of Anglicanism—church law, the set order of doing things—that appeal to them and to their need for definition and regulation in their lives.

These are some of the ways in which I see Christianity as a fulfillment of my people's tradition. Things my grandfather did before me were certainly important to our people; he compared the old rituals and practices to see how well Christian forms would fit them. I have simply carried on his work, trying to compare. When I consider my church's relation to tradition, I find that they fit together very well.

# 7

# Melanesian Cult Movements as Traditional Religious and Ritual Responses to Change

## WILLINGTON JOJOGA OPEBA
### Northern Coast, Papua

Melanesian cults have often been discussed in the context of European contact and colonization assuming that: (1) Melanesian cults were entirely new phenomena with no roots in traditional beliefs and rituals; and (2) it was fitting to describe such cults as millenarian movements of Melanesia or cargo cults, and thus to treat them as strange reactions to foreign intrusion, which pinned group hopes on a great transformation or arrival of wealth.[1]

This paper will attempt to show that such movements, though they did possess some entirely new features, nonetheless had their roots in traditional beliefs and rituals. Cargo cults, or movements with strong emphases on millenarian hopes, emerged when there was consistent failure by both mission and government authorities to honor, respect, and indeed understand the movements in their *traditional* contexts, and when these authorities adopted negative attitudes and suppressive policies.

This study of the Baigona and the Taro cults among the Orokaiva (Oro or Northern Province, Papua New Guinea) attempts to show not only the importance of traditional beliefs and rituals in the cults, nor only the attitudes of the colonial government and missions toward these practices, but also the effects of adverse policies on present and future Melanesian responses to ongoing changes.[2]

In this broad analysis, three general areas of argument or issues will be presented and debated:

1. cults as traditional adaptive and innovative mechanisms in change processes;
2. cults as responses to foreign experiences and phenomena, for example, whites and white civilization;
3. cults as a mission to establishing the truth and the way.

Given this general outline, let us now examine the Baigona and Taro cults.

## THE BAIGONA OR SNAKE CULT

The first cult movement of any sort recorded by Europeans in Papua New Guinea was the Milne Bay prophet movement of 1893.[3] It was some years before other movements were reported. Around 1911 the Baigona or snake cult was reported.[4] This cult was of particular importance to the Orokaiva because, although founded among the members of the Winiafi clan near Wanigela (see map, p. 51), a people living on the extreme south of the Northern Province, it spread as far north as the Binandere in the extreme north and to the inland Orokaiva peoples. Hence it affected most of the Orokaiva. (*Baigona* in the Ubir language, the speakers of which allegedly originated the cult, refers to a woman describing her female counterpart. It is the opposite of *Auou*, a term specially used among males to address their male companions.[5] To discover why and how Baigona, a word meaning "woman," came to be used in the cult would require further study. It is not my intention to delve into terminological analysis here; my main aim is to describe social activities and to analyze the major beliefs behind them.)

Baigona was said to have been started by Maine, a member of the Winiafi clan near Wanigela.[6] Maine was said to have ascended to the summit of Mt. Keroro (Mt. Victory) where he was killed and his heart "smoked."[7] It is said that a snake was responsible for this ritual act.[8] Hence Maine was initiated into the "mysteries of Baigona science, and given certain medicines that would cure old diseases."[9] On completion of the act, he was allowed to return to his village, not only to practice the newly acquired knowledge but also to spread it far and wide throughout his neighborhood. This he accomplished quite successfully with his disciples or Baigona men.[10]

Maine's prophecies and beliefs varied but they mainly concerned agricultural and curative knowledge. The religious and ritual ceremonies he advocated were directed first toward agricultural activities (food production, control of climatic conditions, especially rain), and second toward ensuring protection against sickness and death. Because a snake was responsible for initiating Maine, all snakes were held sacred and were not allowed to be killed. The killing of snakes was thought to result in heavy rain and subsequent flooding, something most people wanted to avoid because of the major rivers that surrounded their villages. Insofar as illness and other calamities were concerned, the Baigona men (that is, the prophet and his followers or converts), assisted those who suffered and who required medication. The curing process consisted mainly in using betel nut and prescribed herbs and ginger, which had been chewed into a compound to massage evil substances out of the patients.[11] Cures were carried out in elaborate and dignified ceremonies.

The most important ritual required in all the practices or ceremonies was a special dance called *Poroga*. *Poroga* literally means "cloud." During the healing process, either young men would beat their drums, singing songs around the patient while the Baigona doctor performed his work, or else lines

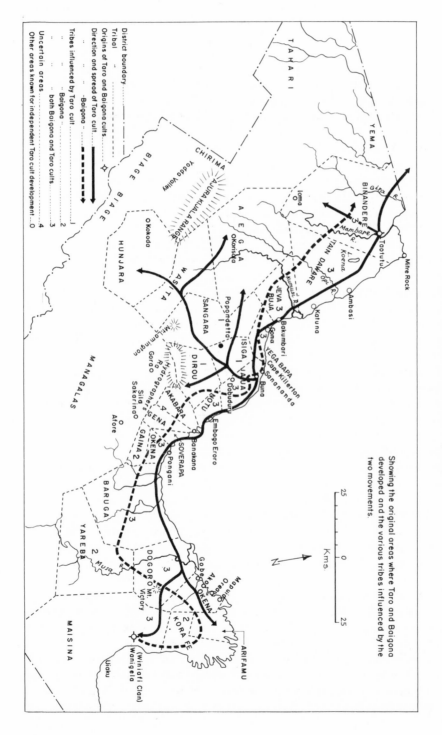

# THE NORTHERN DISTRICT, PAPUA

Showing the original areas where Taro and Baigona
developed and the various tribes influenced by the
two movements.

Kms.

25 0 25

**Key (legend):**

| | |
|---|---|
| District boundary | ......... |
| Tribal | ......... |
| Origins of Taro and Baigona cults | ......... ☆ |
| Direction and spread of Taro cult: | |
| Baigona | ⟶ |
| Tribes influenced by Taro cult | ......... |
| Baigona | ......... 2 |
| both Baigona and Taro cults | ......... 3 |
| Uncertain areas | ......... 4 |
| Other areas known for independent Taro cult development | ......... O |

**Labels on map:**

TAHARI
YEMA
CHIRIMA
BIAGE
BIAGE
Yodda Valley
KUMUSI RANGE
O Kokoda
HUNJARA
MANAGALAS
AEGA
O Okorosia
WASITA
SANGARA
Popondetta
MELANGIN
Hydrographer's Ra.
Goro
DIROU
AKABARA
GENA
O'OKENA
GAINA 2
Sila Sakaringo
O Afore
BARUGA
YAREBA
Musa
MAISINA
Uiaku
DOGORO Mt. Victory
OKENA
KORA FE
(Winiaffi Clan) Wanigela
ARIFAMU
Gobege
Akogunu
O Mapuno
Oreresi
SOVERAPA
O Pongani
Sanakana
Embogo Eroro
O Dobuduru
TOTU
'ISIGA I VAUA'
JEVA 3
BUJA
YEGA BAPA
Gona
Cape Killerton
Sanananda
Bakumbori
Buna
Kumusi R.
ITAIN DAWARE
L. Koena
Mambare R.
Opie R.
BINANDERE
Gira R.
Tootutu
Mitre Rock
Ambasi
Katuna
IOMA

of drummers would accompany the doctor while others danced. The Anglican Bishop Copland King's observation of a Baigona doctor enlightens us as to this important Baigona ritual:

> He [the Baigona doctor] gave the patient various herbs to take in differ-
> ent ways. Another thing [herb] was soaked in the water and the water
> drunk. Another was made into a lotion in which he washed. Then Eroro
> [the doctor] chewed betel nut [with possibly other ingredients], and the
> red matter was plastered all over the sick man's body. Then, while an
> assistant stood behind him chewing ginger and spluttering it all over the
> place and yelling out in sympathy, Eroro knelt in front and snatched at
> the man's body with finger and thumb, pulling the red mass off and
> calling "Baigona, come out! Baigona, come out!" at the top of his voice.
> This naturally exhausted the patient. Some leaves were given to him to
> stuff up his nose and the treatment ended.[12]

## OFFICIAL ATTITUDES TOWARD BAIGONA

Baigona was stopped by the authorities in 1914,[13] but the reasons advanced for doing so were actually unjustified in view of official policies regarding the customs of local peoples. "It has been the policy of the Administration," runs a government report, "not to interfere in native customs except where the custom is obviously harmful or repugnant."[14]

Baigona was really a fertility cult. Since the people were agriculturalists and lived near the tributaries of big rivers, the cults naturally emphasized rain. Their efforts to cure the sick and dying formed a significant part of their duty to maintain the well-being of their society. There were no signs of external influence on Baigona, nor was it a millenarian, cargoist movement. It was clearly traditional, originating from traditional experiences and background. Peter Worsley, even with his crude analysis of the beliefs behind the cult, sensed this:

> On the whole the cult appears to have been characterized by the use of
> simple traditional types of magical techniques for the solution of limited
> and minor personal problems. It was also passive, having no millenarian
> goal or expectation, and tended to lay the responsibility for the misfor-
> tunes of life at the door of the people themselves.[15]

Colonial authorities had come to grips with the traditional importance of Baigona. A. E. Oelrichs, the Resident Magistrate of the time, found it hard to decide whether to eradicate it or not "because they only had drugs that are beneficial. It is a very subtle move on the part of Maine, because how can the government interfere under these circumstances?"[16] He found it impossible to get witnesses to give evidence against the Baigona men or to lay charges. Oelrichs himself might even have been converted to Baigona; he admits that when a snake was killed by a Mr. Oates, the rain fell despite the fact that it was a fine day.[17]

It was hard for both mission and government, then, to find reasons for removing the movement. This is evident in Oelrich's forced justification:

> The people recognize that the men themselves have nothing in the way of drugs to harm them, but they fear the Baigona itself which is all powerful and is quick to revenge anything done to one of its people.[18]

It was surely not possible for him to prove such a fear was shared by the people, but the authorities sought to rationalize their suppression of the cult.

Governor Murray (Governor of Papua, 1907–1940) saw Baigona as a threat to his rule because the movement was developing a large following. Given the uncertain relationship between natives and whites, Baigona's influence among so many tribes seemed dangerous. He concluded: "Baigona is interesting as far as the growth of the movement—which is developing into a new religion before our eyes—is concerned, but there is a danger that it may develop into systematic extortion."[19] They saw Baigona thought as stemming from indigenous beliefs, and therefore government officials were afraid it would develop an undercurrent of rebellion. Because of this, many Baigona men were sent to prison.[20] When E. W. Chinnery (A. R. M. Mambare) brought fifteen Baigona men before the court, he described them as "the most cunning rogues with a craving for power."[21]

The traditional spiritual possession exhibited in trances, fits, and speaking in tongues worried the government. All this was just unacceptable, and, as one statement reads,

> The administration advanced as a principal reason for the suppression of the Baigona movement its use of thoroughly obnoxious paroxysms of a peculiarly horrible nature.[22]

In other words, the spiritual, mental, and physical expressions of the people that were typical of their ritual performances were considered dangerous to their health, or abnormal and insane.

The government was concerned about the political and sociopsychological implications of the movement, but the Anglican Church saw Baigona as a "superstitious and a rival religion, cribbing certain practices from Christianity but offering no material or tangible gain."[23] King was especially critical because he thought he had seen Baigona members baptizing and giving new names to the cult's adherents. He maintained that it was a heathen cult, arguing strongly:

> Some people talk about using the native beliefs as a stepping stone to Christian teaching. I, on the other hand, am rather pleased to have something which I can show is entirely opposed to Christianity. The quitting of a heathen cult is a great step to take. It means more than a

simple enquiring into Christianity because there is something else. The Baigona took up certain practices cribbed from us . . . they baptized their people and gave new names. The whole matter is extraordinarily interesting.[24]

Because of their experience with Baigona, government officials and missionaries kept watch for other movements of a similar nature. After this movement was brought under control, in fact, strong warnings were issued to field staff to watch for future outbreaks. One such statement read:

The further development of the Baigona movement will be carefully watched, for it may be of great value in throwing light upon the origin of other similar movements, although of course, an allowance must be made for the influence which Christianity and foreign civilization in general must infallibly exercise upon many of the details.[25]

Then came the Taro cult, at a time when the church and the government were prepared to go all-out to deal with any traditional or semitraditional religious or ritual movement.

## THE TARO OR JIPARI CULT

When the Taro cult was first observed in 1919 among the Orokaiva and reported, the government anthropologist F. E. Williams was given the task of studying it.[26] Among other things, his study was to "determine how much good 'was in the new activities,' and how much evil, and to decide what treatment they deserved at the hands of the government."[27] This was because, like Baigona, "the cult has occurred with such a frequency and has exerted so wide and powerful an influence upon the natives"[28] that it was regarded as dangerous. Williams's report noted the popularity, influence, and expansion of the movement among the Orokaiva:

It has so far made a more general appeal and displayed greater tenacity than any other of the new religious cults of Papua.[29]

Indeed the cult had spread as far inland as the Hydrographer's Valley inhabited by people quite distinct from the Orokaiva and along the southern coast as far as Wanigela and Uiaku, where Baigona had been born.[30]

The Taro cult, like Baigona, was founded by a prophet. His name was Buninia, and through a visionary dream he became possessed by the Taro spirits (ancestral spirits).[31] The major revelation in this encounter was of rites that would ensure an ample taro crop and generally fertile gardens. The penalty for not performing these rituals was the ultimate destruction of crops.[32]

While the agents of the cult's dissemination were Buninia's disciples, especially Yaviripa and Yavevi,[33] countless individual prophets also emerged who claimed personal inspirations and initiation from specific Taro spirits (such as *Gaiva, Ovivi, Porove, Orori*.[34] From them, new cults took their names. Other related cults, though also initiated by Taro spirits, took their names from some physical detail. *Diroga (Riroga)*, for instance, a cult that was prominent among some coastal and inland Orokaiva (the Jaua and the Waseta), manifested itself by the carrying of and dancing with spears (*kiembo*). This ritual symbol made it a movement quite distinct from others.[35] *Diroga* or *Riroga-bari*, incidentally, meant pay-back killing in its original sense.

Among the Orokaiva of the central and southern regions the *Hohora* or rooster cult was important, its major ritual being a distinctive dance in imitation of the roosters.[36] Other coastal and inland Orokaiva followed the *Eriri* or rainbow cult, initiated by Aragata and extolling the spirit of Orori Taro. Its followers carried spears as symbols in their ritual dances.[37] Still others, such as the Sebaga Andere, one of the coastal Jaua, the *Gaiva*, and *Kekesi*, believed the Taro spirits to be important.[38]

A plethora of related cults emerged soon after the original movement did.[39] This was not surprising since there were so many species of taro among the Orokaiva. Because of this multiplicity of taro types[40] numerous movements could arise independently without direct influence from the Taro prophet Buninia. They appeared to Williams like sects and variant cults worth exploring individually.[41]

Like the Baigona, however, in which *Poroga* was an important dance ritual, the Taro cults also had a main ritual in common—a dance called *kasamba*. With the exception of the Riroga and Eriri activities, in which spears and weapons were prominent, most Taro cults used drums (*sino*) extensively.[42] Whereas the more mobile Riroga and Eriri dances were entertaining and were gracefully performed, *kasamba* dancing was usually performed in one of three positions—standing, kneeling, or sitting. *Kasamba* was in fact unique; it did not resemble any traditional Orokaiva dance-drama.[43] The songs composed by the Taro prophets, as well as the style and manner of their performance were unique. They were classified as new and foreign.[44] Integral to the dance ritual, furthermore, and an essential part of the cermony, was *Jipari*. *Jipari* means "to shake" or "tremble" in the Orokaiva language. Shaking fits and speaking in tongues (or speaking in unintelligible languages either through excitement or as part of their ritual obligations) were common features of these cults.

## OFFICIAL ATTITUDES TO THE TARO CULT

Williams conceded that the cult was not particularly radical, and not so millenarian as to disappoint its followers with unfulfilled promises.[45] The cult gave no evidence of anti-white feeling, and it seemed to him to be "independent both originally and ideologically."[46] He did emphasize the fact that it was potentially political,[47] though to what extent he did not say.

The movement's critics took it to be animistic,[48] and as a result attempts were made to persuade the people to abandon the practices. Strong measures were taken against the prophets for "so long as the prophets exist, similar cults will occur from time to time."⁴⁹

Although Williams's study was meant to be "more description than analysis"⁵⁰ and to allow his readers to draw their own conclusions,⁵¹ his report was pro-government. He was clearly looking for characteristics in the cult that could give sufficient excuse, cause, or reason to suppress it. He also represented the view that cults in Melanesia emerged as a result of socioeconomic factors due to white influence and civilization.⁵² *Jipari*, or shaking fits, speaking in tongues, dreams and visions of the prophet(s), let alone *kasamba*, the dance ritual, were all worrying, if not evil. Williams even took *Jipari* and speaking in tongues "to be violently contagious and . . . caused by an imbalanced nervous organization."⁵³ The tongues spoken were unintelligible— and thus, madness.⁵⁴ He argued that in the long run the cultic activity would cause wasting and physical deterioration.⁵⁵ As for the prophetic aspect, it was "based on a baseless fabric of dreams or even the hallucinations of the insane."⁵⁶ He recommended that the authorities take certain measures. He suggested that education would get rid of *Jipari*. The people could be persuaded that it was shameful. He maintained that it should be treated as a disease or a form of madness, and that anyone who practiced it should be removed to hospital and kept under temporary supervision.⁵⁷ Williams concluded that the Taro cult was an "undesirable practice and should if possible be stamped out."⁵⁸

With regard to the various ceremonial practices of the cult, he argued that they were either derived from white culture⁵⁹ or had nothing constructive to offer to Orokaiva society. Against the people's claim that the cult promoted the fertility of the land, he maintained:

> We have seen that the ostensible purpose of the cult is to promote the fertility of the garden. In reality, the rites which are most directly aimed at this result seem on the whole useless and in one or two cases destructive.⁶⁰

This criticism stemmed from the fact that *kasamba* dances were actually performed in the gardens, where the Taro leaders gave their blessings and enacted rituals to enhance new growth. Stamping on the ground or on the crops was an essential part of the ritual, but it undoubtedly appeared destructive and detrimental.⁶¹

Other things worried outside observers. Old leaders in traditional societies were said to have been challenged by the cult leaders, and it was feared that older ceremonial dances would suffer a serious setback.⁶² In addition, the people spent much of their time and effort on the cult activities instead of attending to government and mission duties. Since so many cult leaders apparently ceased working in the gardens and lived on the expense and labor of their fellows, it was concluded that they were trying to adopt the roles, status, and lifestyle of government officials—sitting down and commanding others to do physical work for them. The destruction of the crops and the prophecies connected with it[63] looked like a ritual preparation for receiving the white settlers' cargo from ships.[64]

So much of the description by Williams and his contemporaries was in the interests of colonial authorities. They made little or no effort to analyze the ritualistic or symbolic essence of the numerous ceremonies. Thus the outsiders' evaluation was neither fair, objective, nor balanced.

## TARO AND BAIGONA:
## AN ASSESSMENT AND ANALYSIS OF BELIEFS

The approach of Williams and his contemporaries was highly selective and indeed "defective" in its pursuit of sabotage and elimination. They inevitably made mistakes because they operated on false assumptions. They thought *Kesi*, for example, to be the name of a ship in the *Kekesi* cult,[65] and they latched on to many ritual phrases in "unknown tongues," which they suspected to be from foreign influences: "halleluyah" or something similar; "a shun man" or "shun shen sha"; "alleluah sal omi"; military-sounding commands to get people to the gardens;[66] the slogan "Alla same Jesus Christ" (all same government);[67] "kaikai" for "kikia"[68] and "eating with forks."[69] These are a few examples illustrating the selective, defective, and distorting nature of the white observers' approach.

Although the Taro cult was reported to have been completely wiped out by 1928,[70] in fact it left behind a rich culture and a way of life (in many ways different from previous habits) that can help us uncover the errors of the older commentators.

*Kaikai* for *kikia* led to a complete misapprehension. *Kikia* sounds like *kaikai*, which means "to eat." Actually *kikia* or *Akikia* (the correct pronunciation is *Akikia; kikia* may have been a shortened form) is not *kaikai*. It is an important ritual chorus recited or prescribed by Taro prophets to obtain maximum physical and mental control of their followers in anticipation of *Jipari* or the shaking fit.[71]

*Kesi* of the Kekesi cult noted earlier also indicates this dramatic experience. Westerners described *Kesi* as a ship,[72] but they also saw a special eating habit in the use of carved forks to eat taro in the *kekesi* rituals. *Kesi* and the use of the forks were the perfect combination to fit the white theory of outside influence! To the Orokaiva, however, eating in the manner described was a long-established tradition, and they would have been insulted to have been told otherwise. The tradition was particularly important for the magicians and sorcerers at the time of their initiation or before some act of magic or sorcery,[73] when they followed strict dietary regulations and eating habits. This habit continued, yet unlike past practice, it was no longer restricted only to sorcerers or magicians. It became an important ritual for *kasamba*, the Taro dance and the feasts accompanying it. At the beginning of the *bondo* (feast) and *kasamba*, a few taro were selected and cooked by the members of the host village. After the taro was cooked, it was carefully sliced into small portions and distributed among the guests who had arrived for the ceremony. The visitors had to pick up the sliced pieces with special forks similar to those used by sorcerers. These were made from either black palm or ribs of coconuts and sago leaves. The ceremonial slicing of taro into pieces is called *Kesisi*.[74]

As indicated earlier, the feasting and dancing, let alone the exhaustion and destruction of gardens and the accompanying rituals, were regarded by outsiders as a waste of time, an irrational activity. It seemed like a ritual act meant to destroy traditional property in order to secure the arrival of the white settlers' goods. In reality, however, most rituals had objectives quite contrary to the motives so attributed to them. Part of the *kasamba*, for instance, was performed in a sitting position, all the participants singing *kasamba* songs in accompaniment to the drums (*sino*). The ritual significance relates to the fertility of the taro plant. Taro should sprout upwards with healthy leaves, but the tuber (*babe*) could only grow sitting well in the ground. In Orokaiva garden ritual the people would utter "O' ha anubeio, O' taro sit'."If the taro does not sit firmly on the ground it will produce more leaves instead of a large tuber. Similarly, it appeared destructive that young taro suckers were destroyed by dancing and stamping on the plots, but the Orokaiva believed that by physical contact with the new plants, or by throwing taro or banana suckers down on the ground, one awakened the plants' spirits so that they would grow faster, be healthier, and mature more quickly than otherwise.

That all this was a waste of time, energy, and community resources simply is not true.[75] Traditionally those participating in special ritual ceremonies had to abstain from ordinary physical activities. They observed a strict diet, eating little and drinking boiled coconut juice instead of water. This was acceptable to the community. Those involved did not just sit there, enjoying life at the expense of the people, as if anticipating a time when *kiap-kanaka* ("ruler-ruled") relationships would be reversed.

Furthermore, the destruction of property and the numerous feasts during which food supplies are exhausted are not unusual. In some Melanesian societies such events occur annually and may last for days, weeks, or even a month.[76] In others they may occur randomly—perhaps over intervals of many years—but the communal feasts last for months.[77] A great feast might appear to exhaust completely the food resources of the people; in reality it is a justified investment guaranteeing security, confidence, and the prospect for future prosperity. In the fertility ritual the people offered praise and thanksgiving to the spirits to mark the end of a successful (or particular) period and the beginning of a new life and adventure. In the case of the Orokaiva, initiations, death feasts, and other ceremonies took place annually because taro (*ba*) normally took one year (*duberi*) to mature. And with their concept that success and prosperity depended so much on *kando*—that is, on giving away, sharing—the exhaustion of their resources every year was a normal practice and an acceptable part of life.

The prophets of the cults cannot be said to have been mad, insane, or confused. They did not emerge from nowhere, but had preconceived plans, and these corresponded with their group's desires and aspirations at a particular point in time. This was why the people accepted the leaders, their prophecies, rituals, and instructions, and took them all very seriously. The language spoken and the words used in the composition of various *kasamba* songs, though at times difficult to understand, had meaning. Had they been unintelligible or unfulfilling, the songs would not have been learned, understood, or appreciated, nor for that matter would they have survived so long among the Orokaiva.[78]

Not everyone is expected to be a prophetic leader. Not everyone is a dreamer or visionary who comes into contact with spiritual phenomena miraculously—whether it be dead ancestors or animals—at a time when the revelation of rituals and spiritual power for cultural innovation is necessary. Dreams, visions, and spiritual contacts are not to be taken lightly. For the Orokaiva they are disclosures of reality. Why should we take them to be gestures of the confused? There are many communication channels between human beings and their surroundings; there are means of interaction between the known and the unknown, the living and the dead, the physical and the spiritual, the spiritual and the supernatural world. What is more, prophets or cult leaders were considered spiritual beings because they were believed to have become *binei*, spirits or spirits of the dead. They were no longer natural beings but were both natural and supernatural (spirit-being), enjoying the privileges of both worlds. In other words, by miracle or initiation, they have become so special, powerful, sacred, and even potentially cruel, that they no longer lived normal lives. Thus they would serve the community or alternatively could try to break down the community and turn it in a new direction, depending on the given situation. This helps to explain the extraordinary autonomy of the leaders and the respect they enjoyed from their followers.

The adoption of new names by prophets and the conferring of such on their followers was nothing new; it was an established part of the Orokaiva culture. To name was to have power and strength. Names did not come out of the blue. The community, clan, or tribe ensured that their offspring were named after their ancestors or clan or tribal chiefs in order to maintain continuity. Naming was related to the laws of succession, to land right, and to property inheritance, so of course parents were carefully selective about choosing their children's names.

The desire among the Orokaiva to obtain new names from abroad, particularly from distinguished warriors among enemy tribes, was a common feature of ongoing tribal conflict. An Orokaiva warrior would often attempt to capture and kill enemy fight-leaders or warriors in order to obtain two trophies: the name (*javo*) and the heart (*gamo-poporo*). He would confer the name(s) on his young warrior(s), and these young men would roast and feast on the heart(s) of the enemy. The practice of obtaining the names of victims seemed to have also served as a count or record of wins over the enemy. It was part of an important ritual. The ceremonial eating of the heart and adoption of new names were symbolic. They endowed the recipients with the power, strength, wisdom, and all the identifiable qualities of their namesake. This was vital, and it is why a captured victim would immediately know his fate. It was in fact the practice for the captive to give his name, tribe, clan, recall the number of people he had killed (if possible naming them individually), and then insult his captors by insisting on his own quick death.

Thus even if some names of persons or objects in the Taro and Baigona cults were apparently of European origin, this is not to be construed as "misguided." The people probably had good reasons for taking such names, and the rationale was traditional, not foreign. To allege that the people copied a Christian confirmation ceremony, for instance, is absurd and denies the people's own culture and their ability to respond to different situations.

The Taro and Baigona cults were traditional religious movements of vital significance. Of a non-millenarian nature, they were simply devoted to the prosperity of the Orokaiva. The *jipari, kasamba,* and various other rituals embodied in the cults had positive and beneficial effects. Among other things, it was widely accepted that these rituals produced ample food, particularly taro. Edmond Donoba, a Gaiva prophet of the Sebaga Andere who supported the Taro movements, stated that "there was more taro and more food" as a result of them.[79] In fact, some of the Orokaiva people of Kokoda revived Taro cult activity in 1924, when they had a severe taro shortage. This shows how important the Taro cult was to the people.[80] Since few radical changes in Orokaiva dance and drama have taken place apart from the innovations brought by these cults, and since certain eating habits derived from the cults' rituals and tabus for planting, harvesting, and feasting are still maintained, we can see how significant the movements still are to the people.[81] This leaves us with some interesting issues to consider.

I consider these issues under four headings: social change, foreign influences, the impetus to missionize, and the role of symbols. I would like now to discuss them as general issues and not as pertaining to the Orokaiva people alone.

## CENTRAL ISSUES

*1. Cults as traditional adaptive and innovative mechanisms in the process of social change.* Change is a universal phenomenon. As changes begin, develop, reach a climax, and recede people experience them and react to the situations they bring. It is unnatural for people or communities to be unresponsive to change. The people coped with change in Melanesia by means of ritual and thus eventually assimilated and incorporated the new idea into the overall repertoire of their traditional culture.[82] The need to renew, review, or explore new supernatural formulas in ritual response to a particular situation is an important part of Melanesian culture. Melanesian societies were not static—as one is often led to believe—but dynamic, with room for maneuvering and flexibility.[83] Hence, ritual change, experiments with new magic and sorcery substances, the application of new practices and techniques—all often deriving from dreams, visions, and spiritual revelations—were common and clearly traditional throughout Melanesia.

It is often argued that the so-called cargo cults in Melanesia occurred because of the arrival of whites and their civilization. According to this view, confusion, envy, or the desire to obtain material wealth and power precipitated Melanesian cult activities. If Melanesians swallow this distinctly expatriate approach, they are virtually treating themselves as a kind of recent migrant, or as if they had begun to exist as total beings only recently, unable to adapt or to develop in themselves qualities of life or insights necessary for the creation of a worthwhile, civilized society.

This type of preconception is all too prevalent. Many Melanesians have come to think that traditionally their peoples were not truly social, political, or religious beings nor able to interact wholesomely with others. "Cannibals," "savages," and "primitives" are terms expressing the whites' attitude toward the indigenous cultures, and they set an unfortunate precedent for modern Melanesian self-consciousness. Hence even Melanesians can find it hard to accept that certain important and interesting practices are original to them, without reference to white influences.

Cults and religious ceremonies were hardly new. They were crucial means of responding to ongoing changes and of sustaining continuity. Feasts and dances, through which goods and services were exchanged, payments and tribute offered to ancestors, initiation ceremonies carried out—all were familiar practices. They were part and parcel of the religious cult activities. Similarly, when any society experienced natural disasters—epidemics, floods, or calamities of comparable nature—traditional religious and ritual approaches were applied, or new ones explored and initiated in response to these situations. In these cases the chances of applying new ritual and religious formulas were very good. The fact remains, however, that while the outward rituals might have been innovative, the general practice and approach were almost always neither new nor foreign, but an original part of the people's cultural and religious life. Melanesian societies, we must stress, were dynamic and flexible; not only were the people able to reach for new ways and means when the original religious and ritual responses failed or proved unproductive, but the rate and frequency of religious innovation and adaptive cult activity in these societies were quite high.

2. *Cults as response to foreign experience and phenomena; whites and their civilization.* Let me illustrate some of my previous observations under a new heading. When the first white persons came to Orokaiva and Binandere country, they brought with them a thing called soap. On it were engraved two words: P-U-R-E S-O-A-P. Some of my ancestors thought, "Well, this is our clan." Among the people there was an Orobe clan called *Pure.* While this might have been a coincidence, the people were confident that they had now finally found some clue to their questions about whites. Not only were the people envious about the whites' material wealth but, more importantly, they were curious about their superior strength and fighting ability. It had not been long

before that their warriors had been beaten and humiliated.[84] The whites' supremacy and indeed their physical appearance raised unsolved mysteries. There was something weird about the whole thing!

To me this attitude indicates a highly sensitive, sophisticated, indeed healthy progression. The people were able to confront a situation that was both mysterious and unknown and relate and explain it in terms of their overall physical, spiritual, and cosmic world. There is nothing sinful, heretical, or mad about their approach; it was quite normal and acceptable. After all, what a Melanesian sees and treasures as important is not necessarily the same as what the white sees, feels, interprets, and understands to be important. Both score equal points because both are culturally biased. The invading whites win in the end because of their suppressive policies, leaving the Melanesians terribly dissatisfied, yet more inquisitive and determined to pursue their inquiry further. This dissatisfaction and discouragement have often led to other developments, in which the responses become more aggressive, rebellious, anti-white, and millenarian, although even these still remain part of the adaptive process, the traditional way of handling ongoing changes.

The early cults or movements were traditionally inspired and oriented, "natural" religious and ritual approaches to changes in their societies, but the consistent suppressive policies and attitudes of whites made it impossible to maintain older forms and functions. Instead, Melanesians adopted a new strategy, and although traditional beliefs remained relatively undisturbed, ceremonial practices, organization, and orientation of the newer movements were changed to accommodate the new challenges. Newer cults became, as stated earlier, rebellious, anti-white, and millenarian. During this later phase, a concern for the whites' cargo and material wealth manifested itself. We should not interpret this as a rejection of the past in favor of the new. Ritualistic and symbolic attempts to procure cargo were really just a part of the Melanesians' continuing inquiry into how a group can overcome the frustrations and struggles of its day.

In some cases Melanesians were willing to accept what was offered by the whites as a possible solution to the growing number of problems in the post-contact situation. In the Madang area, for instance, law and order had the backing of both mission teaching and government policy (and many Melanesians accepted the colonial order because of this connection). Yet when experience proved later that "toeing the line" failed to resolve their problems or adequately adapt them to the changing needs and requirements of the day, they responded, often aggressively.

The Siar insurrection of 1904 in Madang is a classic example.[85] The people of Siar, Riwo, Garaged, and Biliar had accepted the German Lutheran missionaries. Suddenly the government decided to drive them off their land. Forced labor and land alienation were also at fault, but dissatisfaction with the performance of the Christian church to which they were originally attracted was the major reason for the uprising. The people complained that, although they had accepted Christianity at the expense of their traditional religious and ritual beliefs and practices, Christianity had failed to fulfill its obligations, let alone satisfy the peoples' aspirations. Whereas in the past many gods represented particular aspects of human lives and the environment (gods/spirits of the garden, rivers, seas, mountains, bushes, each with its own distinctive religious and ritual characteristics and each responsive and answerable to the people), the one God of the Christian religion was seen to be inadequate and had failed significantly. The people therefore wanted to revert to their original religion. The Mission refused to allow this and this led to a crisis and the revolt.

It must be emphasized that a cargoist and millenarian mentality should not be taken as a confused, misconceptualizing, even envious attempt by Melanesians to obtain the whites' culture and civilization. Each movement should be analyzed carefully, looking for the kinds of adaptation that reflect the repertoires of the past. Cargo cults were not really deviations from age-old methods of problem solving. The *Asisi* (Spirit) cult of the Orokaiva in the 1930s, which involved mass killings of pigs and followed prophecies that were millenarian, hostile, and cargoist, is an example of a movement in that direction.[86] When the original Taro movement among the Orokaiva was suppressed, they had to take a new stand.

3. *Cults as missions to establish the truth and the way.* Even after the people had tried to accommodate to the expatriates' civilization, white authorities seemed reluctant to accept Melanesian attitudes and approaches. There seemed no logic in white attitudes, and thus further inquiry became an urgent task for the Melanesians. The people had, in their view, done all they could, to no avail. They could only conclude that there must be something wrong, weird, or secret about the whole colonial situation.

Melanesians had had contacts among their own racial and cultural groups for generations through trade, warfare, and migrations, but their contact with whites and their civilization was unique. Whites were racially different, physically and culturally superior. Such differences posed deep questions as to the whites' origins and presence. Some took whites as spirits of their dead ancestors or as culture heroes, and therefore felt obliged to assist and cooperate with them out of fear. Others took them simply as human, treating them as such from the outset. Whatever the responses and reactions, one thing was obvious: the ultimate defeat of the Melanesians and the consequent new lifestyle, with the distinct cultural, ethical, moral, and religious standards, would have to be accepted and observed by the people. Despite this, however, we can detect a search for the "truth and the way" in the Orokaiva religious cult activities at the threshold of a new time.

Foreign opposition or condemnation of their initiatives was viewed by the people as a kind of sabotage, as attempts to prevent Melanesians from discerning the truth or the secret about new mysterious experiences. Anti-white, cargoist, and millenarianist reactions were early alternatives, yet as time went on, people became still more inquisitive and demanded the *truth* (or the sources of the truth) and the *way* to everything. They wanted to analyze the parts in order to understand the whole, and interaction with the missions made them look to particular parts of their tradition and to the Bible to explore possible relationships.

It is therefore not surprising to find some Melanesians, such as the Paliau of Baluan Island (New Guinea), accepting the Bible and proceeding through it thoroughly and systematically to see if there were any resemblances between their traditional religion and Christianity.[87] The Bible came to be a resource base for their enquiry into truth. Not only did the Bible reveal information about creation (a subject of vital importance considering Melanesian interest in the whites' origins) but it contained humanitarian principles as well— compassion, equality, and so on. These principles demanded close examination because, while the whites' civilization seemed to derive from the one source, there were enormous differences between the policies of the church and those of the government, each apparently representing different moral standards. The Mission seemed to be more generous and its teaching offered the best explanations and reassurances. Not only did the Bible uphold and prophesy a good and attractive way of life, but there were also points of continuity in Melanesian tradition and in the biblical message (as the Paliau discovered). Given this continuity, Melanesian thinkers supposed that fundamental principles governed both Melanesian and biblical traditions. Thus they could use both biblical and traditional means to inquire and establish facts about the origin of whites and their differences. The matter at stake was the search for truth and the path to it. However imperfect and questionable their arguments, they were out to solve a genuine puzzle. Let us probe this matter further.

4. *Cults and the role of symbols and symbolism.* One characteristic common to Melanesians is self-consciousness or caution. They take care and reassure themselves before they leap. They are wary of offending another or even the spirits by some impetuous comment. In other words, they are selective in their choice of words and in the way they approach each other. Every network of social and kin relationship in the community is governed by carefully defined or prescribed patterns of social behavior. Special modes of speech govern the approach to one's brothers- and sisters-in-law, to parents-in-law, and so on. Any violation of these tabus brings heavy penalties: death by sorcery, misfortune incited by spirits, or fines in the form of feast contributions. Constant vigilance is necessary, then, even with people in whom one has implicit faith.

The Orokaiva have a saying: "Your brother is your killer; never trust him. He is the last person in your company of companions." Your brother-in-law, even though he comes from another tribe, is the one expected to have the highest respect for you. This is still a cherished understanding today. We fear our brothers more than we do our other relatives, even though we respect each other. "One that eats with you in the same pot, sleeps with you on the same mat is your killer," goes the Orokaiva proverb, a saying that expresses the uncertainties or curiosities we have about each other.

Consequently, the Orokaiva have a system of checks and balances to ensure safety and confidentiality. We have in our tradition, for instance, various symbols and signs used in linguistic expressions. These may be paralleled with the biblical parables. The appropriate Orokaiva term is *enia-ge* and literally means "hidden language" or "hidden truth." If somebody calls you "smart," "bright," "handsome," "good-looking," you do not immediately accept the compliment; rather, you assess yourself and the other thoroughly to test if the statement is valid, and if the one complimenting you might in fact be saying the opposite—that you are unkind, selfish, and introverted. Similarly, a reference to your kindness and hospitality might really be advice for you—to pull yourself together or bear the consequences.

An Orokaiva, then, does not accept any verbal or physical expression (an angry look, let us say) at its face value, but ponders it from two opposing views before arriving at a decision as to its true meaning. A person who is kind and hospitable could be as bad as a person who is not. Each has his or her own motives. Indeed, we are likely to be more suspicious of a person who is generally good, generous, and hospitable than of one who is generally bad and hostile. Good is bad and bad is good among the Orokaiva and one cannot be too selective or cautious!

I was once asked by my grandfather—a magician of some repute—to accompany him to the garden. I accompanied him in the belief that he was going to teach me some of his magical powers (with vines, trees, leaves) because he so rarely asked me or other members of the family to accompany him on his walks. After scouting the forest and the jungle, we returned home. On our return, he asked me if I had seen, noted, and located all the things he had shown me. I was surprised at this and asked him to repeat himself. "Oh!" he replied, "didn't you know that you were taken specially to see certain things of importance which I use?" I admitted that I was aware of that and said I was not shown appropriate trees, shrubs, vines, and other paraphernalia, except in odd cases when I remembered his utterances on short and apparently unrelated matters. He rebuked me: "Sorry, but you have just had your turn! The next opportunity will not come for some time!"[88]

You can imagine how I felt! But at least I learned a fundamental point. In our little adventure, almost all communication was by sign or symbol. I remembered him tramping on a vine and falling, breaking a branch of a tree, asking me to verify the name of a bird whose voice we could hear from a distance, and so on. I failed to take serious account of these things because I assumed that there was nothing new or unusual about them. But he had made special gestures of communicating important knowledge and skills to a potential inheritor.

The thinking behind symbolic expressions is that if anything is sacred or important it has to be maintained in a hidden form. This not only ensures its vitality, but also avoids both the chances of unauthorized dissemination by potential inheritors and the possibility of outsiders obtaining the knowledge. Symbolism also implies confidence, discipline, trust, and patience in the potential successor. The secret is inviolable. If potential successors give away something of what they have learned because of bribery or temptation, they can only give a part or an exaggerated version of the reality. The truth is still hidden, and they—as the Orokaiva say—have only imparted half (*mendo*) or none (*puti*) of it.

Colonialism and modernization have had an impact on Melanesia—serious effects at some levels and limited material consequences at the village level. The impact has been like one great nonverbal mystery, a symbolic form or *enia*, to use the Orokaiva term. The truth has been hidden, so the search for the way to the secret was pressing. The search has often been manifested in religious and cult activities.

The essential function of all the activities from traditionalist cults to anti-white, cargoist, and millenarian movements is the same. The problem of the coming of the whites is crucial. The resources of traditional knowledge, however, have never been forgotten. Ideas were circulating that the whites were deceiving the people by hiding the truth, the core, the meat, and only exposing *puti* (the "empty skin" or "shell"). Many argue that resorting to traditional institutions and activities would eventually bring the right understanding. For them patience and the performance of proper rituals have been paramount, and they insist that the inquiry can never reach reality unless it involves the traditional spirits.

In conclusion, we should note that cult activities of the Melanesians reflect their access to a rich body of religious knowledge. These cults, indeed, reveal the essentially religious nature of Melanesian societies,[89] societies that are clearly not pagan, evil-dominated, or lacking in morality, even if made to look that way by the early missions and the government. The prophets or cultic leaders who have sought to protect pre-Christian religious forms, moreover, far from being mentally sick, are worthy of praise as true prophets for refusing to accept their people's loss of their own destiny in the face of Western civilization.

I realize that some Melanesians now join with their white compatriots in denouncing cargo cults and other comparable religious activities as sheer madness, but they should be warned against acting unfairly against our cultural heritage. There may be good reason for condemnation in some cases, but good reasons derive from detailed study and sound assessment, not from impetuous reactions against what is apparently unnatural and strange. Governments and churches of today should adopt a policy of minimum interference lest they destroy important traditions and ritualistic initiatives that enable Melanesia to harness ongoing changes into their village-oriented societies.

# 8

# The Demolition of Church Buildings by the Ancestors

## ESAU TUZA
### Choiseul Island, Solomon Islands

"Our ancestors in the *hope* ('ancestral shrines') are not dead. They are asleep (literally, 'we made them sleep')." This is what I was told in two different places[1] in the Solomons (March/April 1981). In other words, the spirits in the *hope*[2] (or *sope*) were made to sleep when people covered up the *hope* with *nedara,* a wide-shaped coral from the sea. Nusa Simbo and Nusa Roviana are two places in the New Georgia Group (Solomon Islands) where I noticed *hope* of such description (see map, p. 68).

In Nusa Roviana a virgin bush area is left uncleared because a spirit is said to have inhabited a clamshell located in the village. People are afraid to clear the area; if they did the spirit would cause a strong gale, which would destroy all the houses.[3] The clamshell is still there, old and disintegrating, but the spirit will not be awakened.

Respect or fear for the *hope* (Roviana) or *sope* (Choiseul), where the spirits are kept, is still strong today. In June 1977, I asked Lamech Pitavoga of Boe Village, Choiseul, chief of a group that owns a *sope* at Vanaboboro, about three miles inland from the village, if I could collect one of the heads from it.[4] He looked at me, startled and a bit apprehensive, and said, "I have no objections to your request. If it (the *sope*) were mine, I could give you permission right away, but since it belongs to my lineage, I have to call a meeting and see what their reactions are to your request." I learned later, however, that it would not be possible to collect the head there and I was encouraged to contact another person related to another *sope* nearby.

Can our ancestors be awakened, if they really are asleep? If so, where do we see them up and about? This article suggests that our ancestors are very much alive—in church buildings, in us, and in our communities.

First, some background as to where one can point to ancestral presence.

# THE WESTERN SOLOMONS

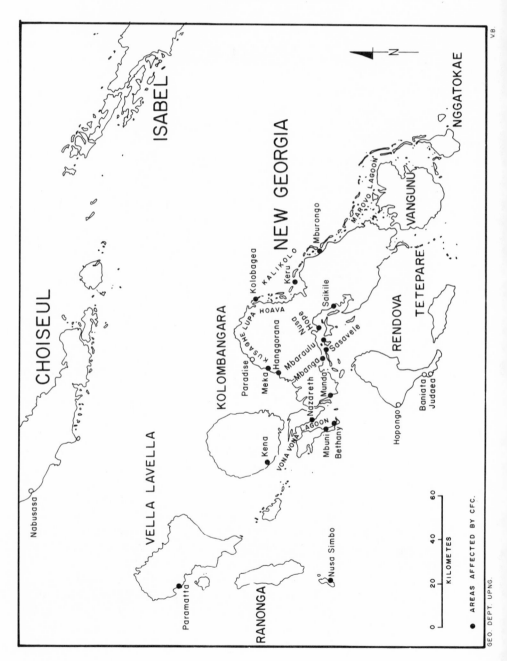

GEO. DEPT. UPNG.

Graveyards, the cross, and church buildings will be assessed in this respect. Then the early worship development of the Christian Fellowship Church (CFC), an independent church of New Georgia will be examined, with special reference to its church buildings and its founder, Silas Eto, the "Holy Mama" (or Holy Father). Finally, I look at the present emphasis of CFC worship, which suggests the devolution of liturgical ritual in the church, worship being relocated "in the body of Holy Mama." The ideas I discuss may seem somewhat strange, but they are important for showing how at least one Melanesian group, with its own distinctive culture, has come to understand and apply Christian worship.

## THE ANCESTORS' EXODUS TO THE CHURCH BUILDINGS

Answers to my inquiries about whose heads were kept in the *hope* suggested that they were mainly the heads of chiefs.[5] Those who took part in the *hope* ritual[6] claim that heads of chiefs and in some cases family heads[7] were deposited in the *hope*. The reason given for this was that chiefs were "people of courage,"[8] who were once warriors, rich autocrats, born organizers, and people of great generosity.[9] People of such qualities or ideals, chiefs, are idealized into the world of our ancestors. Codrington is partly right when he writes:

> Among living men, there are some who stood out distinguished for capacity in affairs, success in life, valour in fighting, and influence over others; and these are so, it is believed, because the supernatural and mysterious powers which they have . . . are derived from communications with those ghosts gone before them who are full of these same powers. On the death of a distinguished man, his ghost retains the powers that belonged to him in life, in greater activity and with stronger force; his ghost therefore is powerful and worshipped, and so long as he is remembered, the aid of his power is sought and worship offered him: he is the *tindalo* [spirit][10] of Florida and Lio'a [spirit] of Sa'a.[11]

Codrington recognizes "qualities" of people who stood out "distinguished" from others, but he gets so bogged down with the idea that such qualities are only available in the realm of the abstract, that is, the realm of the supernatural, that he places too little value on how these qualities become operative and alive with the people themselves.

In the western Solomons,[12] ancestral ideals are very important, for they delineate two types of people: chiefs and warriors. Chiefs not only include people of high authority and prestige,[13] but also those who are generous and loving. Such people become trustees of the land,[14] managers in tribal groups,[15] and peace negotiators in tribal feuds. Without such persons, indeed, managing village affairs would have been impossible and community harmony difficult.

Community living was confined to small scattered villages where clans and family heads controlled social relationships. Relations within the clans were considered a family affair and thus subject to family and clan heads, but outside social relationships were under constant threat of warfare. This necessitated the rise of warriors who could emerge as victors in tribal battles. Such men are called *tie varane* in Roviana or *palata* in Choiseul.

Chiefs and warriors represented a set of ideals that sanctioned the continuity of the village communities. These ideals were not only the ideals of the dead, but also of the living. They were incorporated in two ways—through the funeral and the *sope* rituals.

After death the bodies of the common people were cremated, buried in ordinary graveyards, or else thrown into the sea; the bodies of the chiefs were left in one place to decay and their heads were deposited in the place of worship *(sope)*. Reuben Rukana of Choiseul[16] states "that commoners were often neglected in funeral rites, while the chief, if he died, they carried his body in public in a coffin, blew panpipes and danced around it before cremation."[17] This was also the custom in Simbo,[18] New Georgia,[19] and Vella Lavella.[20]

Edge-Partington describes the funeral of Hiqava or Ingava,[21] a warrior-chief:

> Immediately he was dead, they strapped him into a rough sort of chair that they had made, so that he was in a sitting position. Then they put on all his shell arm rings, amounting to about thirty on each arm—and on his breast his large "Bakhia"—all around him they arranged his po-ota or money, and by his side they laid his shield, spears, and tomahawks. He was left in this sitting position for two days; hundreds of natives came down to take a last look at their great fighting king. It was a real "lying in state" or "sitting in state." Ingava was known to have been the biggest fighter in the group. The mourning arrangement was as follows. His two chief relations, Gumi and Gemu,[22] and their children, all have to shave their heads and are supposed to remain on Ingava's island for 100 days. His widow has to remain in Ingava's house for the same period and is not only not allowed to go outside but is not allowed to put her feet to the ground for the whole of that time. These rules are not strictly observed now as formerly—they do the 100 days mourning on the island and shave their heads but they do not remain on the island all that time, for I saw some of them in the villages. The successor is Gemu, Ingava's eldest cousin. At the death of Ingava they had a big feast which is repeated every thirty days. Ingava was buried next to his father and brother at the end of his own island. Their form of burial is to leave the body in the fork of a tree until the flesh is rotted away, after which they remove the skull and put it into the Tamate[23] house where all the relatives' skulls are kept.[24]

Hiqava's head would have been deposited in the *hope* house[25] if Methodist missionaries, who started work there in 1902,[26] had not condemned it, and if the government had not undermined Hiqava's leadership in 1900[27] by destroying his war canoes and burning his houses (in retaliation for a head-hunting raid he had led on Ysabel Island).

Hiqava, who was known as king of Rubiana, had a canoe house *(paele)* with seven war canoes *(tomoko)* in 1890.[28] He was the son of Pequ Vovoso and brother of Izomo, both of chiefly descent.[29] Because of his chiefly descent and his ability, he became friends with the traders. He "had a knack of making Europeans feel at ease." He was described by a visitor "as a pleasant intellectual man."[30] He was also a merciless killer and headhunter. Through the acquisition of boats, guns, and European wealth, he became a *bangara* (chief) and *tie varane* (a brave fighting man). On Hiqava's head-hunting expeditions he took two English-built boats and five hundred men. Between three and four hundred of his warriors carried rifles and they had nine thousand rounds of ammunition.[31]

By gradually extending his conquest, Hiqava was accepted by the people of Simbo, New Georgia, and Vella Lavella as their *ngati bangara* (paramount chief). His sphere of conquest included Guadalcanal, Ysabel, Florida, Choiseul, and Buin. He was the *ngati bangara,* "known to all Naval Officers and traders who have been in that part of the world as the 'King of the western Solomons.' "[32]

Why was this Hiqava given such attention at his funeral? Simply put, his funeral was a reminder to his people. A person of such calibre had to be frequently recalled so that with him and through him the society would remain intact. The recalling to life of ancestral ideals came through the *sope* ritual. This ritual, described elsewhere,[33] is a way through which *mana* (blessings?), as exemplified by ancestors during their life as human beings, can be retained. Because *mana* belongs to the realm of the spirits represented by the ancestors, their place of worship, the *hope* or *sope,* is a sacred place.

> No ordinary man is ever allowed to enter a *sope.* Anyone can look towards it, but to enter, not at all. Since this is the house of the spirit, only the owner of the *sope* can enter. But even to see, one has to see it only from a distance. The law concerning *sope* is this—"If you want to look towards it, do not look sideways, but look straight on. But if you do not want to look towards it, don't look towards its direction at all. To look sideways is forbidden."[34]

The *sope,* set apart for the *sisiama* or *hiama* (priest), demands proper respect. Side glances, which are interpreted as halfheartedness, as escape or avoidance, are not acceptable. Only the *hiama,* whose life experience makes him the expert on ritual, can offer sacrifice there.

Sacrifice, if rightly performed, can bring *mana*[35] to people. Puddings (made out of *ngali* nut and taro), yams, taro, pigs, and acceptable garden produce are burnt in front of the *sope.* These offerings recall the generosity of chiefs in providing food to their people when they were alive and remind the people that both they and nature should continue to provide for the needs of people. When the fire was still smoking the worshipper recalled good deeds performed by ancestors, from the recent past to the distant past. Invocative prayers followed, asking the spirits to protect the *hiama* and the people:

> When the fire is in smoke, we pray like this—"These (in reference to gifts offered) belong to you spirits. Give us good health. Take good care and grow things in our gardens. Give wholeness to our clan *(butubutu),* drive sickness and accidents away. Bless us all to be healthy.[36]

Physical well-being, nature's growth, productivity, and wholeness are considered as resources coming from ancestral spirits. Sickness, death, misfortunes, famines, and accidents are said to come from evil spirits or from sorcerers. To find causes for any of these, *vore* or *sabusabukae* rituals are performed. *Vore* ritual involves waving armlets about and calling on different spirits to reveal the people or causes responsible for human misfortunes. The answer is said to be given when the arms become heavy and suddenly drop. Then and there the *hiama,* having no control of himself, not knowing what he says, speaks to the people from his religious ecstasy and tells them hidden answers. This shamanistic state experienced by the *hiama* is called *sabusabukae,* the "possession of spirits."

Is *hope* ritual dead? Or does it function in other areas of human life?

Today we continue the tradition of our ancestors by burying important people near the church buildings. The grave of James Pitu,[37] the son of chief Bela of Nusa Roviana, who pioneered the work of the Lotu there, is located at the right side of the church.[38] At Sepa, Choiseul, Andrew Nulakana's grave is placed in front of the church building. Andrew, of chiefly rank, pioneered the work of the Lotu at Sepa, for he wanted peace, wholeness, and freedom for his people, who lived under the threat of tribal warfare, disease, and sorcery.[39] The grave of Stephen Gadepeta,[40] one of the first converts in Choiseul and the person who was mainly responsible for the spread of Christianity in Choiseul for fifty years, is located at the back of Sasamuqa church in southwestern Choiseul. The body of Luke Zale,[41] a Choiseul teacher/catechist who worked many years as a missionary in Buka, is to be dug up and buried in a grave beside the new iron-roofed church building at Petats.[42]

More investigation has yet to be done on why people want to bury chiefs so close to church buildings and on the impact these burials have on the people. I am familiar with one case concerning Abel Pitakömöki[43] whose grave is located at Boe village, Choiseul. Abel was a teacher/catechist there from 1941 to 1975. His teaching ability and his love for people live on and shine through many hearts.[44] Because of his ideals the people decided to bury him in front of the concrete church building. It was said that on the day of the burial a heavy rain fell and then suddenly stopped.[45] The rain was a sign that Abel looks down on his people and weeps over them. In other words, he qualified as an ancestor, for around his death myths appeared. In realization of this and at the request of many people, I wrote the following words in reference to his death:

That call came on Monday, 10th November, 1975. There and then Abel was called to his rest—"forever with the Lord." His tomb is located at Maröe hill in front of the church . . . facing east. That tomb will remain an abiding pillar for those who felt Abel's impact in their lives. It remains there as a symbol of the man who forever said "farewell" to his beloved people, but constantly reminding them that "Boe village belongs to God and so are its people." With this note, the living continue the living tradition of the dead.[46]

Abel is dead, but his love for each person, his faith in others and his ability and patience as a teacher, live on in the hearts of his people.[47]

Not only are graves located near church buildings, but crosses are also attached to them. Except for Luke Zale's grave (which is to be removed), all the other graves mentioned above have a cross on top. A cross, symbol of Christ crucified and risen, is also located in front of most of the church buildings in the western Solomons. Jesus is the point of reference for the cross. It is possible that belief about him as an ancestor exists. This belief is reflected in church buildings that were built in order to remember the local people.[48] The cross is situated above the front doors of Peter Izu's memorial church at Namatoa, Teop, Bougainville, and the words "Izu Memorial Church, Namatoa" are placed on the right, under the cross. The same is true of Barthemeus Nodoro's memorial church at Boe, Choiseul—the cross is above the memorial. If the grave and the cross have anything to say to us, it is that the ancestors have already entered our churches and we, as worshippers, "tune in" with them.

Respect for the church building as a holy place is central to the thinking of our people. In Elijah Dalisaru's church at Kaqologa, northeast Choiseul, four statements printed on a cardboard sign hung almost directly above the pulpit call the people to be quiet and worship God:

Preacher: Do you know about this house?
People: Yes I know it is God's house.
Preacher: Are you able to be quiet?
People: Yes, I will be quiet to worship God.[49]

To be quiet and worship God is a feature in most congregations in the western Solomons. Before the preacher enters, the church steward stands up in front of the congregation and reminds the people that the house in which they are now gathered is God's house. To worship God truly, they must keep quiet, be attentive to what the preacher has to say, and receive God's word through the power of the Holy Spirit. After this announcement the preacher enters and the call to worship begins.

The prayers offered in worship services resemble the prayers offered to traditional gods. In Choiseul, the phrase used in reference to God is "He who sits with legs folded cross-wise in heaven."[50] In Roviana, the phrase is "the one who looks or bows down from heaven."[51] The concept expressed in these two phrases is that of "old" people sitting above their own people and advising them about what to do. After these phrases are offered to God as an "old" person (the older one gets, the closer one is to supernatural forces), the petition for the spirits to give *mana* (dynamics to life) follows. In the early 1950s a man prayed thus:

> Send us your hundred spirits to watch over us and protect us over the night, and bring us safely to a new day so that we will give you our praise.[52]

The number one hundred is associated with Perotovumbi ("one who kills a hundred"),[53] an ancestral warrior spirit. This was the god to whom Liliboe, a Choiseul chief, prayed before he went to capture Jijipele during the Senga-Vurulata feud in the early part of this century.[54]

Morning and evening prayers are daily pleas for protection made to the spirits: "Protect us, O God, throughout this day and bring us safely to the evening in order that we may worship you"; or "Send us your spirits to protect us throughout the night and bring us safely to a new day so that we will give you our praise."[55] Protection is needed, for each day people are threatened by tribal warfare, sorcery, accidents, and other forms of misfortunes. When night draws near, the threats of roaming spirits, sudden attacks by enemies, and the sorcerers' search for their victims cannot be ignored.

If, then, the ancestors have been summoned to make their dwelling places in the churches, so to speak, can we experience their spirits?

## CHURCH BUILDINGS, ART, AND THE HOLY SPIRIT IN CFC's EARLY LITURGICAL DEVELOPMENT

If any Melanesian was particular about church buildings, it was Silas Eto of Dive village, Kusage, north New Georgia, the church founder (to be called "Holy Mama" later) of the CFC. At least he was particular before the outpouring of the Holy Spirit in religious ecstasy *(taturu)*. His church building at Kolobagea was a striking example. It was completed in 1934. A missionary who visited the place three years later noted in his diary:

> We anchored at a place called Kolobagea. The church was a sight to behold. I have never seen a native church so ornate. On either side of the central roof were two smaller ones. The whole place was built with leaf and other materials but in front of the church door was a big cross. With a crown on top of it and written on the arm of the cross were the words in the Roviana, "We are saved from all sins and the law of Moses." At the front porch were two little gates on which were written the 10 commandments. On each side of the gates were texts, some of them written in bad English, like "Grace and True came from Jesus Christ." . . . The inside of the church was just as wonderful. The pulpit was a masterpiece, and

warranted to put any man off his sermon! It was in the "V" shape, very nicely worked with native plaiting.[56]

This is but a description of one of Holy Mama's many church buildings in the CFC villages.[57]

Holy Mama once believed that humans could receive the spirit of God in the church buildings through worship. Apart from singing, Bible readings, and preaching (which were and still are characteristics of Methodist worship), Holy Mama put the greatest emphasis on prayer. His prayer life was combined with fasts, which at one time made him very thin and weak and because of which he was hospitalized.

> In my prayer life Mr. Goldie[58] asked me, "Are you sick? Is that why you look so thin?" I said, "No. I pray all the time in the bush. Day and night." Mr. Goldie said, "That is all right, but you should pray only in the house." He put me in the hospital and he asked the doctor from Tulagi, the former capital of the BSIP, to come and see me. He examined me and said, "He is not sick." Mr. Goldie asked the doctor to feel my heart. The doctor said he was sorry. Then he went away. That afternoon Mr. Goldie asked me, "What are you worrying about?" I told him that I was worried because I wondered how to become the true servant of Jesus Christ. I did not eat and drink properly, and could not sleep well at night. Mr. Goldie said, "I will help you son." So I thanked him.[59]

Holy Mama's prayer life, which began in earnest in 1918, continued until the outpouring of the Holy Spirit at Kolobagea in 1934. In 1977 he recalled:

> Man (addressing me), I did not really understand what came over me between 1918 and 1934. I prayed every day everywhere non-stop for new life in the spirit. It was almost like being mad. Now of course, I do not need to pray, for I have already become spirit.[60]

The outpouring of the Holy Spirit would have been impossible had Holy Mama not been able to introduce his liturgical innovation in the church. This came about through the use of art. Eto was, and still is, an artistic genius.[61] In the church at Kolobagea he carved a crucifix on a huge post at the center of the church. Under the crucifix he carved a Solomon Islander holding a shield and spear. Above the crucifix, he wrote "I am the Light of the World" and at the bottom he inscribed: "Let us shelter beneath the cross of Jesus Christ, who cleanses our sins and takes away the darkness of the people who believe in Him. . . . For God so loved the world that he gave his only son, that whosoever believeth in him should not perish but shall have everlasting life."[62]

By the use of art, Holy Mama evokes two lively responses from his congregations. First, he arouses in people the strong feeling that they are now one with and subject to Jesus Christ. Missionaries often called on people to give their lives to Christ and to renounce their heathen wicked ways. Holy Mama's worshipper cannot escape the "real encounter" that explodes in emotional outbursts.[63]

Second, Holy Mama preserves the basic traditional structure of worship which centers on faith in the ancestors, as exemplified in the preservation of heads. In former days heads were preserved in the *sope:* Jesus on the crucifix becomes the substitute. In this way, Jesus, the crucified and the risen, becomes "alive." Thir Jesus, "in the spirit," so to speak, has come with power and touched his people through religious ecstatic experience, often wrongly labeled *taturu* (see below), a replica of spirit possession, the so-called *sabusabukae.* *Sabusabukae* entailed possession by spirits who revealed hidden causes of sickness, death, and misfortunes, and helped people to predict in advance the outcomes of certain ventures undertaken in life (for example, going on a head-hunting expedition, or moving into a new area to live, or organizing a feast).

Spirit possessions in traditional societies were similar in some ways to those experienced by Holy Mama's followers and thus to those that caused the schism in 1960.[64] Sam Rove,[65] an old Methodist catechist who used to go with his father to offer sacrifice to "Foolish God,"[66] recalls that his own experience of *sabusabukae* [67] is similar to his experience of the spirit with the CFC. Sam says that when he waves armlets and shell money about, requesting his ancestral spirits to answer his requests, the answer comes when he feels a great weight moving from his arm toward his body. He experienced this same feeling at Sasavele, a CFC village.

> I have already proved that Eto's *taturu* experience was similar to those of *sabusabukae* experience. I began to feel the cold and the weight right through my body and my arms began to shake. That is exactly the same feeling as that of *sabusabukae* experience.[68]

The feeling of being cold (*ibu*) is also similar to the experience of Naule, an old catechist at Marovo. Naule was a very sick man, but when he heard that Holy Mama could cure people of their diseases, he decided to attend a CFC service.

> As he sat through a CFC service, he began to feel the cold "touching" his head. Immediately after that, the *ibu* ran through his whole body down to his feet. As soon as he recalled his past experience of *sabusabukae,* he fled the church and ran outside to his . . . house.[69]

A number of CFC followers have had similar experiences. "From the legs up my body would go cold like a dead person. When the Holy Spirit comes exceedingly strong, it can cause a man to die and then to live again."[70]

Unfortunately, the word *taturu,* which was used to describe the CFC religious experience, is in fact an inaccurate word to use on two counts. First, traditionally it has no association with spirit possession in the good sense of the term. It is a word used mainly in reference to people who have no common sense and who act irrationally before they die, or in reference to people with epilepsy. The Choiseul equivalent is *mamaqila.*[71] In either case, the experience is said to have been caused by evil spirits or sorcerers. Second, the ecstatic experience that we call *taturu* has two features: gibberish, often accompanied by excessive salivation, and wall climbing. But these features are not common to all CFC villages. They have only been witnessed in Madou, Ha'apai Hindu, and Sasavele in the New Georgia group and Nabusasa in Choiseul. These villages faced much opposition from the Methodist loyalists. In the other twenty-three (now twenty-two) CFC villages, the ecstatic religious experience includes crying outbursts, in which one asks for forgiveness of sins, visions of Jesus and heaven, trances, seizures, and glossolalia, all of which are quite common in Melanesian ecstatic/spirit experiences.[72] Hence to say that *taturu* is common to all CFC villages is inaccurate.

Because they were afraid of *taturu,* Sam Rove and Naule thought the CFC ecstatic experience was caused by evil spirits. This fear was enhanced by missionaries' condemnation of *sabusabukae* as a part of traditional worship.[73] The term *sabusabukae,* however, in reference to spirit-possesion, fell out of use. Hence, there was no other word in common and recent use to refer to spirit-possession except *taturu,* which the Methodist loyalists naturally applied to various ecstatic experiences and therefore to the unusual happenings in CFC worship. The Holy Mama and his followers, however, see these happenings as the outpourings of the Holy Spirit in the midst of the people.

After the ecstatic experience, it is said, people receive new life. The process and the end results of the experience are what count for the CFC followers. Alex Naqu of Rarumana is one of many who received a new lease on life after an ecstatic religious experience. Educated in Fiji, Alex became the first forestry officer in the Solomons. As a Methodist, he finds worship patterns inhibiting, boring, without life. His knowledge of John Wesley, who went through the "warmed-heart" experience, made him wonder whether people could indeed experience the power of the Holy Spirit in their lives. He heard about the CFC experiences.

> Out of curiosity, he went to observe the New Way[74] services. On the first few occasions, he was not moved at all. All he could say was that they were crazy! He decided to go for the last time. He went and sat down and gradually people began to go through *taturu* in varying stages. All of a sudden, "his heart was shut" and pain began to surge in. He then could no longer breathe. Then he raised his arms up to heaven and began to scream. For the first time in his life he was lifted higher than himself. While in that state of mind, he realized his sins and at the same time God's forgiving love through the spirit. After that state was over, he came to experience "release."[75]

The "warmed-heart," "the heart that is hot," and weeping—all quite common in the mission in the late 1930s,[76] no longer happen only in church services.[77]

They also happen when people come face to face with Holy Mama.

A woman in her mid-twenties experienced a "hotness" (*manini*) in her heart and an "outburst of crying" when she was forgiven by Holy Mama. She was accused of adultery at a certain circuit's quarterly meeting. The man who was suspected was a good friend of her family. The woman knew she had not committed adultery, but church leaders pressured her to confess her "sin." She heard through friends that Holy Mama could forgive sins, and so with her husband's permission, they went to Paradise, CFC's headquarters. Holy Mama listened attentively to the woman's story and said that, according to her story, she was innocent and would be forgiven, but the church leaders would have to face the judgment of God. With such words from Holy Mama, she felt "her heart was hot," her burden taken away, and "tears" set in.

> Minister (addressing me), if I were still in the United Church now, I would not experience forgiveness. Holy Mama . . . was able to give you something of God. Through him I am able to learn of God's love and care for every sinful man. Every time I recall that confrontation with Holy Mama, I cannot help but shed tears. It is a moment which I will never forget until I die.[78]

"New life" for the individual, a result of ecstatic experiences, is reflected in the way villages are kept tidy and clean and in the people's sense of religious life—participating in singing, clapping, praying, and giving testimonies during worship services at CFC villages. In contrast to this the Methodist villages are "poor and scraggy . . . where people . . . do not hold worship unless the catechist is there."[79]

Although this liberating experience initially comes through worship services within the walls of church buildings, when it becomes incarnated in the people, there is no further need to worship God in any church buildings!

### THE BODY OF HOLY MAMA: THE TRUE WORSHIP

> The body of Holy Mama
> Has become the spirit,
> He is just like Christ
> Inside the new life [Hymn 55, verse 1B].[80]

"I go to prepare a place for you, and when I return, I will see that you are received, and where I will be, there you also will be" [John 14:13]. Jesus Christ is God. Let us be prepared so that he receives us. It is true, people! Jesus Christ is God loving. His birth incarnate is true. His death on the cross is factual. This is to show us the life he lived and his rising again.

"Where I will be, you also will be." Anyone who is already in the place where Jesus is, has already seen all things. . . . Such a man has everything that Christ has. In Christ's place, there is no jealousy, no enmity, no wild thoughts. Where Christ is, there you will find the place of love of the Spirit. Isn't it exciting to know that the things belonging to God in the spirit can really work where we are and live?[81]

After the *taturu* we slept at Sasavele (renamed New Eden). The people did not allow me to sleep at anyone else's house. Instead, they told me to sleep inside the church building. Many children and girls came to spend the night with me there. Where I am, there you will find children and girls. . . . The girls are just like my beds and blankets. . . . They bit my legs, my face, my tongue, and my body. I was shocked, but they said, "You are the one whose scent is not human. Your scent is better than cream and *seda*. That is why we want to be with you so that we may inherit your nature. That is why we bit your body, for your body has already become the tree of the Holy Spirit."[82]

The first time Silas Eto, the Holy Mama, was viewed as a spirit through religious ecstasy was in 1960.[83] In other words, he was deified.

This is the reason why we deified Holy Mama in 1960. The Holy Spirit first became known in 1928[84] and Holy Mama came down with the Holy Spirit in all the CFC villages in 1960. This is why we sing of and preach about Holy Mama as God. Some people do not believe this, so they left us. Other churches in New Georgia think we are liars and so they mock us. But in 1970, 1971, and 1972 it was proved that Holy Mama is God. Holy Mama and Jesus are seen together at every evening devotion in CFC villages.[85]

When Holy Mama became the Holy Spirit, he became the substitute for church buildings. This is important as a starting point for discussion. Before 1960, church buildings had been holy places set aside for worship services. But after 1960 it was a different matter altogether.

Between 1960 and the early 1970s Holy Mama's rest houses were built very close to church buildings—in Madou, Paradise, and Kolobagea. After 1970, when Holy Mama was seen in visions (*dodogoro*) with Jesus, Moses, Elijah, and the Holy Spirit, Mama's place came to be in the church buildings. In Tamaneke, his own village, Holy Mama and members of his household live in part of the large church there. Holy Mama's own house used to be on a little hill behind the church building, but he left this and came to reside in the church.

The pulpit, which used to be central as a place of preaching in the 1930s, is no longer used. Instead, Holy Mama seats himself on a chair in the middle of the church, surrounded by his people. By doing this, he turns the place of worship into a place of meeting, where people's needs are dealt with.

In July 1977, Mama called his people in Paradise to an evening devotion. He had heard the previous day that students of a nearby high school were short of food. We went to the church, and the Holy Mama seated himself on a chair surrounded by his people. He recited John 15:1-15 from memory. After this, he explained to us that one's life is dependent on what one eats and drinks. To give food to the hungry and water to the thirsty is to give one's life to another. He then went on to say that the students at Banga High School were short of food, a necessity for living, and if we loved as Jesus commands us to, we would collect food the next day and take it to the students at Banga, an island about four hours' trip by motorized canoe from Paradise village. At dawn the next day, when it was still quite dark, Holy Mama and his people went to their bush gardens to collect food. By about 10:30 in the morning four large canoes were filled with baskets of sweet potatoes, yams, and other garden produce for the students at Banga High School.

Visitors can sleep in church buildings. When three United Church members and I visited New Tiberius, a CFC village, Silas Lezituni, the village chief spent the night with us in the church.[86] At Tamaneke, I slept beside the huge pulpit for two nights.[87]

Such uses of the church buildings point toward the destruction of worship services centered on church buildings. This is in accord with the view of Holy Mama:

> Prayer is finished with, faith is no longer needful and Bible reading is done away with. I no longer need to pray, I no longer need to have faith. I have already received my reward. Jesus Christ is already in my heart. . . .[88] For if in us we have all the commandments of Christ, in us there is also God, for this is what He intends us to be. We, in our faith should know Christ is in us. If we do not know this, we are nothing. But if we know that He is in us, we are worth a lot in God.[89]

Occasional glimpses of Jesus, Elijah, Moses, and Holy Mama and other biblical characters must be seen through *dodogoro* (visions).[90] *Dodogoro* in the CFC became established in the early 1970s, when it was claimed that visions of Moses, Elijah, Jesus, and Holy Mama "just happened" (*vura va hodahodaka*). These visions were initially confined to church buildings where people sang, prayed, gave testimonies, and preached. Normally the lights were dimmed and the people meditated in the semidark while focusing their eyes on the pulpit or a special chair where it was hoped that visions would appear. This all came to an end in 1980.

That year, according to Holy Mama, people saw visions above the strings attached to two poles outside the church buildings. The strings' movement is interpreted to mean the presence of the Holy Spirit. Traditionally in Choiseul, the *sinipi*[91] or *manuru sinipi*,[92] a good spirit, helpful to humans, especially those who are oppressed, is said to reside on the strings in the bush. He has pointed buttocks so he cannot sit on hard flat surfaces. He therefore pierces the string with his buttock and sits on it. Whether this has any connection with the presence of the Holy Spirit on the strings is hard to determine. But the connection between breathing, the spirit, the wind, and *mana* is certain. Life exists when people breathe. They become spirit when they stop breathing. But the spirit blows like a wind—hence movement, activity. Activity gives force or *mana*.

> Although the spirits may be identified as distant spirits of the dead or other spirits located in specific areas, common belief states that their force and movements are often discerned locally by detecting things moved by the wind.
>
> This belief is perhaps initially related to the idea that when a person dies, his "wind" leaves him. This belief is also fostered by the fact that wind is movement, and hence activity. . . . We may now say that wherever there is a spirit, there is activity, movement, and the wind. In other words there is force and *mana*.[93]

If my interpretation of the presence of the spirit is correct, then simple meditation in front of the strings is a substitute for morning and evening devotions for CFC. "These days we no longer observe morning and evening devotions. Instead we have occasional *dodogoro* just outside of the church."[94]

During these *dodogoro*, a variation of a liturgical pattern that was used for the worship services of the CFC in its initial stages is used. It is called "The First Exercise,"[95] and is merely a third of the order of worship for the CFC. It is as follows:

Pastor: Christian Fellowship.
People: Yes Sir.
Pastor: Repentance.
People: Halleluia Trust.
Pastor: Forgiveness.
People: Halleluia Obey.
Pastor: Salvation.
People: Halleluia Gladness.
Pastor: Faithful.
People: Halleluia Everlasting Life.
Pastor: Honor.
People: Halleluia Holiness.
Pastor: Born again.
People: Halleluia Hossan.
Pastor: New Life.
People: Halleluia Trinity.

At the end of the response to "New Life," people and pastor clap their hands. When the clapping is over, the people may sing, or pray, or be quiet, or repeat aspects of the exercise, whatever they feel led to do. This, to them, is worship.

Is it really possible to worship God as a church without church buildings?

During the war years (1942–45), people experienced a church without church buildings. Most missionaries left the country and church buildings were either deserted because people were told to flee to the bush, or demolished by the allied forces. During those years people's houses or bush shelters were used for Christian gatherings. A chief writes:

> It was impossible for us to gather in any great numbers for public worship, but God was with us in our homes—although they were only bush shelters. I arranged with the teachers that wherever they found themselves, they were to burden themselves with the care of Christ's flock in that locality.[96]

On his return after the war, Goldie, the pioneering missionary/chairperson, was asked if it had not been a very painful experience to see one's lifetime effort destroyed by the war. In reply Goldie said, "It is not destroyed; the buildings are gone, yes! but the real work lives on in the hearts of the people"[97]

What was true for the church during the war years is also true for the CFC as a church today. It is difficult to document changes chronologically, but a few things need explanation. First, after the ecstatic religious experience, "New Life" is equated with the life of Christ, which is said to be "incarnated" in Holy Mama. When you receive this new life in the spirit, your life is a prayer life, which is already a service to God and to others. This does away with church buildings. As I have noted above, Holy Mama, symbolizing the life of God, lives in the church buildings. This "life of God" has taken human form in the Nine Graces (fruits of the Holy Spirit?) (see figure, p. 89).[98] This is done through art. The heart is love; right ear, goodness; right side of nose, long-suffering; right eye, faith; mouth, peace; brain, joy; left eye, temperance; left side of nose, meekness; and left ear, gentleness. Leaving aside what actual impact this might have on the people, it is interesting to suggest that Holy Mama localizes "nine graces," or fruits of the Holy Spirit, within the physical human realm, and by doing so he places them within easy reach.

Second, Holy Mama is both man and God. This is clear in that both people and Holy Mama want to see visions of "Holy Mama."[99] "Holy Mama" the spirit, to speak traditionally, has already qualified for the ancestral realm (the realm of the supernatural) and Holy Mama the man helps his people to understand and aspire to the view that, being human, they can strive for the realm of God.

Third, the "Holy Mama," who is already idealizèd, is the same Holy Mama who brings to being a community of independent and loving people, without which there is no church in the true sense of the word. Through the use of art in his liturgical innovations (see above), he brings about freedom from individual sins to a new life, and from the oppressions of Methodist leadership and worship to a worship that is spiritual. Through sheer hard work, he has helped his people to plant fifteen coconut plantations, giving them an annual income of between $12,000 and $15,000,[100] and thus financial independence, which is lacking in other established churches. Not only are coconut plantations used for the church as a whole, but individuals who need financial assistance may make copra out of them, earn for themselves the amount they need, and give the church any surplus.[101] Tax rates and children's school fees are paid by the church by making copra once a year out of the church's coconut plantations. This is done through communal work.

Just as coconut plantations provide financial independence, land provides a sense of security for people living in community. Within each CFC village, a certain amount of virgin bush is reserved "for those who are yet to be born or for anyone wanting to come and live in the village."[102] Beyond this reserved area people can make their bush gardens or work on developmental projects. In this way, land is available to create communities where people can live together as brothers and sisters. This is basic to traditional societies in the Solomons. It goes against individual ownership, which gives priority to a money economy and to capitalism and pushes people off the land. Land is for the benefit of people living in community and therefore the CFC as a church becomes a trustee of all the lands belonging to CFC people. In this way the church, or Holy Mama, takes the place of a traditional chief who knows that land is important for the people.

Holy Mama would have achieved little had he not been able to have a strong sense of identification with his people. This came through to me in July 1977 at Paradise. When we walked around the plantation there, I noticed that the secondary growth needed clearing. I therefore asked Holy Mama whether he ever considered employing laborers to keep the plantation clean. He looked at me and said, "In the CFC we do not need laborers. It is either we all are rich or poor together."[103] Although Holy Mama has a special fund for himself, which goes toward fuel for his pastoral visists and to anyone who comes to ask money from him for any cause he thinks worthy of support, his everyday dress is but a piece of material covering the lower part of his body. In this way, he identifies with the majority of his people, who, in comparison with other people around the Roviana Lagoon, are generally poor. The only times when he is well dressed are during occasional big church gatherings or when meeting important visitors. During such occasions he wears "a variety of garbs, including a special mitre and decorated white robes."[104] By using wealth and land for his people by identifying with them, the Holy Mama is saved from the arrogance, boasts, and manipulations of many traditional chiefs in Melanesia.

Overall, therefore, the life of God incarnated in the body of Holy Mama has become incarnated in the people. Holy Mama is both God and man. He represents qualities or ideals of constant value reminiscent of ancestral qualities, and yet he remains man in the midst of his people. This helps them to strive for better things in the direction of God. Direction to God is rooted in the realm of the "spirit" (new life, life of God) seen in *dodogoro* (visions) and in our own environment—coconut plantations, wealth, and land. This is because the Holy Mama, god/man and rich/poor, has identified with his own people as a human being.

Such a church, a community of people "alive," becomes the worshipping community, offering to God and to the people what is their respective due. This is the spiritual worship that does away with church buildings and progresses in the temple of the human heart, exhibiting itself in human life and witness.

## CONCLUSION

Our worship based on ancestral belief is not dead. Our ancestors are very much alive and thriving. They make their way to the church buildings via the grave and the cross. We pay them the traditional respect through reverence and prayer. They follow us from the church buildings to the world where we live and witness with the rest of God's people, knit together in love and service. Only Christian colonialists, who seek to find God in Western garb, will not be able to see this truth. Despite this, of course, we consciously or unconsciously live side by side with our ancestors.

If this first point can be accepted, then it follows that Christianity as a religion has close affinities with ancestral worship, at least in its early New Testament phase. There people lived in a community, believing in a man (Jesus) as God and Savior. Through this man Jesus, they were forgiven their sins and were freed from the rituals of the temple and the legalism of the Pharisees. This freedom does not come through worship in the temple, but is experienced through following and believing in the man/God Jesus. Is not this alone a glimpse of a temple within a "body"? When I think of the CFC liturgical development, I recall Vincent van Nuffel's words, as he reflected on decentralization of the temple rituals:

The temple has been built as a pedagogy. It was necessary yet transitory means to self-knowledge and self-realisation, in a given community. It was the place where I put on my new body. Once I have discovered that, I felt free to move away from my temple. It did not matter any more if it was empty or not. The Spirit, God, the Heavenly Christ, was no longer in it, for me. Through the use of the temple, I discovered that God was inside me, and that the Heavenly Christ was indeed my better Self. Now that my temple is left behind, I am able to share my daily consecrated bread with everyone, of whatever temple. I understand that the temple, the priest, the victim, the sacrifice, are indeed articulations of my heart. This was the revelation in Jesus the Christ; as it was the revelation of many people before and after Him. Moses, Jeremiah, Second-Isaiah, the Buddha, Pythagoras and scores of others "prophesied" the end of their temple, and they invited people to form a New Community, international in outlook.[105]

The CFC shows certain affinities with Christianity, so we should not only talk of independent churches as caused by the interaction between Christianity and our cultures,[106] but we should also speak about experiences in both sets of tradition having similarities.[107] Thus Western Christianity is not our only criterion, but we can assume a large part of our culture is already basically in line with Christian tradition. So we can speak authentically about our own churches.

Finally, if we set any store by this authenticity, we are required to take indigenous expressions of worship, church life, and theology seriously. The CFC, claiming to be the church initiated by the outpouring of the Holy Spirit, is a homegrown church. It is the church of the black people. This means, therefore, that it must be recognized on its own merit, not passed off as failing to square with Western expectations.

When it comes to church structure, what should count is how the people are affected, not the historical (Western) precedents of a given model. The Holy Mama, as the head of the church, cannot fit into the post of a president of a Methodist conference or a bishop of a diocese in which policies are dealt with or resolutions passed. Such "big shots" have few contacts with their own people. Holy Mama is essentially love at work, and all his people know and experience him. He gives his people visions to go by and power over wealth and land. His people see these as dynamic, Godward experiences. All decisions therefore must be directed by this dynamo. Although twenty-two villages are divided into four sections, each under a pastor, working in communities under the direction of Holy Mama is their conscious effort. Holy Mama therefore is a "service," both to God and to people.

Theologically, thinkers in Western churches may be tempted to draw an analogy between the Solomonese advocacy of the Holy Mama and their own belief in Jesus as the only one to be acclaimed God,[108] and so regard the CFC as heretical. I believe it is futile to apply theological criteria or concepts that have been systematized and philosophized for hundreds of years to situations that have arisen only in the past twenty years. The situations are incompatible in any case. But even if you demand that people should believe in the "correct" doctrines of the church, are you able to ascertain that every member within your congregation believes in God in the same way that you do? I doubt it. Yet this is exactly what church-growth theorists want to achieve for "established churches" in Melanesia. By attempting this, of course, they alienate church establishments, for theological imports do not necessarily cater to religious experience in the actual context.

I am increasingly aware that belief in God is dependent on how one experiences God in one's life, and I assume the CFC's belief about Holy Mama is an affirmation of religious experience rather than a theological commodity. This, then, raises the question as to how we approach religious affirmations theologically. Leaving aside the intricacies of the doctrine of Incarnation, the belief that God is within and among the people is the best starting point for achieving a truly local church. But God-with-us for the CFC is God's self-revelation through a person, through art, through religious ecstasty, through the use of land and coconut plantations, and through communities. Hence the belief in special revelation, a term often employed by missionaries, which uproots and alienates local people from their environment, especially from their land, has to be balanced (if not done away with) with a theology of God's self-revelation in the immediate context. While the former often alienates the person and so the context, the latter brings God down to earth and sees God in all human affairs. This in itself is worship. Without it we may have many church buildings, but neither God nor our ancestors will be there!

# Appendix to Chapter 8

(Note: The sevenfold responses in the First Exercise are referred to as seven steps necessary for healing in Christ. The order written here is the continuation of the First Exercise.)

Pastor: Jesus Christ.
People: Halleluia, win for Christ.
Pastor: Christian Fellowship.
People: Yes Sir.
Pastor: Now you are the body of Christ.
People: Halleluia, love one another.
Pastor: Christian Fellowship.
People: Yes Sir.
All: Honor the Lord. Halleluia Almighty God.
Pastor: Christian Fellowship.
People: Yes Sir.
(First Exercise repetition here, after which the following is recited by all.)
    Jesus Christ before me.
    Jesus Christ in my heart.
    Jesus Christ in my head.
    Jesus Christ above me.
    Jesus Christ behind me.
    Jesus Christ around me.
    Jesus Christ in my brain.
    Jesus Christ in my mind.
    Jesus Christ with my whole life.
All bow down to pray.
Pastor: Christian Fellowship.
People: Yes Sir.
All: Honor, Halleluia, Holiness.
Pastor: Follow, the Christ.
All: Halleluia prayer. Father, Son, Holy Spirit, Holy Mama be with us, or help us, or bless us. Halleluia Father, Halleluia Father to the Son. Halleluia Son to the Holy Spirit. Halleluia Holy Spirit to the Holy Mama. Halleluia Holy Mama to the CFC. Halleluia, Amen. (Clapping follows here.)

(Actual service in church building starts here.)
Hymn
Prayer
Hymn
Scripture reading
Choirs
Hymn
Texts (or brief sermon)
Hymn
Benediction

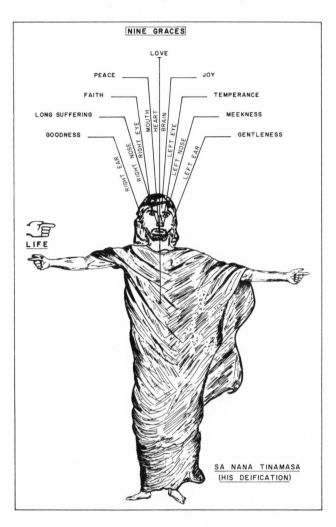

NINE GRACES

LOVE

PEACE — JOY

FAITH — TEMPERANCE

LONG SUFFERING — MEEKNESS

GOODNESS — GENTLENESS

RIGHT EAR — RIGHT NOSE — RIGHT EYE — MOUTH — HEART — BRAIN — LEFT EYE — LEFT NOSE — LEFT EAR

LIFE

SA NANA TINAMASA
(HIS DEIFICATION)

*FIRE.*

Smoke from the brain.
Smoke from two ears.
Smoke from two eyes.
Smoke from two nose holes.
Smoke from the mouth.
Smoke from the heart.
These are seen in Holy Mama, the
   person of prayer.
The life of the flesh disappears.

*INSIDE THE HEART OF A PERSON
OF PRAYER.*

1. Person becoming God.
2. Born again.
3. Life in the spirit.
4. Living in the New Life.
5. Be true to Christianity.
6. Not being born from woman.
7. Person can become God.

These show the life of the spirit.

# 9

# The Land Is Sacred:
# Renewing the Dreaming in Modern Australia

## GUBOO TED THOMAS
## Southeastern Australia

I want you to walk with me through the valley of Omona in southeastern New South Wales. I will show you some sacred places. Only then will you begin to see the spiritual significance of Aboriginal culture, or the culture of the Koories (as Aborigines often call themselves in eastern Australia). As I walk through the bush I get a strong feeling when I'm coming to sacred space. I know I have an advantage even over archaeologists and anthropologists. I know inside that it is the Aboriginal who is the real expert on these matters because I'm a "bloke" who feels it in his bones when approaching any sacred site. So why not come with me to share the wonderful blessings from such places?

To get the best impression of my area, we can start from an island called Marimanga in the middle of the Wallaga Lakes. As I stand with my feet in the water, holding two spears, a *nulla-nulla* and a *woomera*,[1] I can look up toward Mount Dromedary. When Captain Cook sailed along this part of the Australian coastline he saw so many humps that he named the area Dromedary, and the white people still call it that. The Aboriginal people named it Gourga. On the lake you can see black swans (*gunyu*) and ducks. The island is shaped like a duck, the totem for my people being the black duck. Stretching for eighty-four miles around the lake is our country—Wallaga Lakes. That bush belongs to us; it is our "property" now, according to the whites' way.[2] The mountains attached to Dromedary at the back are ours too. One special little mountain is of granite, not sandstone. We call this Najinoka, for the old Aboriginals used to go to its western side to collect birds' eggs. Only the tribal elders could go and take one or two eggs out of each nest, never cleaning the whole lot out.

Aboriginal occupation of this area goes back thousands of years. Just out to sea lies the island called Montague Lighthouse. At the end of the last ice age the coastline, fourteen or fifteen miles out from the present one, receded to separate the island from the mainland. Out on that island are places where the Aboriginals camped long ago, ate shellfish, and made implements.[3] In the beautiful bush up on Mount Dromedary, too, you will see some leftovers from Noah's ark. Our people spoke about the ark in the early days of our great ancestors, of how it was afloat on the great flood. Up there on the mountain among the trees, you can sense the presence of its remains. Because the spirit is there all the time, and especially a large rock that sits on top of a still larger one, we know that the ark came to an end there in the heights. We hear of this in a story that goes back for generations. So the old people spoke about Noah. They spoke about the Bible; it was exactly the same for them as it is for us now. And the Aboriginal children, they all thought about Jesus, and about God. We call God Darama, the Great Spirit. It is the same Jesus, the same God.

Consider some of the beautiful rocks of the Dromedary. Some of them are very special, and again, because of their relation to trees, one can sense spiritual significance and the presence of spirits. A huge round one has been cut away all around the underside. The power in it, the energy! If you touch the underneath part, your hand will be pushed down toward the ground. That's Koorie power. But these rocks were not made by human hands; the Almighty made these for the Koorie, the Aboriginal people. One wonderful rock has a long, massive form; it rears its head out of the ground, broader at the summit than at the base. This is the Rainbow Serpent, which is important for our ancient connections with other Koorie peoples. We, the people of the Yuwin tribe, or nation,[4] are related to the Aborigines of Arakun in the Gulf of Carpentaria, a people said to have migrated along the eastern side of Australia. We have a place at Wallaga Lakes called Kaihola; there is a man by that very name at Arnhem who knows a good deal about this serpent. Down at Wallaga we can show you holes where the serpent came up out of the water, where the old people saw it and it spoke in their own language. Farther to the west of New South Wales is a lake where the Koories claim the serpent lives; it is also supposed to come out of a lake on the eastern side of Canberra.[5] People ask themselves why the water goes away so quickly; it is because the serpent has come up. And so the serpent comes where I live—through the big holes in the ground and even to the smaller versions of the big rearing rock I spoke of, which all mark the serpent's spiritual presence and freedom to move across the land at will.

I can take you to other places. Near present-day Bateman's Bay, Ulladulla, and Milton you can see a beautiful mountain with a box-shaped formation on top. When Captain Cook saw it he called it Pigeon House: perhaps it looked like that from a distance. But the Aboriginal people were closer to it and took it to be a woman's breast. In the valley below it food is abundant and there they obtained all the nourishment they wanted, all the food they needed for forty thousand years. They were not often sick and had many medicines in that valley. They survived for so long, and yet now you see the difference. We are eating whites' food today and becoming smaller and smaller! The Aboriginal people were once wonderfully strong people living off game and feeding from the berries women harvested in abundance.

Strange and beautiful places in Australia have deeply spiritual qualities that cannot be separated from their beauty and richness. I think of the mountains overlooking Monolong. There are actually pebbles and fish bones in the rocks high up there; and if you look into some of the rocks properly you will see faces—noses, mouths, eyes—in the shapes talked about in the stories still passed down by my black brothers and sisters. Seeing these faces in the rocks is what I call the spirit. When you are there you get a feeling of our ancestors roaming all through the area thirty or forty thousand years ago. Down in the valleys of the Wallaga Lakes areas, you will see beautiful rain forests, filled with giant gum trees (eucalyptus), ferns, creepers, flowers. In the dampness everything seems quiet, untouched. There is a Presence there—in a spiritual sense—because God, Darama the Great Spirit, has touched everything, from the smallest hanging moth to the oxygen that keeps us alive.

The rain forest explains why I oppose the timber companies, whose workers are cutting down the last remains of the Aborigines' forest and threatening the land once roamed by our ancestors. I fight even for the Yowie, the long-armed bush spirit, who to the Americans would be equivalent to Bigfoot or to the Abominable Snowman. The Yowie is a spirit involved in our tribal initiations. You can see traces of the Yowie in the rocks. This spirit has existed for fifty thousand years or more in our bush; yet once I saw the Yowie out there in the mountains but I did not interfere and just came straight back. The white people, though, are coming down here to try and catch the Yowie, taking all the land and trees away at the same time. But old Yowie knows that the whites are approaching and moves away. As for myself, I have had to stay and fight.

The Japanese chip mill industry was started in my area. They brought in their bulldozers and logging trucks. They desecrated our sacred sites and cut a great deal of timber down. I protested. I went to Sydney. I gave three television talks from Paddington Town Hall and took part in two talk-shows on radio. I did not know what I was stirring up, until representatives of the Department of Parks and Wildlife came down to our mountains—the Mumbulla mountains we name them, after old Jack Mumbulla, a very spiritual man who was one of the great tribal elders of the southeast coast, and who would certainly not want his land and his culture disturbed.[6] So I had got through on the media, and I was able to help stop the timber milling from going any further, along with a lot of white people, I might add, who were behind me in what I was doing and who understood something of the meaning of Aboriginal culture.

I took representatives of the Department of Forestry down to our valleys and into our mountains and told them where the areas sacred to my people were, even the place where young initiates sit and learn about our culture, have Dreamtime, everything. But they did not really understand, and I could see in their eyes they had no clue as to what I was talking about. They wanted to see stained-glass windows or statues of angels: something like that would make a place sacred. But the Aboriginals do not even set up stones to make any spot sacred. Certain significant, beautiful rocks are enough—as Nature put them there—to call a place a cathedral. Such a place is made by God, not by human hands (like a big church in Sydney).

Working with others (including a Catholic priest, Fr. Terry Fox), we won back 11,000 hectares from the milling invasion and kept our sacred site intact. Now it is important to know that once you spoil an Aboriginal sacred site it is no longer a site. You can knock down a church and build it up again and it remains a sacred place. But an Aboriginal sacred space is made by the Master. It is out there where the Aboriginals worshiped, closed their eyes, talked about Jesus, and enjoyed the particular spot as part of their communication with God, with their friends all around.

The special places are usually in the mountains. And why is that? The law comes from the mountain. The commandments were given there, in the mountains. Moses went up on a great rock, and struck it, and water gushed out. Jesus himself went up into the mountains to pray, saying to his disciples, "You wait here." What is more, you will find that most churches have been built on hills—the whites have had the same idea as the Aborigines. Well, the Koories had their mountain cathedrals for centuries. That is according to their oral history, anyhow, and there is nothing to say it is wrong.

Eventually, of course, the Koories and the whites met in Australia. When the whites first came to this land, though, they did not come to it as proper human beings. They came in here bloodthirsty. They fought their way across the whole island of Australia. The missionaries, also, who took up positions here—they were not real Christians because most had hatred in their hearts for the Aboriginal people. When I think back over the stories of my grandfather and great-grandfather, which have been handed down over the generations and which will pass on to my children's children, I know the whites did not have love in their hearts. They were mostly convicts, often with balls and chains on their legs. Sadly, New South Wales bore the full brunt of the invasion of the Europeans, who murdered our people, poisoned them, and much more. Even the missionaries said, "Look, do away with your sacred sites. This is your book, the Bible." But we knew about God the Spirit, about Darama, already. I have told you so before.

We have been steadily losing our land ever since those times. They put us on reserves, which the missionaries took over. Even some of the missionaries, I have heard, shot the Aborigines in the same way others did. The moment missionaries left the reserves, the land was classed as "commons" and went back to the government. Racism, you can tell, is everywhere here. There are good white people and bad, I admit, yet Australia is a very, very racist country—to me just as bad as South Africa. There are Christians among the racists, who somehow reckon Jesus to be a white man.

We do not want to be overtaken like and with all this. We are simply asking for a bit of land; still they will not listen. We are not asking for Sydney Harbour Bridge or the Sydney Opera House, or any of the big impressive places like that; we are asking for the land where our sacred sites are and can still be preserved, the land that was handed down to us by our ancestors. After all, we were in Australia before the whites came here. We are truly part of this land—it is Mother Earth to us. We do not own it; the land owns us.

Aboriginal culture was in Australia long before Christ lived, over 100,000 years before he lived. Yet Aboriginal culture is an extremely spiritual culture. It is based on the Bible, you might say, or it has the same pattern as the Bible, as I showed in connection with mountains and the spiritual understanding that comes from them according to both our oral history and the Bible. It is about time the whites learned these old truths. There are too many churchgoers and not enough Christians. There needs to be a revival among the whites so they can break through the old barriers, so they can walk more closely with the Aboriginal people. This is part of my work—not only to stop the bulldozers, but also to take white folk into a Renewing of the Dreaming ceremony at Wallaga Lakes. In spring and summer over a hundred whites come to participate in this revival at the lakes and in the mountains. I try to show them that we are part of the trees, part of the bush, part of everything, and it is wonderful, because this is what so many whites are searching for in Australia. This wholeness and this walking together is exactly the same thing we find in the Bible.

It is no good saying that Aboriginal culture is finished in Australia. It is not. The culture will still live. It has to come out through us, the Aborigines. We should be telling our young people more about our culture. I try to do a lot of talking in schools, to teach white children, too, because they must learn to respect our culture. Apart from education and renewing the Dreaming, the fight must still go on—the fight for land rights in Australia. I reckon I am just as good as any young fellow to keep it up.

# 10

# Aboriginal and Christian Healing

## AN INTERVIEW WITH MICK FAZELDEAN
### Western Australia

*Mick Fazeldean*: First let me say I cannot read or write. I was born on a cattle station outbush south of Onslow, on the coast of western Australia. My father was an Afghan, my mother was part Pommie (English), but my mother's mother was a full-blooded Aboriginal. After my parents had brought me up I used to make visits to a cook on the station. He was a Filipino.

When I was about ten years old he showed me all sorts of different, magical things with his handkerchief, making butterflies coming out of it for a start. I was very interested because I felt something special was going on. He also showed me how to remove objects from sick people's bodies. Later on he asked me, "Would you like to know how to do these things, my son?" I said, "Yes." "Well," he went on, "you must believe the Lord and think of the Lord in your mind." I thought about these words, but never got involved with a church. It was only when I was almost thirty years of age that the church became important for me. That is when I started speaking the way I do to explain the method of spiritual healing. Many of my people, the Aborigines, can do the same sorts of things I do but they have not studied healing as much as I have, and because I love this work so much I think the Lord is telling me to do something for many different people in Australia.

At first my gift made me worried. I even had to run away from the hospital at Derby (well east of Onslow) because, when I was a mere handyman there, I saved a person's life. He only had seven hours to live, yet I had him walking within two hours. Just with my concentration, without any operation—just with a touch, not with their prayers or anything—he lived. News eventually spread. So I came down to Melbourne. I was called by a lady who was a nurse and had a breast complaint. They were going to remove her breast but she did not want it removed. The doctor told her she had nine months to live if she did nothing. I healed her. Through Aboriginal brothers and sisters down in Victoria, I met other needy people. So I began a work of healing with whites. I found

European persons very, very hard to work on for a while, but since those early days it has become easier. They find it hard to relax, their bodies are very tense and it's hard to work through with my mind. But now, in time and with much more prayer, they do relax and I can heal. Would someone like to ask some questions to keep me going?

*Garry Trompf (GT)*: Could you tell us a little about what you have learned from Aboriginal healers?

*Mick*: I have learned much from the Aborigines. Actually four different nationalities of people have taught me. I have studied long, longer than other Aboriginal healers, and for what reason it is hard to say; I just followed it all up constantly, and I'm still on it now. An important happening led me to heal more people: I had to raise a horse! I thought if I could heal a horse I could heal a European person! And it happened. I think God is with me, continually telling me what to do and taking me around to meet different people, to share what I have done with many sick persons.

*Polonhou Pokawin (PP)*: How did you raise the horse?

*Mick*: Well, I just thought in my mind, made a small prayer, and felt here and there on the sick animal. It was difficult to concentrate! You've got to concentrate on the body and it is very, very hard to concentrate. As I understand it, to get down to concentration your mind goes up. Go to God and God gives you the power to work on the problem, through religion or whatever means are helpful. I am still looking forward to a complete understanding. I just know it is so true as I do it, and yet I myself would like to know how I really do these works. Perhaps someone else could explain it, using Christian words I mean. But Aborigines are Christians themselves, even if they use their own language and songs and so forth. Their ceremony of initiation is a church, and they have special songs for it, just as Europeans have English hymns.

*Wendy Flannery (WF)*: Could you say something about how you first realized that you had healing power and how you felt it coming to you?

*Mick*: That goes back to the time I met this Filipino gentleman, the cook who was working on the station. I used to go to him every night to hear about his healing methods, and I went so deeply into it that my mind felt like a thousand miles away at times. In fact sometimes I could be talking to him and yet be many thousand miles away at the same time. I could not tell you what happened because I did not see it in my ordinary state. Somehow I met people down in Melbourne, and an Aboriginal brother or two down there, long before I went to heal that nurse.

*Bernard Narokobi (BN)*: Could you say how many people you have healed?

*Mick*: Thousands of them. I simply could not tell you, there are so many of them. I am sixty now, and I have been healing since I was about fifteen. When I first started I could not believe what had happened. Everywhere I went some person would come; everything came rushing down on me. They arrived by land or else I was flown by air to help them. At times I often thought: Why? There were surely many who could do the same thing. Through all this, though, I have learned fourteen different languages.

[Published accounts of case histories were then read. In May 1981, for example, there were three healings: Keith Aldrich, aged 36 (from chronic asthma), Christian Pratt, aged 24 (from viral meningitis), and Jack Thomas, aged 45 (from bronchiostasis).]

*Mick*: These case histories were written down by a European lady who saw me working on a person. I said I would like her to record the happenings in English words so that when I got back to Derby I could continue all the more. Many people would like me to work in a hospital, but God tells me to just pick up individuals here and there where I am called to go, to help any people at all. It is not for the money I do it; I do it for the love of it, because the Lord seems to tell me to help many people. A man once offered me a large sum of money. He said, "I could pay you $A500 or $600 if you work on a few cases." I said I was happy with $30, which is enough to keep me going while I am traveling. If I needed help, though, I know I could just write to these persons and they would collect money for me.

*WF*: I'm trying to get a sense of what you experience as a healer. Do you concentrate on a particular sickness or a particular part of the body, or do you just concentrate on the power going through you?

*Mick*: The whole body. So if I'm looking at something down here or down there all my work is on the whole body. As I'm working there my mind is inside that body, and yet I am not doing any physical operation. So therefore my mind is within but it is up on a high level as well. Usually it is clearer before I touch the body. We seem to work together somehow, the patient and myself, a matter I would like to know more about. I would like it explained by someone.

*PP*: You don't use anything?

*Mick*: Nothing. Just my mind and a small prayer, and that touch. It's not a press, or squeeze, but just a touch or whatever. As I put my hand down to touch this body, the body feels a kind of electricity. Electricity comes from down deep. And I don't tell the person when to rise or when he or she is ready to get up; they will tell me how they feel within thirty minutes. A sort of a relief results, and I can then say, "All right, I will see you in a couple of days."

*GT*: But if it takes longer?

*Mick*: If it takes long—if it takes over thirty minutes, let us say—then I will come back and work on the person again from another angle, to take him or her up to another floor in my mind.

*GT*: Perhaps you could tell us a little more about the background to all this. We are interested in the fact that there are gifts already known in Aboriginal tradition and other traditions, quite apart from Christianity. You say you had this gift before you really knew the church, is that so?

*Mick*: Yes, for many years, long before I met the church. I was told secrets about healing by my stepfather, and he was a full-blooded Aboriginal. He was always telling me to be careful, to follow the track as to how you look after the people and the sick. That went on and on. Later I went to church and I found how most of the words in the church were very close to the ones used in our Aboriginal ceremonies. The words they use go back to the words used by Christians.

In many places I have heard stories about a lost tribe many thousand years ago. One such lost tribe was the Injibandi tribe. Up on a mountain, everyone is told, and near Millstream, far west of Derby, there was once a people before we Aborigines landed. These people had their own initiations, but one little group did the wrong thing. After a flood rose up and washed these people away, they became the lost tribe. They were swept away by the flood and came to Millstream, arriving via an underground river. Down there they started another little group: the Injibandi tribe.[1] They had their own initiations, ceremonies, and so forth. A lot of their tradition is dying out, mainly through the mixing with different tribes. It is interesting that everything they say is just like the Christian church, and it means the same thing. Possibly it is so close that it is only the difference in language that prevents Aboriginals from getting close to the church—because they don't study enough. Somehow I have been better able to study even though I cannot read. I have come to see where I am going to go and what was going to happen to me and how to do it. I believe that in the past you would find the same source of healing behind the Aboriginal tradition and Christianity.

*GT*: What about cases of pointing the bone or sorcery? Such cases mean that some other person is involved who is trying to bring on the sickness or that there is a bad relationship between two people. What happens with the healing in that case? Is it important for you to make contact with the person who is actually pointing the bone or bringing on the bad effects?

*Mick*: No. We just take the problem away from the sick person. We take it away and of course nothing of the evil effect remains. Then if the pointer or sorcerer does the same thing to someone else, the effect must be taken away again.

*PP*: In your healing, when you touch a person, do you extract something out of the body—like bones?

*Mick*: Yes.

*PP*: But do you see the bones?

*Mick*: No. I don't see it, but I can feel it—just that feeling in my fingers when I'm working on it.

*PP*: But you don't specifically bring out a bone or some object?

*Mick*: No.

*GT*: Yet there are traditional Aboriginal healers you know who would do this?

*Mick*: Yes, some certainly would.

*GT*: Earlier on, would you have done anything like that, or is it that right from the beginning you healed the way you've been healing—just by touch?

*Mick*: By touch, with a touch. I can take whatever is inside away.[2]

*Simeon Namunu (SN)*: You said something began happening when you were ten.

*Mick*: At ten I started studying, thinking. I was getting so close to the goal. At fifteen I started healing.

*SN*: When did you come to know the Lord, or the church as you call it?

*Mick*: That was some twenty-five years ago.

*SN*: Twenty-five years ago. Twenty-five years ago, what sort of powers do you think you had?

*Mick*: I had that feel, it was in my mind. He just talked to me in my own language through a small prayer. I didn't understand it was a proper thing; I didn't know it was a prayer when I first started. It was in a dialect. You would say *Nirudanda urugungar ngalagu gnalamaliu*. Well, *nirudanda*, that means "you come with Me." It was in Aboriginal language. That language is Taragu. If I said it in my Narriuyindi language I would say something like this: *neregari neregari ma mama*, "Let the Father come down to me. I am holding this person." Then, as now, when I work on a body, after I've finished I have to have about twenty-five minutes of rest because my mind becomes heavy. It tightens up.

These are prayers I learned only from Aboriginal people, but it really all started back with the Filipino man. Then I spoke to Aboriginal people and they instructed me further and told me, "You talk to God in that language. God will help."

*BN*: Have you worked on someone with a medically permanent disability, like a paraplegic?

*Mick*: Well, I worked on a European gentleman in Melbourne. He was a paraplegic. He would be about sixty-five or seventy years of age. Within four weeks all his skin and limbs were coming back nicely. You'd think he was about fifty or so now. But I can't believe now that I did it! I concentrated while he was sitting down on the other side of the room and he calmed down. Later on he asked me if I'd mind having a look at his back. He had arthritis, and I helped him out with that for three weeks as well.

*GT*: What about terminal cancer patients?

*Mick*: That's what was happening to the woman with breast cancer. That's what she thought she had and strangely, as I was working on her, I somehow realized that the whole problem had to do with the top of her foot, and a vein coming out of it. That was the whole problem. So I said to her, "There's something wrong with your foot," and she said, "It gets itchy there, and I put some Vaseline on it, but it's still there." So I touched that, and I worked on it and found it was the whole problem. Three weeks later I got through to it completely. She's well now. She's out pushing a lawn mower! She likes cutting lawns and now she has started again.

That was the case of a European woman. Now let me tell you about a white man I am starting to train! I am looking forward to this training, although I don't know how it will go. Once I helped the man concerned. He used to go to the hospital in Canberra. I examined his kidneys and bladder and in three weeks he was completely well. He was a European chap, but quite unable to understand how I did it. He tried to ask me how it was possible, but I said I did not really know the answer. It was in my mind, I said, and there were no words to explain.

He insisted on getting a chart to show me the parts of the body. I pointed out to him on the chart where the problem really lay. "But, that's the throat," he said, "and, anyway how do you see all this with your naked eyes?" "Well," I answered, "I talk to God, and God shows me." He said he would like to learn the same secrets. "Well, if you'd like to learn to be like me," I told him, "I'll take you down to an [Aboriginal] elder and let you learn from him just as I did earlier." So I have been taking him down to Onslow to see my uncle there, and I believe if I could get him to work like I do—on cancer especially—he could explain more clearly than I can what goes on, and even write it all down.

*Fred Wandmaker*: You mentioned that a woman said she had something wrong with her breast, and the problem was in her foot. Does that happen often? That you find out where the problem is without them telling?

*Mick*: Yes, but I do ask them what is wrong with them. I do not like to say "your problem is down there" without them saying what they think is wrong. Yet with every person I have worked on who is going to pass away—the very serious cases—I have always worked on their toes first. From the small toe I then work upwards. I worked on a very sick girl this way. I saw her in the hospital; she was skin and bones. You could see every joint of the bone. My wife said, "I know you're very clever, Mick, but I'll bet you five pounds you will never fix her!" So I said to one of my friends—she was an Aboriginal nurse—"Look, go in the morning and touch that girl on the mouth. She's going to open her mouth and receive some food." Now the doctor said she was going to pass away that night around midnight. In fourteen days she rose and walked around the bed. On the twenty-third day she was discharged and went back home.

I suppose I ought to tell you about other types of help I have been asked to give. You see I have brought twenty-five children into this world! I've had two breeches. There are many other healers among our people who have not been able to do anything for a mother with a child in a breech cross. One time a family came over twenty-five miles to get me for a birth. We got to the scene just in time because the woman was all dry, and that meant she was just about leaving [this earth]. We were only there five minutes and I touched her just like that across the hips, and down here in the back, and underneath the hip bone. The baby just came nicely around and straightened, and in about five minutes the baby was born. Well, there it is. But I wouldn't like anyone to call me a doctor because I'm not!

*PP*: Have you ever felt a sense of failure? Have you ever felt that you've failed?

*Mick*: At times I do, but then I work harder. I have only got two chances, one to raise, another one to lose. Let me tell you about an Aboriginal chap who was in hospital for almost a year and who had only two weeks to live.

He was lying day in and day out on his bed, and he developed a heart problem as well. I worked on him over Sunday, recently. The following week, on a Monday, he was walking. He met the doctor on the path coming down from the hospital. The doctor asked, "Isn't your name Raymond Clement?" "Yes." "Then how come you are out of bed?" The patient did not know my name, which was one good thing, and simply said, "Oh, my uncle came down here, and was sitting down here, and was sitting down talking to me. I soon felt better." He was discharged the following week.

I look forward to learning one day how this all comes about and where the power of strength comes from. But I at least understand it comes from "up there."

*PP*: Can you explain what is going through you and what makes you perform the healing in your vernacular language rather than English?

*Mick*: No, it is too difficult for me. That is why I'd like to meet someone—a [Catholic] Father, let us say—who could explain it well. I would like to learn from someone like that and come to a clearer understanding. At least I can say a few things. With any person, no matter what the sickness or who it is, my first act is to come along and just have a look. As I look at him I give my small prayer, then there is a power just like electricity that comes through from the switchboard on the other side. It is like plugging a wire in, if you see what I mean.

*Guboo Ted Thomas (fellow Aboriginal)*: It is very hard for brothers and sisters to answer questions like that. Sometimes it is a matter of a very special contact between the Healer up there and the one down here, and it is a very strong, personal business. Sometimes the Aboriginal people meditate, or use special words, as he does, or dream. We contact God, just as do so many other people. My mind, my meditation goes up to heaven, to God, for guidance.

[South Asian] Indians have some philosophies whereby the mind goes out and contacts "the Other." We have very much the same traditions as the Indians do. In Aboriginal culture something is very strong. Our character and our faith in our part of Australia, down in the southeast, produce exactly the same activity. My grandmother, for example, was a healer. Healing is a wonderful gift.

*Mick*: Thank you for adding that, brother.

*PP*: Can you heal yourself, supposing you ever get sick?

*Mick*: To a certain extent, yes. But in one sense, no. I'd first have to go and see another healer. Then, as the other person is healing me, I would use my power and we would work together to take something away from me—some pain, or whatever it was.

*Guboo*: Faith has a lot to do with it, too. If you have faith, God will heal you. If you ask, "Do you believe I can heal you?" and the person says, yes, then the brother can do it.

*PP*: What if they say they do not have faith?

*Mick*: Then it would make it harder for me as a healer. I would have to go to my second prayer to work on that body. To make the body well in that case I would not touch it. I would just sit; but when I sit I would have to be sitting looking straight toward the person. My soul has to be dead square on him or her; centered on that body. I could be sitting down talking, even drinking tea or coffee. Within an hour the person's mind would change. They would say,

"Could you please help me? I would like you to help me." It's the same thing as healing. It is very simple to do that, but it is very hard to explain it. It is God's way to use many languages to get to one goal.

*PP*: In your communication you have to be speaking in different languages. How do you receive the message from God? In fact, do you actually receive a message? If you do, do you understand it? Do you feel the power?

*Mick*: I feel the power. And even when I come to something very serious it is not only just "up there." It is here as well; and then your breath counts for so much as well. If I am working on someone who is seriously ill, and if I feel sure it means I have got to change my prayer in my own mind, I go up to another level to work on that body. I try to get to that other level to work first and work on it just with the mind. Then the appropriate power will come down strongly the moment I go on to touch the body concerned. There's no squeeze, no touch, but an electricity goes through and takes away from the body whatever is causing the pain. Electricity—that is the word that comes closest to explaining the workings of my healing.

*Esau Tuza*: I in my small corner, I find it sometimes very difficult to touch a person. So I never think to heal them. Sometimes I don't know when to touch them. Do you ever have that experience?

*Mick*: Yes. Sometimes I come along and I'd have to be there five minutes before I touch that body, because that way I look at the person and sum up which direction to approach things. Not until you get that all straightened out can you put your hands right there on the right spot.

*Esau*: So yours has much more to do with location and "geography?"

*Mick*: Yes.

*Esau*: I have been aware of that, of a small feeling and spacing. It's very interesting.

*Mick (and others, in surprise)*: Have you healed anybody?

*Esau*: I have, yes. I couldn't tell that I had sometimes. And I'm not aware of the psychological side yet. I use more feeling than location; in fact I was not aware of this understanding of location before.

*FW*: Now, what about other types of special power in your society? Do you know anyone in the tribe who has other special powers, let us say for rain-making?

*Mick*: Yes, there are rainmakers among the tribes. They are different from me; I couldn't do that.

*FM*: Yes, but when you talk to rainmakers, are you able to communicate, and are you able to talk to each other about how you feel when you do what you do?

*Mick*: Ah, yes. A couple of times I have talked things over with rainmakers. They do practically the same that I do in reaching levels, but a bit lower down. I work a bit further up in the levels of the mind.

*WF*: As I understand it, when you say you have been studying and thinking and so on, you are really talking about these different levels, and about moving up and down. Could you try to go deeper into that?

*Mick*: As I have already said, if the sickness to be healed is only a small matter, I go up these levels only to a certain [or limited] extent. But if there is something really big to be done, that's when I go on up to the other levels. My mind goes up there; it goes higher and higher to another level.

*WF*: Now you were saying that rainmakers were on a certain level?

*Mick*: Yes, but they work down there on a lower rung.

*WF*: Right, and you are above, where you find power. And are there some in-between levels too?

*Mick*: Well, it depends on what you mean. You come to a first level, and second level, and you are still not very far. Three levels, and you are on a high one—on the rainmaking level—but you can go on, until you reach the point where you can go no further.

*GT*: How do you describe those levels to yourself in words?

*Mick*: Well, it's not so much to do with words; it's what your mind says, what you think without words. Sometimes the healer and the sick person can get onto the same level, or healers can help each other by going up the levels together.

*GT*: You mean all this is done silently?

*Mick*: Silently. You only need to get two persons together and they do not have to tell one another what they are doing.

*SN*: So is it more dreaming than thinking with words?

*Mick*: No, we are talking about something that is just now in the mind; you yourself could see it with your mind. You sort of feel and see at the same time with your mind—and that is the beginning of finding the levels.

*SN*: Do you see pictures?

*Mick*: Yes, in one spot, yes. I do.

*SN*: So you *see* something, too?

*Mick*: That's right; but not all the time. A picture just comes at a certain time. When you come to each level you will sense it, and as you get more deeply down, something like a flash comes out when you know you are at the right point for healing. It is not so different from looking at a TV screen, but the flash doesn't stay long.

*BN*: What about other preparations for your work? Before your healing do you go through certain rituals? Do you make certain sacrifices, abstain from eating some kinds of food, as I understand rainmakers do?

*Mick*: No.

*BN*: What about the body of the sick persons you want to heal; do you require them to do certain things in preparation?

*Mick*: Well, yes, in the sense that I could give them that [preparation]. Somehow in me my body goes into them, and by thinking, that [approach] will relieve their trouble and make them feel lighter or whatever.

*Michael Maeliau*: Your body goes into someone else's?

*Mick*: In or on to the part of them needing help.

*GT*: A sort of incarnation?

*Mick*: I'm not sure about the word, but maybe you say the right one there.

*GT*: What about diet? What do you—does it enable you to know what these persons need in their diet?

*Mick*: That's right, yes. You can tell what should be the first meal after the work you have been doing on a person.

*WF*: So you can actually feel what is inside that person and what they need?

*Mick*: That's right. You come to the edge of a certain point through using the levels of the mind, and that point is just like a light switch. You realize that when you get to it and touch it, you will put the light on.

*Esau*: I find that very, very interesting. Especially the combining of healing with pastoral care. For me, it is not until I touch, I feel, what you might call the electric cord, that the moment of healing really happens.

*Mick*: Yes, as I say, it is something like a switchboard!

*Esau*: For me, too, the prayer to say comes automatically. It just comes—the way you want it. You're not ready for it—it's there as soon as the feeling calls for it between you and the patient.

*Mick*: Right. And sometimes I'm not ready, but God is ready at all times. I could be asleep and someone would come along and get me up, saying, "Look, we need help over there!" I would have to try and wake up. Even when tired, though, as soon as I touch that person in need, the contact you are talking about will be sent down.

*Esau*: But I have two problems. One is that I cannot cure myself, you know. While I can cure others, I simply can't cure myself. I have terrible migraine headaches sometimes, but I can do nothing by myself for them.

*Mick*: It's the same with me.

*Esau*: Another problem is that I have a tendency to escape from the person whom I heal, because sometimes their pains and suffering come on to me myself; I want to go away.

*Mick*: I know what you're trying to say. Sometimes when I am fairly close to a problem, it affects me like a needle injection.

*GT*: Healing can hurt you, then?

*Mick*: Well, sometimes and in the end, yes. I get dizzy after working on someone very deeply. I've got to rest for about twenty-five minutes. Because of what I use "in there," in the mind and in the body, and because using my eyes, feet, all of myself together—it affects me. I need about twenty-five to thirty minutes to have a break and calm down my mind.

*SN*: The next thing is return to prayer then?

*Mick*: Yes.

*SN*: Now, when you pray, what word do you use for God?

*Mick*: Any of the Aboriginal words for God; whichever ones come spontaneously from above.

*Esau*: I also pray in my language. I say *mamma* or *da*, which simply means, "Father or mother, you are here." *Da* implies more than that, but these words are my only connection from above. When I contact a sick person that's my only link. I go through a time when I forget myself completely. I even forget all I have learned about pastoral care and ministry at the moment.

*Mick*: Interesting. That time of blotting out is the same for me.

*Esau*: It seems to me, too, with that forgetfulness, that I could be watching what is going on outside myself and the other person. I don't use the name Jesus; I use the word *Da*. That's all. That is my singular kind of relationship, *seulement*, as you might say.

*SN*: Esau, tell us, how many people have you healed?

*Esau*: Not many. I would say twenty-four people. But, as I say, I have difficulty, because I tend to run away after healing the people and have a problem over the whole thing! So I cannot cure myself.

*Mick*: But why do you have to run away?

*Esau*: Well, let's take my last case. It was a mental case in May this year [1981]. I was with my friends Caleb Kotan and Matthew Harper and some others. We had been all praying for this man out of Honiara [in the Solomons]. He had been in a hospital for three months, and there his ailment was so unpredictable that the doctor could not see anything wrong and did not want him to stay around anymore. "Let him go back," he insisted.

He was back in the Solomons, and fellow students had stopped praying over this man for some time. They were out of the ward when I came in. They had been very concerned for the man for a long while and Caleb was particularly worried that his complaint—of being *long long* as we say in pidgin—would always return. He had a sickness which often drove him to run away from home and led him to do things irrationally.

Anyway, I happened to be there and for some unknown reason the father asked me to go and pray over him. In a strange way I felt called to him, so I fetched back Matthew and Caleb to come with me. It took us about one hour just to talk to the sick man. This was simply because I found it difficult to touch him. After that hour was up I had simply run out of things to say! But then I began to recognize through counseling—just counseling and feeling—what was needed. Steadily I came to a situation where I was "not there." I was there physically, I admit, but perhaps I could say not mentally, if you gather what I mean.

In that situation I normally use water, not water that comes from rivers, but rain water. I don't know why, it just comes from the feeling. In his case I just wet my hands, put them over his head, the place where he was thinking and the source of his worrying actions, and I prayed over him. Then, immediately after the prayer, I went outside. When I was standing in the open, my head was spinning. It had happened various times and I don't really know why.

*Mick*: Your mind was working so quickly and you prayed so hard, that it made you start "running." When you come to the task you just have to be normal; everything's all got to work together.

*Esau*: True, but at least the spinning does not always last long, often only a few minutes.

*SN*: And what happened to the person you were praying over?

*Esau*: That person? It happened that Caleb came up to Honiara and brought the message from the father that, well, I healed him on that night. I always run away from people I heal. And so the message from the father was later passed on: "Will you please thank Esau? My son is completely cured. He's gone back to the village and lives happily." That's all I heard, and that, as I said, was my last case. I was actually asked by the doctor to send my case matter, and I was glad to make contact with him because we seem to have been working together.

I should add here that I have learned much from my father, who was also a healer. Traditionally he had tremendous power—which those of us who have gone through school or even theological college do not easily obtain. It's in the culture. We don't have it.

*Mick*: That's right.

*SN*: Your healing, Esau, does it have any connection with traditional healers?

*Esau*: I think I learned from the traditional healers, but it seemed to me that the Spirit is also embodied in them. Over and above the traditional healers I also learned from the Holy Mama[3] that one must become both man and God and the healing must be mediated from that kind of person. Do you know what I mean? It seems to me as if the Spirit can be specially embodied in a person. Don't ask me how or why, because I still don't know! I am still thinking things out.

*GT*: Could I ask you, Mick, whether you've had cases like the one Esau cited, of people who were mentally disturbed.

*Mick*: Hardly at all. I have almost never worked on that sort of thing.

*SN*: And could I ask you, Mick, where does the Holy Spirit come into your healing? Let's go back to your earlier days, connections, and early personal history. Has anybody ever talked to you about the Holy Spirit or God?

*Mick*: Yes, well that's putting this Power into the English language isn't it? And I do accept the Holy Spirit. I admit I have learned a lot from the Methodist Church, and from the Church of Christ.

In all the little things I've studied—on and on—I am still praising and praying to the Lord. And the Lord is still asking me to press on to meet many more people I can help in the future.

*PP*: So, you would not turn your power to work against other people? In fact, can you also use your power to hurt anyone?

*Mick*: No, I couldn't. I have been offered money to harm others, but I have said, no, I can't do it, because God has told me not to do it. God gives me the power to raise people, and when the devil comes into the middle, God tells me how to avoid the devil. It has happened a couple of times that somebody has offered me a thousand dollars to hurt someone—children actually—and I've refused. Why should I hurt a living child? I should like to see children grow and live, and to see all people well!

# Part IV

## Theological Horizons and Adjustments

# 11

# Spirits in Melanesian Tradition and Spirit in Christianity

## SIMEON NAMUNU
### Eastern Papuan Islands

I recall vividly an experience from my upbringing with my grandmother. I had started school when my parents were sent to a very remote village to look after a church there. Because my parents did not want to interrupt my education they decided to leave me and my brother with our grandmother.

The school we were attending was three miles away from where we were living. Each day we would walk to school carrying our food for lunch in a basket made from coconut leaves. As we entered the school area we would hide our basket of food in a tree, making sure no one saw it, because we feared someone might make magic on it and poison us.

Our grandmother was a faithful church member and a local preacher. She was keen for us to attend Sunday School and regular church services. In spite of her Christian convictions, however, she did not hesitate to tell us about the spirits living in trees, caves, and rocks and about certain areas that could affect us if we were not careful. "These spirits are dangerous and can make you sicken and die," she said. She believed strongly, too, that witches are active at night, roaming about laying traps to harm people against whom they have hostile and vicious feelings. Innocent people can be caught in those traps if they are not careful. Hence we had to be careful and were to return home before dark. When any of us got ill my grandmother would send for a sorcerer to drive out the evil power or objects in our bodies.

How should the church in Melanesia address itself to such outlooks? If the church is the "called out one" by God through the work of Jesus Christ, it is surely here on earth to manifest the living and powerful God, as well as to proclaim the Good News of Salvation in Christ. Surely it has arisen to throw into question every human-made belief and practice, let alone old fears about magic and spooky places.

I do believe that Melanesian traditions have many good values that are deep and meaningful. These values can be theologically, intellectually, and emotionally inspiring. These values, then, should not be overlooked and forgotten. At the same time I also do believe that some Melanesian traditional practices are not useful from the Christian point of view. Clearly no single social tradition is perfect and without trace of sin. As the Bible has it "all have sinned and fall short of the glory of God" (Rom 3:23), although, since we try to do our very best, God appreciates and accepts.

Thus we are left with a problematic relationship between the church and complex human culture, and are naturally concerned to ask whether indigenizing the church's theology might help. In one small paper, however, I can hardly compare the Christian viewpoint(s) with the multitude of different practices in Melanesia. Thus I am going to confine my attention to the issue of spirit, first looking at the spirits believed in by my own people, then turning to the biblical concept of Spirit, to show how the Old Testament lays the foundations on which Christian views about Spirit or the Spirit of God are developed.

## MELANESIAN SPIRITS

Melanesians see themselves and their social life in relation to nature, to other humans, and to spirit-beings. They recognize that their social life is not limited only to the perceived physical world but extends into the invisible part of the universe as well. The Christian also acknowledges the invisible life. In Melanesia this outlook derives from a mixture of feelings and ritual practice. Within that framework of Melanesian belief is the certainty that human beings exist not by their own power and for their own ends. Human beings are born, according to the ancient legends, either of themselves or of birds and animals or other entities. Upon their birth or creation Melanesians are endowed with a sense of history, purpose, a set of values, and a vision of the physical world by which they are guided.

They are also born into the world of the spirits and much of their life is spent maintaining and promoting that spiritual order. Thus wholeness for Melanesians depends largely on the spirit world within which they live and work. So when they depart from that spiritual order of existence, some kind of immediate physical punishment will be inflicted upon them. In the event of these consequences they have to set to work and try to restore the broken relationships. They may kill a pig and offer part of it to the spirit, and for them that would be a religious experience.

Like Christianity, Melanesian religions describe classes of spirits. For most Christians there is the Supreme Spirit-Being known as God, and then classes of angels—the spirit-beings who are delegated with various responsibilities—and also Satan and the order of spirits opposed to the Supreme Being. So also Melanesians claim comparable classes of spirit-entities.

In my society on Panaeati Island (Misima District, Papua), our Supreme Being was called Yabowaine and was invoked well before the coming of

Christian teaching.[1] Yabowaine is the person of "the above," and is the creator, sustainer, and giver of all good things. Yabowaine helps people in trouble, especially during the tribal fights of olden days. We give Yabowaine a masculine gender.

Of lesser importance are the *Totowoko*. They are believed to abide in trees, rocks, and specific areas. They are numerous, live everywhere, and are held to be male and female spirit-beings. Most of them are believed to be helpful and friendly, but others are vicious and fearful and can make the living sick or ill. They can even be owned by particular individuals within a given village. They are then known as protective spirits because they protect their owners wherever they go. They are kind and helpful to their owners when invoked for courage, strength, endurance, and other qualities.

Next, we have the garden spirit, who is believed to be a female. She is the producer of our garden yams. At planting time she is invoked for favor and good harvest. She abides in an unknown place said to be in a mountain where the sun sets.

Important also are the spirits of the dead, especially of the recent dead. These spirits are sometimes known as ghosts or devils. These are what we call the *yayaluwa* or *sevasevan* of the dead people. These spirits are neither male nor female, although the spirit can be identified by the name the dead person used when he or she was alive.

These spirits are believed to live at a known place called Bwebweso on a mountain called Lion. Bwebweso is the last place where all the spirits end up; it is like a paradise for the dead. When people die, they first have to go to a place located at the eastern tip of Misima Island, where they have their ritual bath. When all is well they proceed on to Bwebweso. Here we find something like the belief in purgatory as known among Roman Catholics.

The ritual bathing is closely connected with a pig sacrifice on the day when death occurs. The pig-killing sacrifice is called *tuwan pagapagasisi*. It is believed that the ritual will ensure the dead easy passage to Bwebweso. If persons are known to be rich and important, some of their wealth is buried with them and some may be kept to pay for pig-killing rituals. Although the living consume the sacrifice it is most important that the dead are redeemed spiritually to Bwebweso, the paradise, by rituals practiced. Sorcerers have a part to play in employing magic as part of the ritual, especially if the dead person was known to be a witch. They have to ensure that his or her spirit does not turn into a devil we call *piwapiwa*, who comes out at night or in lonely places and frightens the living, especially the deceased person's close relatives. The living can receive strength and protection from the dead. Often a small portion of the dead person's hair is kept to ensure such help and protection. That in itself shows that all this is religious experience.

The dead spirit, it is believed, can re-enter living persons and throw them into a severe fit with a loss of consciousness. That reaction is called *ala sevasevan*. It is really a spirit-possession of the living. When that happens a sorcerer may be called to use magic ritually and release the person from the spirit's possession.

That again is a religious experience, and not unlike some pentecostal religious experiences or exorcism in the Catholic tradition.

The last category of spirits consists of birds, animals, reptiles, and fish. This may sound strange to the Westerner, but for Melanesians it is not difficult to conceive of a spirit taking on any shape or form, giving it life to move about with ease. This is not so different from some of the strange phenomena in the apocalyptic writings of the Bible (Daniel or Revelation) in which rather unbelievable figures of animals, birds, and humans are given life, their strange behavior fulfilling the divine purpose and will.

## THE SPIRIT IN THE OLD TESTAMENT

The word used for spirit in both Hebrew and Greek is significant. In his book *I Believe in the Holy Spirit*, Michael Green tells us that *ruach* (Hebrew) and *pneuma* (Greek) have three primary meanings: "wind," "breath," and "spirit" (see Ezek 37:1–14).[2] In both the Old and New Testaments *ruach* and *pneuma* are used to denote the life-giving breath that God gives and without which a human being is spiritually lifeless and inactive. That is why the Deuteronomist affirmed that "man does not live by bread alone, but . . . by everything that proceeds out of the mouth of the Lord"(Deut 8:3). The emphasis here is that all life belongs to and reflects the divine, sustaining principle. Jesus quoted this very passage (Mt 4:4) and the form he gave to it made the original meaning still clearer. Instead of using the word "everything" he used the phrase "every word" in order to teach us that we have to depend on another life, which is of "a higher kind than that which is nourished by bread, and that that life is nourished by the total self-communication of God."[3]

*Ruach* in the Old Testament connotes the wind or spirit of life, without which humans cease to exist. *Ruach* is not indigenous to human beings but is on loan, a kind of present. The *ruach* is the life that emanates from God and must return to God at death. The two meanings of the word tend to merge: first, wind, or the elementary act of breathing in and out through the nose; and second, spirit, or the life-giving breath of God to the innermost being of a person. In both senses, faith is necessary for us to share this mysterious gift of God.

I want to make one more point here. The Hebrews did not divide human beings into spirit, mind, and body as moderns often tend to do. They thought of the human being as an entity, an animated body, and a living person. They also employed another word—an evocative one—to "describe our human vitality, the quality that marks a living person from a dead one: and that was *nephesh*."[4] *Nephesh*, in contrast to *ruach*, is equated with a person's life. It may even be identified with blood, which the Hebrews deemed absolutely basic to physical existence (see Gen 9:4; Lev 17:10–14; Deut 12:22–24).

The Old Testament teaching is that this powerful, life-giving, mysterious Spirit belongs to God and to God alone. To the Hebrews it is essentially the personal God, Yahweh, in action. It is from this background that the Christian doctrine of the Holy Spirit can be understood.

## CREATOR SPIRIT?

The Old Testament teaching on the Creator Spirit is not at all clear. Although there are allusions in Genesis 1:2 ("the Spirit of God was moving over the face of the waters") and Job 33:4 ( "The spirit of God has made me, and the breath of the Almighty gives me life"), the idea of a Creator Spirit seems somewhat alien to Hebrew thought. These and other references are usually wrongly interpreted in any case. What the Old Testament teaches on this subject of Spirit is restricted almost exclusively to the relationship between God and human beings.

Such a restriction suggests that the Hebrews wanted to be careful about what they said concerning the Spirit as Creator. In those days there were many nature mysticisms in pagan religions. The Hebrews had consistently maintained that God the Creator transcended all things; they emphasized the otherness of God. They wanted to speak of the Spirit of God as the energizer rather than the Creator; thus the Spirit is portrayed as actively involved in God's ongoing creative work. In Genesis 2:7 we see that God breathes life into the already moulded forms of animals and the human being. There is little evidence to show that the Spirit creates, but we do see that the Spirit gives life. In Psalm 104:30 we read: "When thou sendest forth thy Spirit, they [God's creatures] are created; and thou renewest the face of the ground." Yet even here, in a psalm thought to be an adaptation of an Egyptian and therefore a foreign hymn, it may not mean that the Spirit is understood to be the actual creator of the animals and "things innumerable."[5]

Most pertinent passages seem careful to place the Spirit as an accompanying energizer of God's creative acts. That is in line with what the Old Testament teaches about *ruach* as breath. Thus we have in Psalm 33:6 the statement: "By the Word of the Lord the heavens were made, and all their host by the breath of his mouth." The spirit comes into operation as the result of God's decree or command. God's Word is more distinctively creative, as in Genesis 1:3: "God said, 'Let there be light'; and there was light" (cf. Gen. l:6, 9, 14, 20, 24, 26).

It must be conceded that there are certainly some hints of a Creator Spirit in the Old Testament, and certainly this idea is present in the period leading to the New Testament. But rather than build on something about which we are not so certain because of the slight evidence, it is preferable for us to say that the Spirit written of in both the Old and New Testaments is more the energizer than the creator, and thus more the animating principle of life, especially in the relationship between God and humanity.[6]

## THE SPIRIT AS THE PRINCIPLE OF LIFE

In the New Testament the word "life" is prominent. The early Christians did not hesitate to attribute life to the Spirit. The Spirit plays the significant part in the Christian's life. Here life depends entirely on the Spirit whose presence mysteriously changes, reforms, and builds the person in the unity of love.

The Spirit, as we have seen, is the highest element in redeemed persons. This element does not belong to the person; it is on loan and therefore must be received by faith in Jesus Christ. The Spirit is God's gift and the Christian should not disregard it (1 Thess 4:6). The Spirit's presence creates unity and the Christian's job is to preserve that unity by the bond of peace (Eph 4:3).

Right from the beginning, according to Genesis, the action of the Spirit was recognized to be chiefly to give humans the power to rule, to be good craftspeople, to have insight, and to manifest prophetic utterances. If in the Old Testament the Spirit of God gives life, so we see in the New Testament the life of the Christian is to be found in the Spirit. Here the point is that for the Christian the indwelling of the Spirit of God raises the level of experience in life and is linked to Christ in the new birth. The Christian is then enabled by the Spirit to know the truth about God. Hence character, initiative, purposive action, ethical qualities and the like all together point to what is called personality (see 2 Cor 5:17-19).

All in all, life in Christian experience points to the principle that the risen Christ and the Spirit are practically interchangeable in respect of their operations in human experience.

In the Gospel of John, Spirit is the intrinsic nature of God. One cannot fully know God unless one is "born anew" (Jn 3:3); only then will the door open to the glory of heaven. John means that there is spiritual birth and light illuminating one's surroundings and showing something beyond oneself of God, who is Spirit (Jn 4:24). The Spirit is the Spirit of God or the Holy Spirit, who is the principle of the life that is synonymous with salvation.

The Holy Spirit of whom we speak here as the principle of life is the God who is deeply involved in human affairs, who gives light to see life as it really is, and who gives us the power to take up the challenge of making decisions. The early Christians saw the Holy Spirit, the breath of God, consoling and revitalizing them to enter into life's full force.

## THE HOLY SPIRIT MOVEMENTS OF MELANESIA

In the light of my comments about spirits in Melanesian tradition and the Spirit of God as represented in the Bible, it is of interest that there are now arising in many and varied Melanesian contexts (particularly in Papua New Guinea) so-called Holy Spirit movements. At least one book and one university thesis discuss some of the phenomena of these movements, especially the ecstatic activity—people being filled with the Spirit, speaking in tongues, dancing, shaking, prophesying, healing, discovering and expelling evil. I will tell something of my own experience in this connection.[7]

In 1978, while a student at Rarongo Theological College, I became interested in the renewal movement in New Ireland and decided to do some research on it with a view to making it the subject of my sub-thesis. I went to New Ireland and conducted some surveys. I spent about six days in the village of Sorvun near

Namatanai and talked with various people there about the movement.

The revival on New Ireland is centered in the Kavieng area, but it has spread through individuals and passed through New Ireland down to the Namatanai area. From my interviews with various people I gathered that people see it as a new trend in which they want to share and so they seek involvement.

I stayed for a time at the United Church high school in Manggai. The headmaster was David Odd, a charismatic person, and the school is well known for the activities of the Holy Spirit going on there. With the permission of the headmaster I interviewed some of the students. I gathered different impressions from these young people. Many of them said that they had been forced into the movement by the personality of the headmaster. Others claimed their joining had resulted from a genuine decision on their part. Still others said that they ran away to hide in the bush when they saw the headmaster approaching, and reappeared when he had left.

I finally had the opportunity to talk with the national leader, Ben Lenturut. He told me that he had conducted a week-long camp on Zau Island. Toward the end of that camp he decided to hold a communion service. He told the people that when they went home they must bring back a *kulau* (a green coconut used for drinking). They all came back with *kulaus* and put them in the church. On Sunday he told the people that as they went out of the church they would each receive a *kulau* and then they should stand in an oval-shaped area outside the church. As they went out, someone stood at the door to cut the *kulaus* open, and Ben told them to eat the *kulau* meat as bread and drink the juice as wine. So they went out and stood around in the oval, about a thousand people in all. After they had finished eating and drinking, something like a wind, according to Ben, sprang up. It just blew without any trees moving, and everybody fell flat on the ground, praising and singing. Ben did not know how to stop it and just let them go on for about two hours, when everything returned to normal. That was just one incident he related.

The practice of re-baptism into the church was initiated in New Ireland. Ben Lenturut was involved in this activity, though it seems that the idea was originally somehow forced on him. In the end he accepted it as a call from God when he was asked to re-baptize some students and teachers at Manggai High School. One boy refused when the headmaster spoke to him, saying that all of them had already been baptized into God's family. So Ben went away and decided to contact (United Church) Bishop Gaius about it, saying that he had been asked to conduct the re-baptism but did not know whether he should do it.[8] The bishop gave no definite answer and pressure from the school continued. Eventually the bishop told him just to go ahead and do what God wanted him to do. And so the first re-baptism was held at Manggai. The second occurred a year later in a village called Kandang in central New Ireland, where one other minister was involved. Both Ben and this other minister underwent re-baptism.

I got the impression at the last United Church Assembly that the revival in the United Church is spreading. What is happening in one section of the United

Church is also happening in other sections. I feel that it is supernatural, the work of the Holy Spirit, and that we cannot control what God is doing.

In the Kapuna situation, in the Gulf Province of Papua, a revival surrounds the work of the expatriate Dr. Calvert. The Papuan mainland region of the United Church has not had a good relationship with Dr. Calvert. Dr. Calvert reported that the revival in Kapuna began on the station where he works as a doctor and spread to nearby villages. He said that as a result of the revival each individual Christian had made a personal commitment to Christ, but it took a long debate in the Assembly before the value of his work was acknowledged (1980).

I am personally sympathetic to these developments in my country, and feel that the churches should welcome these transformations born of the Spirit. The Holy Spirit moves through a land dominated by its traditional spirits, and the Spirit replaces and overcomes those that are evil and gathers up into power all those of value for the Kingdom.

Now I want to add some cautionary remarks.

## DISCERNING BETWEEN TRADITIONAL SPIRITS
## AND THE HOLY SPIRIT

Traditionally people in my region see both good and evil as coming from the spirits. All the spirits are believed to have influence for both good and evil. Thus, in Misima, the spirit Tamudulele can be invoked both for killing and for curing. Both good and evil are associated even with Yabowaine. From one and the same spirit may come success, good luck, skill, wealth, and prestige, as well as failure, social disruption, sickness, misfortune, and death. Success and good fortune are viewed as the result of possessing the power of the spirits, especially when it is a matter of creating or transforming something in ways considered beyond human power. Thus, for example, the power to be victorious in a fight is obtained by properly performing the ritual needed to win the favor of a spirit associated with such power. With this attitude, extraordinary results can be expected with little effort.

The power of the spirits is creative and can bring about the effects desired. As far as ordinary Christians are concerned, it makes little difference whether miraculous happenings occur through the power of the Holy Spirit or through that of traditional spirits. Supernatural phenomena are believed to be caused by spiritual power, but whose power they are not always sure of or concerned about. I think this attitude has to do with a pragmatic understanding of spirits. In many contemporary religious movements in Melanesia, people experience the Holy Spirit's power in tangible ways through the manifestation of special gifts and miraculous happenings. In addition, they see that God's power through the Holy Spirit gives them courage to bear difficulties and opposition patiently. They also regard the Holy Spirit's power as available to punish with sickness or misfortune those who oppose them.

Panaeati or Misima tradition knows no clear hierarchy or distinction of good and bad spirits. Christian spirits have a particular hierarchy and distinction. The triune God belongs to the area of sacredness. The separateness of God from creation is stressed. God is the "holy other" and Christians are called upon to aspire to be holy too (see 1 Pet 1:16). In the Panaeati view, the spirits conform to human standards and at the same time maintain their supernatural power. They are not regarded as holy and distinctly "other" in relation to sinful humans. Judgment of wrongdoing is based on whether rituals are correctly performed. If a ritual fails to achieve the intended result, the person is not blamed, but the method of performing the ritual is questioned. Religious piety is based on correct ritual behavior rather than on moral integrity.

When Melanesians substitute the Holy Spirit for their traditional spirits (this seems to be fairly common), they do so from the framework of such beliefs. This is natural, considering that all Melanesian peoples traditionally believed in numerous spirit-beings of both helpful and harmful intent. When the Holy Spirit is identified with traditional spirits, it is understood that God by the Holy Spirit can cause both good and evil, since traditionally all spirits were considered in this way. This presents a difficulty from a Christian viewpoint, since Christians do not believe that the Holy Spirit can be associated with any evil intent. As I have pointed out, the Spirit is God acting now in the place of the Jesus of history and according to Jesus' own characteristic way of acting. As Michael Green puts it, "If we wish to claim the leading of the Spirit of God with any assurance, we shall find that the leading is always toward Jesus."[9]

Why are there so many "split-level" Christians in Melanesia today? It has partly to do with the points I have made above, and one of these pertains to cultural standards of ethical judgment. Traditional religious piety is based on rituals rather than on morals. Traditionally the spirits were not thought of as influencing moral behavior but as manipulable for human needs. Since the spirits were not the basis for morality, the sense of sin was not present. In Christianity, however, the Holy Spirit is the source of power for moral judgment, and good and evil can be clearly distinguished. This causes difficulties for Melanesians, both individually and communally; they tend to have a double standard of belief. They call on the triune God as well as on their traditional spirit-beings. They are most interested in power that manifests itself in supernatural happenings. For this reason they expect the Holy Spirit to manifest power in the same way their traditional spirits do, regardless of their personal moral condition.[10]

## CONCLUSION

Many Melanesians today continue to be involved in practices associated with the power of the spirits, and these surface in spiritualistic movements (see chaps. 7 and 8 above). The Christian message has not essentially changed nor have Christian practices and beliefs in this regard. Traditional spirit worship continues to be seen as a way of experiencing spiritual power in more dramatic and effective ways than people have been able to experience in Christianity.

Christians in the mainline churches of both Catholic and Protestant traditions have begun to take the study of traditional religions in Melanesia seriously. The increase in the number of religious movements in Melanesia has attracted serious attention, partly because these movements draw large numbers of people and seem to be becoming a threat to the churches' traditional theology and liturgy. These movements raise many questions: How have the churches failed to meet the spiritual needs of the people? What special needs do these new movements meet? Could it be that the power of God has not been given freedom of expression because of ecclesiastical barriers?

One reason people are moving toward charismatic groups is that they see their expectations for the manifestation of spiritual power being met. Experiences of such manifestation provide people with a conviction of the reality of the Holy Spirit in their lives. Dramatic experiences similar to the one that occurred in New Ireland could be cited from many other areas of Melanesia. If the churches truly wish to indigenize Christianity in Melanesia, they must take such experiences seriously and examine the meaning of them for people in their lives as Christians.

# 12

# Searching for a Melanesian Way of Worship

*MICHAEL MAELIAU*
*Malaita, Solomon Islands*

Searching for a Melanesian way of worship: By "searching" I do not mean to imply that there are many planned and conscious efforts being made in Melanesia to discover meaningful ways of worship. There are unconscious but nonetheless real searches for such ways, however, and in my remarks here I will strive to be sensitive to the struggles and yearnings that reflect a deeper quest. I begin by making two observations about matters that may seem to point in opposite directions, but in all likelihood are evidence of an identical underlying search.

First, many areas of Melanesia are seeing a decline of interest in church attendance and activities. Religious activities seem to have become mere formalities, to have lost their vitality and excitement. According to various traditional religions, any god who fails to communicate directly with its worshippers is either dead or has transferred to other realms. Such a god deserves little else than a memorial, just to remind its worshippers that there used to be such-and-such a god, or just in case the god decides to return at a later date.

I draw my second observation from the revival movements that are springing up in Melanesian contexts more than ever before. I am not referring to the revival of traditional religions but rather to Christian revivals in already established churches. Certain elements are emerging in the worship of these churches that are unprecedented in Melanesian Christian history. These features can only be accounted for in one of two ways. Either they have been divinely inspired or they are the natural expression of the Melanesian peoples, their spontaneous response to the objects of worship given the spiritual heritages of their pre-Christian past.

Some have stated that there is no such thing as a "Melanesian way" in anything. They say this is true because Melanesia as a whole encompasses such vast differences in traditions, customs, laws, gods, and ways of worship.[1]

Indeed, the forms of worship of any spirit are or have been prescribed by that particular spirit or its venerators and are not the result of some general Melanesian way of worship. It is arguable, however, that underlying those different forms of worship are beliefs, principles, and logics that are basic and common and that could be admitted to be some kind of standard expression.

Before we can go any further, however, it is appropriate to define what we mean by worship and to ask ourselves whether we can pin down such an elusive thing as "Christian worship." Technically worship means to pay reverence to God or to adore God as divine. But "worship" in this context mainly refers to the visible forms or the outward expressions of a respectful and devout attitude toward God. With this in mind we can then ask whether there is any particular way of worship that we can distinctly call "Christian." The various established churches have admitted by the different liturgical practices they teach that there is not one way and one way only that we can call particularly Christian. So we can conclude that the present Christian practices in worship have come to possess their current forms through processes of transmission from one culture to another, beginning with the Jewish culture out of which Christianity was born.

What does the Bible have to say about this? Jesus said to the Samaritan woman, "God is spirit, and those who worship him must worship in spirit and truth" (Jn 4:24). Jesus was saying here that true worship could not be limited to a geographical location. In that same statement he clearly implied that true worship could not be institutionalized either. For "spirit" and "truth," which are the essence of worship according to Jesus, can only be given flesh and form by the individual worshipper. Is it not therefore reasonable to believe that God, the creator of humankind and sustainer of the various cultures in the world, would be most pleased with the worship of any of earth's children when it is expressed in the way that is most natural to them?

Various forms of worship have been introduced to Melanesia by the different churches. It was never thought that the forms of worship could be anything else but Christian—meaning biblically sanctioned. The forms were never questioned, although the fact that different churches practiced differently should have given cause for question. The differences were accounted for since each church announced that their way was the scriptural one and all the others were wrong. This helped to create self-esteem and pride in the particular denomination accepted by a Melanesian group; it also served to keep the followers of the different churches apart.

Another factor made it quite unlikely that questions of this nature should be raised. In traditional religions it was commonly believed that the ways of worshipping any particular spirit had been given and sanctioned by the spirit concerned. So the worshipper was most careful about the correct procedures. Failure to be so rendered the worship ineffective and could even bring on punishment. Many of the practices in Christian worship were accepted without question, then, less out of fear than because what was received was believed to be the divinely ordained way.

It must be conceded, however, that some adoption of indigenous elements of worship was made (missionaries from Polynesia and Fiji brought some of those styles to the southwest Pacific, too). But whatever elements were incorporated into Christian worship were minimal and were included more by chance than by any deliberate or well-calculated effort to indigenize. The more ritualistic churches were more careful to preserve the Western Christian forms actually used in worship. Yet they gave the indigenes more freedom to choose the rules of conduct that governed their day-to-day behavior. The less ritualistic churches were more concerned about the rules of conduct that governed the people's daily lives and allowed more freedom in the forms used in worship.

In recent times it has been realized that Christianity came to Melanesia in the cultural wrappings of its bearers, and that many of these accretions can be discarded without doing injustice to the central message of the Gospel. Because of this realization a sprinkling of national church leaders, missiologists, and theologians began their conscious search for indigenous forms of worship and theology. Those who take this matter seriously will find it a rewarding exercise, but it is by no means as easy a quest as one might think. Two issues should be foremost in our thinking as we carry on the search, and they do not always sit easily with each other. First, we must think of what our findings are going to mean to those who are going to apply them; and second, we must reckon with the uniqueness of the central message of Christianity, which calls out for preservation over and above all cultures.

Let me elaborate on these two issues. When we talk about indigenous ways of worship and theology, what do we mean? Are we merely trying to replace select features of Western culture in Christianity with elements of traditional religions for the sake of change in a changing Melanesia, or is our main concern to make Christian worship become more meaningful and theology more relevant? Some feel there is no real dichotomy behind this question, yet we have to admit that, whereas in some parts of Melanesia direct adaptations from traditional forms could be appropriate, there are places where Christianity has been practiced for more than three or four generations and traditional forms of worship would be more alien than the Western forms, so entrenched and well known have they become. That does not mean that these third- or fourth-generation Christians are content with the status quo. In fact they are often the ones who react most strongly against established forms. The point I want to make here, however, is that our efforts must not be motivated simply out of a reaction to a Westernized Christianity imposed upon us but out of a genuine desire to give meaning and vitality to Christianity in our own context.

If this motivation applies, then we are not doing anything that is new to Christianity at all. Throughout the history of the church theologians have always been dating, updating, and outdating their theologies. Western theologians today continue to do the same thing. They have conveniently divided themselves into two camps: the modern or liberal theologians and the conservative theologians. Both groups have one thing in common, however, and that is to make the Gospel or theology address itself to the people of today in a meaningful and relevant way. Is this not our aim, too? The difference between the two kinds of theologians is not that one is more advanced than the other, but that the liberals want a free hand to give the Bible a greater, more convenient adaptability; the conservatives hold that their theology must be constantly subjected to the authority of the Scriptures.

This brings me to my next point. I believe that the central message of Christianity stands above every culture and yet, paradoxically, can be accommodated to any. Christianity can in fact be adapted to any culture. At the same time it should judge every aspect of that culture, especially if the Bible is the central point of reference for theology. It must be pointed out here that the Bible is not the product of Western Christianity. It was written out of the Hebrew and Greek cultures. So whatever our hang-ups about Western Christianity, they should not affect our serious study of the Bible in this process of discovering our Melanesian identity. We should not reject the study of Western and other forms of theology. We can in fact learn from their mistakes and may even reap some of the good fruits of previous labors. The important thing is not to be bound by Western methods of theology. Our situations are very different, and Western rationalization differs considerably from the Melanesian way of thinking.

I believe in the one supreme God, the creator and sustainer of the universe, eternally existent in the persons of the Father, the Son, and the Holy Spirit. My tribe has no equivalent being who could be identified with God, and thus the English word "God" has been adopted. But where a traditional deity or like concept can be identified with God, then I see no reason why the identification should not be made. There are at least two New Testament examples of this process. First, Paul at Mars Hill in Athens came across an altar to an unknown god. He began to expound the Gospel and tell about Christ. A second example is found in John's Gospel (1:1–3). John adopted the Greek concept of the *logos* and applied it to Christ. If we take our cue from such cases, Christ's uniqueness and preeminence will never be clouded, reduced, or superseded.

This is the central question: If God is the creator of the different human races, would it not be true to say that God must be intimately familiar with every culture in all its components? This does not mean that every part of a culture is good and holy in God's sight. Human beings, left on their own with their sinful nature, will always tend to follow a downward path toward sin unless God mercifully places limits as to how far humankind can go toward its own destruction. We are told in the Bible that this is exactly what God has done. He has a witness in every age and every culture. Romans 1:20 confirms this:

> Ever since the creation of the world his invisible nature, namely, his eternal power and deity, has been clearly perceived in the things that have been made; so they [the nations] are without excuse.

Romans 2:14–16 states:

> When the Gentiles who have not the law do by nature what the law requires, they are a law to themselves, even though they do not have the

law. They show that what the law requires is written on their hearts, while their conscience also bears witness and their conflicting thoughts accuse or perhaps excuse them on that day when, according to my gospel, God judges the secrets of men by Christ Jesus.

We are now talking about God's revelation to humankind. It is necessary to make a distinction between two kinds of revelation. One can be called general revelation, the other particular revelation.[2] General revelation means that God can be perceived through creation and the law written on the human heart. This revelation is available to every person in every culture in every age. Particular revelation refers to God's choice of one particular people, namely Israel, and to God's progressive self-revelation, culminating in the coming of Jesus Christ. This is summed up in Hebrews 1:1-2;

In many and various ways God spoke of old to our fathers by the prophets; but in these last days he has spoken to us by a Son, whom he appointed the heir of all things, through whom also he created the world.

That God chose Israel and not another people should not make anyone jealous. God simply had to pick one people in order to work out the divine purposes.

God was in Melanesia long, long before the Melanesians came, let alone the white missionaries. But the question as to whether the general revelation (as it stood before the actual arrival of the Gospel) was adequate for Melanesians to believe in God, and might have actually led them to worship God "truly," is a debatable one. Several basic questions need to be asked here. Why did God leave the Melanesians for so long before sending the white missionaries? Did God not care that my ancestors might perish? Romans (chaps. 1 and 2) tells us that those who turn against God, deliberately rejecting the knowledge they received through the general revelation, are without excuse on the Day of Judgment. Does not this imply a definite point of moral choice? If rejection leads to adverse judgment, is it not clear that acceptance leads to salvation? Admittedly, the encounter with general revelation cannot be equated with an encounter with the Gospel and its message of salvation. Thus the idea of this pre-Gospel choice must come as a shock to those holding the traditional Christian position, namely, that there is no other name under heaven whereby we can be saved, or that no one can come to the Father except through Jesus Christ, or that a person must be baptized or receive other Christian rites before salvation is possible. Yet I personally know of two Christians, brothers, who were converted before they ever heard about the Lord Jesus Christ or had been confronted with any Christian witness at all.

Historically, biblically, and theologically this position is not without foundation. There was a long period between creation and the time of Abraham when all that was available was general revelation and personal encounters with God.

We read about God's call of Abraham in Ur of the Chaldeans, for example, when he had neither a Bible nor Jesus. During the same period there appeared in Canaan a priest of the Most High called Melchizedek. About five hundred years later, when the children of Israel were approaching the Promised Land, they met a prophet of God called Balaam, who could communicate with God and see an angel and was living in the midst of a wicked and corrupt society that God deemed worthy only of annihilation (Num 22–24).

Until the time of the early church, we have in the Bible only the history of God's dealings with Israel. From then until the West discovered the rest of the world, we only know about the history of the church in Europe and to a certain extent in Asia and Africa. Whatever else God was doing or how God was doing it in other parts of the world we do not know. Were we to hear about God's putative work through the oral traditions of other cultures, moreover, we would probably not be able to recognize it or to admit it to be Christian.

This problem has led some Christians to draw up two doctrines, which I call the "Second Chance" and "Universal Salvation." According to the first doctrine, everyone who has died before hearing the Gospel will somehow, someday, be given a second chance to hear the full Gospel. The second doctrine posits that all peoples, irrespective of the way they have lived and whatever they have done or believed, are going to be saved in the end. To me, neither of these two positions is well founded or logical.

It matters little if readers disagree with me, because whether you are right or I am right we can do nothing now to alter the status of our beloved ancestors. It is important to recognize, however, that God has always been in Melanesia. It is difficult to imagine God remaining inactive and indifferent for all these thousands of years.

It is not that the current talk about the presence and activity of God or Christ within Melanesian culture has been well worked out. Some would-be Melanesian theologians speak of "Christ's incarnation in Melanesian culture"[3]—a phrase I find somewhat misleading. When are we supposed to imagine that Christ became incarnate in Melanesia? Through missionaries or theologians? For me there is only one Incarnation: when God became flesh as Christ, a human being. The Incarnation is unique and can never be repeated. If those who use this phrase mean Christ's living and active presence in the world or among any culture or persons, then terms such as "live" or "dwell" seem more appropriate. If the term refers to the principle of the incarnation, that is, a total identification, then this is understandable but needs an accompanying explanation.

Another phrase that worries me is "Melanesian Christ."[4] The term sounds unnatural, is misleading, and has no special significance. The word "Christ" means "Messiah." Any Melanesian with special abilities could arise and do spectacular things and be called a Melanesian Messiah. I would prefer to speak of "Christ in Melanesia" if it is suggested by the context and avoid trendy slogans.

If we are going to take seriously this notion of God being present in Melanesian cultures, moreover, it would be a grave mistake to conclude that all aspects of these cultures must have been ordained by God. We know that culture is primarily a human creation. And we, in our present problematic state, however noble and honorable are our highest achievements and however much these may resemble God's standards, can never be perfect. Thus an indiscriminate acceptance of traditional Melanesian culture as already Christian would be wrong and makes no sense in the light of the wars and many unwholesome practices of the past. Jesus Christ, who revealed God most fully by his life and teachings, together with the whole revealed word of God in the Bible, must be used to test and challenge our culture, just as it must do to any culture.

After Jesus' death, the whole sacrificial system and other elements of the Jewish culture were thrown out by the Christians, even though these things had been instituted by God. To press this example, who would suggest that all the sacrificial systems within Melanesia ought to be adopted into Christianity? The Word of God must be our yardstick in the endeavor to indigenize Christianity. Christ and the central message of the gospel can be and must be made relevant, but never relative, to the Melanesian culture.

Now I turn to the issue of worship. I said above that worship is a way of expressing oneself to God. In other words, it is the vehicle through which we express our feelings and desires. The main question is this: Can God understand the traditional languages (of worship) that were employed in addressing the spirits? Should the same language now be used to address God since this is the language in which Melanesians express themselves most fully and meaningfully? Can God listen to it, understand it, and accept it?

Let me refer to an incident in my own life as an example. A few years ago a revival movement started within Baptist Church circles in the Baiyer River area (Western Highlands, Papua New Guinea). In 1978 I was asked to go and preach at a revival fellowship meeting there. I was led into the bush, where there were gathered more than two thousand people in small groups. They were all in a state as if they were drunk. Their bodies were shaking backwards and forwards, their tongues were hanging out, and they were panting like someone who has just finished running a race. With all my upbringing and theological training I could have branded them with an appropriate title and walked home. But my heart went out to them—with a deep desire and a prayer that I might come to understand what was going on.

The situation continued until about three o'clock in the afternoon. Then everybody came out of their small groups, joined into one mass of people, and, locking their hands together, charged forward toward a clearing area while chanting their Highlands traditional tunes. They danced round and round and round until sunset in the square. When we dispersed my sermon was still undelivered.

The next day the whole procedure was repeated. At about half past four in the afternoon everybody stopped, sat down, and I finally got to preach my sermon. I am not quite sure now whether it was the original sermon I had prepared or a new one, but I can remember preaching on worshipping with sincerity from the heart before expressing it outwardly, and not just being caught up in the feeling of the crowd. I was thanked most sincerely and warmly, and we dispersed. I went home with a deep burden in my heart and prayed that God would give me some explanation. I was told that this was exactly how these people used to worship their "devils." They admitted to me that this was so, but emphatically reiterated that they had nothing but Jesus in their minds as they were worshipping this way.

I had been through similar movements like this among the Huli and the Sepiks in Papua New Guinea and of course in my own church in the Solomon Islands since 1970.[5] Already I could see that this sort of thing was going to spread throughout Melanesia, so it was important that I come to a clear understanding of these movements.

I returned home, having been away a month, and two small events helped to throw some light on my search. On my arrival, as I stepped out of the car, my family came out to greet me. When my two-year-old daughter saw me, she burst into tears and let out a mighty cry—as if someone had struck her. I picked her up and after quieting her I asked her, "Muina, what made you cry?" "I was crying for Daddy," she replied. "Why? Don't you want me to come home?" "Yes!" and she held on to me more tightly than ever.

On another occasion I came home from work very tired after a hard day. As usual my daughter ran up to meet me, but this time with great enthusiasm. I brought her into the house and sat down with her, but she was still excited. She danced around and around. As I observed her, I noticed that her movements were almost exactly the same as those I had seen at Baiyer! But she had never seen the others' actions; this was a natural expression of her own feelings. It occurred to me then and there that this accounted for some of the things that were happening in the revival movements. A critic might have told my little girl that she was not expressing her love and joy for her daddy in the correct way, by giving him a kiss or a hug. But as her father I knew precisely what she was doing, and it did not matter one bit to me how she expressed it. I responded immediately by taking her into my arms. Does not God, our heavenly parent, also accept whatever form or expression of worship is given by every child, demonstrated in the way most natural to the offerer?

The Bible tells us that God is concerned about the object of our devotion and worship. God wants us to worship the one God only and to do that in spirit and in truth. The meaningful expression of this worship is left to each of God's children. God has not prescribed a particular way, which cannot be altered. All the churches need to recognize this. In some churches or areas a deliberate effort is made to adopt certain traditional elements. I believe that most of the distinctly Melanesian ways of worship and theology are going to arise spontaneously out of the revival movements, which are bound to spread throughout all the churches of the region. The established churches must be flexible enough to accommodate these movements. There is a danger that most of the leaders of Melanesia's established churches, as well as the sponsoring churches in the West, are going to be highly critical and may even consciously seek to stifle such revivalism. They must apply the incarnation principle, which some of their theologians talk about, if they are going to lead, guide, and correct any errors in these movements; otherwise participants in the revivals will break away, either to join other churches that allow them to exercise their freedom or to found Melanesian Independent Churches, comparable to those in black Africa.[6]

I do not think we need to work hard to find indigenous forms of worship. They are now emerging, ready to be identified, encouraged, and refined. I believe that this also applies to indigenous theology. I suggest that we start our search for indigenous theologies wherever new patterns of worship are forthcoming.

# 13

# A Plea for Female Ministries in Melanesia

*ROSE KARA NINKAMA*
*Central New Guinea Highlands*

## THE RELEVANT ISSUES

Today women are trying to free themselves from being *overlooked* by societies, nations, and churches of the world. Their great and gifted responsibilities have always been risky, and they have carried burdens of unfair labels, limitations, and low expectations for centuries.

This article will consider the view, now beginning in some churches, that women be allowed to take up as effective a part in the Christian ministry as men have since Jesus' time. This paper is not without a biblical background and takes into account impressions we have of women and their "roles" in the Old and New Testaments. It has also been written with the contemporary women's movement in mind, a movement that is deeply affecting various societies. The impact of its images and symbols are filtering into the forums of the church in ways both exciting and frightening.

One of the main thrusts of the feminist movement is to re-examine the nature of womanhood. Why is it that women's lives have been so bound by low expectations? Some religious writers and interpreters are discovering that Jesus, surprisingly enough, was far ahead of his time in disregarding negative attitudes toward womanhood and in accepting and affirming women as full human beings. Perhaps Jesus' approach was not brought out so obviously in the Gospels. We are just beginning to understand and appreciate it. The old labels, limitations, and low expectations stunting male-female relations are now being radically questioned, and will continue to be so, through this process of rediscovery.

In most societies, women have been considered inferior, passive, and unintelligent; men have thus been conditioned to feel superior, aggressive, and intelligent. By so polarizing the sexes, each one is actually limited to a "proper sphere." Now the human mind's expectations are based on past experiences.

Each person tries to fit impressions and stimuli into this framework of expectations. Each person tends to resist any attempts to make one change one's already conditioned mind and attitudes. If one believes women are nonassertive and that they do not possess the same motivation as men to achieve, to use their skills and abilities, or to be recognized in their jobs and professions and be well paid for their work, then it comes as a shock to discover that many women do have the same motivations as men.

Today many healthy controversies are focused on genuine problems faced by women. One concerns discrimination—in employment, in education, and in the churches. Another concerns the need for adequate child-care. The problems involved are being seriously confronted, and both women and men are coming to grips with them.

Not only are political, legal, and societal changes taking place in the relations between women and men; changes are also occurring in the churches. Traditional Christian religion has tended to confine women, yet various Protestant churches are now ordaining them, even though some of these institutions are ambivalent in their commitment. Others, by contrast, such as the Roman Catholics and some branches of Lutheranism, have not wanted to discuss the issue of ordaining ministers or priests, yet discussion and a decision are being pressed out of them.

I write as a Lutheran woman theological student from Melanesia, watching the developments around me. In these days, and I think especially of America and Germany, few Lutheran women are ordained pastors. But many work and serve God's people in the same way as the male pastors. We are persons created in God's own image; each one of us is unique. Why then, should such unsound distinctions apply? Martin Luther once said:

> the godless knave, forgetful of his mother and his sisters, dares to blaspheme God's creature through whom he was himself born. It would be tolerable if he were to find fault with the behaviour of women, but to defile them as creation and nature is most godless. God himself must allow all prayer and worship to take place under this privy.[1]

This might have something to be said for it, considering the historical context, yet an even broader vista of possibilities is now opening up for human beings. No longer do women see themselves as limited only to having babies, nor is it seen necessary for women to be excluded from the priesthood because of unclean bodily functions. No longer do women accept that their possibilities should be circumscribed by family and childbearing and limited to narrow, low-paying jobs.

Over the centuries the church has largely conformed to pre-existing cultural ideas about women. Anthropologists have noted that religion usually reflects the traditional beliefs of the society. Since the repression and oppression of women date back so many centuries, in fact, it is all the more surprising that Jesus did not internalize the prejudices of his period. It is helpful at this point to go back to Jesus, not only to show how the churches have fallen out of tune with his vision of life, because of cultural influences, but also to provide a working basis for a sound feminist theology.

Jesus never belittled women in any of his comments or treatment, and what is more, he actually stood up against some of his contemporaries to defend women. He acted naturally toward women, accepting them as full persons who could understand what he was saying and could respond intelligently to him. He discussed his mission with them and trusted women to go out and take the message to others. Women numbered among his disciples (see Lk 8: 2-3), and many of the women who supported him are made known to us through the Scriptures.

Jesus was so different from his male disciples that, as John puts it, "They marveled that he was talking with a woman" (Jn 4:27). Jesus neither put women down nor put them up on a pedestal. Either way, up or down, they can be effective in their own way, and need to be taken seriously as full persons. Jesus never treated women as sex objects, as empty-headed robots, or as beings created to serve male needs.

What happened after Jesus? The church regressed after the freedom of the Gospel. In spite of the positive attitudes of Jesus toward women, repressive rules and judgments of Paul and the Church Fathers have been singled out and followed over the centuries of Christendom. Although Paul authored the magnificent theological statement of equality in Galatians 3:28 ("There is neither Jew nor Greek, there is neither slave nor free, there is neither male nor female; for you are all one in Christ Jesus"), he seemed to revert to his Jewish patriarchal training whenever he laid down rules for specific congregations. I admit that there are certain differences of opinion about what Paul did or did not write,[2] since his writings were probably edited as a body of letters useful for various churches, but there are certain repressive and all too adaptive statements in the letters associated with his name that reveal how the early church began conforming to surrounding social expectations for women. Certain passages place an especially heavy burden on them. The pronouncement that "women should keep silence in the churches" (1 Cor 14:34) and the contention of the writer of Timothy that Adam was not deceived but the woman "was deceived . . . [and] woman will be saved through bearing children" (1 Tim 2:14-15) have done immeasurable damage to women.

One damaging instruction (Eph 5:22) has been enshrined in many traditional wedding services. "Wives, be subject to your husbands, as to the Lord. For the husband is the head of the wife as Christ is the head of the church." This directive gives a literal, churchly sanction to women's subordination. Traditionally this admonition has been regarded as an exact, unmodifiable instruction for marital relations and as normative for all time. Through biblical literalism the husband gets the God-position, the woman the servant-position. Over generations subsequent to the New Testament too many writers were prepared to capitalize on this cut-and-dried inequality.

Even at the time of the Reformation, distinctions invidious to women were made. John Calvin wrote: "Because Eve had given fatal advice it was right that she should be deprived of all liberty and placed under the yoke of obedience to Adam." Calvin thought that obeying was somehow natural to the woman, but that after the garden incident, her subjection became less voluntary and agreeable than before. Adam, by contrast, was rewarded with more authority.[3]

Although Martin Luther married, he retained some very negative ideas about women and sex. "We can hardly speak of woman without a feeling of shame, and surely we cannot make use of her without shame," he asserted. He considered that the punishment of women in pregnancy and childbirth was far worse than the punishment men had to bear (according to Gen 3:14–19). "For what is there of such things a man suffers?" he wonders in his *Lectures on Genesis*, surmising the curse against Adam to be comparatively light.[4] Further-more, like Paul (1 Cor 7), Luther regarded marriage as a protection against sin, a sort of secondary option. "It is a great favour that God has preserved woman for us against our wish and will," he wrote. "It were both for protection and also as a medicine against the sin of fornication."[5]

How is it that such attitudes arose that hardly square with the attitude of Jesus? Although the Scriptures bring out clearly that Jesus sought out and enjoyed women as persons, that they were his close friends, and that he discussed theology with them, all this has become so familiar a story, filtered down through the traditional process so completely, that we Christians do not perceive what has happened to our judgments. Our minds have been shaped by ancient biases. Historical interpretations have manipulated and limited our imaginations. The barriers in our minds and emotions are so real that if they are removed the unveiling surprises us. We feel naked and uncertain. Some biblical stories involving women have been explained from the pulpits with such a sin-oriented twist that what the women do or who they are in special relation to God or Jesus is almost ignored. Here we can cite the stories of the woman at Simon's house and the Samaritan woman at the well (Mk 14:3–8 and parallels, Jn 4:1–41). By dwelling on these women's histories (Lk 7:37, Jn 4:17–18), what they do in the stories is virtually overlooked. Such obscuring and twisting of matters should be brought to an end.

Jesus was disturbed that Martha was distracted with much serving. Unfortu-nately the servant tasks of the church today fall primarily on women and thus are against the spirit of Jesus' approach. Jesus' mother-hen imagery referred to feminine characteristics in God with which women could identify, but which also involve us all. Above all, Jesus used no set and firm words to delineate high-caste church functions for men and low-caste functions for women. There were no firm levels of ecclesiastical structure limiting the talents of the faithful. Both exceptional and ordinary women and men could be the communicators of the Gospel of Christ in a nonhierarchical community. Whenever people were open to the message, at least before the unfortunate reactions we mentioned above, both sexes were among the prophets of the first Christian congre-gations—slaves, women, laborers, street-sweepers, and all.

All this should be of vital interest to women today. We need to recover values that have been obscured and set our sights on the future. Perhaps it is time to go even further back—to the Old Testament—to see what such a recovery might mean.

## WOMEN IN THE OLD TESTAMENT

### *Created in God's Image*

So God created man in his own image, in the image of God he created him; male and female he created them (Gen 1:27.)

According to Genesis, God created male and female in the divine image, after the divine likeness. This creation of man and woman, although it is recorded as taking place on the same day when the land animals were formed, is a completely separate creative act. It constitutes the climax and the crown of creation. It is therefore described with special fullness. There is no formula. The creator said, "Let there be man," not "let the earth bring forth man," as in the case of the previous creative acts. We observe, first, that God prefaces the creation of the human being with a declaration concerning the divine purpose—about the human sphere of authority and influence (vs. 26). Second, in a direct and special manner God creates man in the divine image, *both* male and female (vs. 27). Third, God blesses both of them and entrusts them with duties and power upon the earth (vs. 28).

In God's own image, God created man and woman. This image, it seems, means a production—in form and substance, physically or spiritually—that conveys the idea of resemblance and outward similarity to the divine. Man and woman's nature, then, is made "after the likeness" of God; they possess divine (or potentially divine) qualities (beyond the power of description), and these qualities—which cannot be taken away—are not possessed by the animals. Thus both man and woman are capable of approaching, or receding from, the likeness of God. No distinction between male and female is made in terms of importance, and this clearly indicates that God did indeed create them equal.

It is not good that the man should be alone; I will make him a helper fit for him [Gen 2:18].

God created woman for a purpose. Here we see that man by himself is less than fully human and not complete. He needs another in order to reflect truly God's image and fulfill God's pupose. This other is woman, the only companion really "fit for him." The image of God clearly consists of and requires both male and female (although each, we should add, in different terms and with different emphases). "Male and female he created them," it is stated, and in this assertion there is no implication of woman's inferiority simply because she was created second. On the contrary, God made things starting from an apparently lower form to a higher form. God started by creating light, something very basic, and finished with human beings, both male and female being the highest form of creation. We now understand that man is incomplete and alone, without suitable companionship, and until the woman is created true humanity does not exist.

Both man and woman are to be the supreme caretakers over the fishes, the birds, and the beasts, a task that requires courage, skill, observation, and judgment. From all this comes the blessing of fruitfulness.

It is common in Melanesia and elsewhere for men to use the Genesis material as a way of putting women down, and that is why I spend time with it. One important general point I am making here with these prejudices in mind is that Adam is a collective term for humankind and includes women. Woman is the feminine of man. Woman is not only man's helper, but also his complement, and is most essential to the completion of his being. Eve was Adam's other half and different from him in sex only, not in nature. Priority of creation gave Adam the headship but not superiority. Both man and woman were endowed for equality and for mutual interdependence. Often woman excels man in her capacity to endure ill-treatment, sorrow, pain, and separation. Throughout history, men, in their pride, ignorance, or moral perversion have treated women as greatly inferior, and have enslaved or degraded them accordingly. Among many tribes and clans today women are mere chattels, the burden-bearers, with no right whatever to equality with man. But the opening pages of the Bible simply lend no justification for this.

If some argue that woman is inferior because she disobeyed God first and was responsible for Adam's fall (Gen 3:6), let it be pointed out that Genesis never actually had God order Eve in particular to abstain from the fruit of the tree of knowledge. The command was given before she was specially created (2:15–17), and this is why she suffers no patent curse in the way both the serpent and Adam do (3:14–19).

*Various Figures*

What about the rest of the Old Testament on women? The position of woman in Israel was in marked contrast to her status in surrounding heathen nations. Israelite law was designed to protect woman's physical weakness, safeguard her rights, and preserve her freedom (Deut 21:10–14; 22:13–30). Under divine law her liberties were greater, her tasks more varied and important, and her social standing more respected and commanding than those of her heathen sisters. The Holy Bible has also preserved the memory of women whose wisdom, skill, and dignity it willingly acknowledged. Numerous names of devout and eminent Hebrew women adorn the pages of the Old Testament. To some extent, admittedly, a woman was considered her husband's property (Gen 12:18; Ex 20:17; 21:3) and owed him absolute fidelity. While the husband had no formal rights over the person of his wife, he was nevertheless recognized as lord and master. By her chastity, diligence, and love, however, woman created an honorable position for herself within family and community circles.

Any prominence women attained was obtained by force of character. I think first of Miriam. She apparently saved her baby brother whom the princess called Moses. Miriam was the first Hebrew prophetess raised up by God and was inspired by the Spirit to proclaim God's will and purpose. Her responsibility as prophetess was the same as any of the male prophets to come. There is no distinction. Miriam stood at the Red Sea proclaiming and singing the power and faithfulness of God, and she led the Israelite women in dancing (Ex 15:20–21).

Other women achieved comparable greatness. God raised up Deborah and endowed her with a remarkable personality and varied gifts for the deliverance of the distressed and defeated people. With extraordinary resoluteness she occupied several positions. She stood among the warriors (a difficult and important role when put in its ancient context); she declared the whole counsel of God; she was the fourth of the Leaders or Judges of Israel and thus a remarkable ruler (Jg 4–5).

Esther, one of the last women appearing in the Old Testament, had greatness thrust upon her. God chose her to be the queen of Persia and to save the Jews from destruction under foreign rule. In risking her life on behalf of her people, she won deliverance for her nation and was thus an instrument of God's providence (Es 7–10).

In giving such space to the accomplishments of women, the Jews reveal that they lived under social arrangements in which the sexes were much more evenly balanced than in the other ancient societies we can document. This relative balance looks ahead to the coming of Jesus and the earliest Christians.

## WOMEN IN THE NEW TESTAMENT

I have discussed the understanding and sympathy Jesus manifested toward women (see also Mk 5:25–34 and parallels; Lk 10:38–42; Jn 11:20–45). In the great Sermon on the Mount, moreover, Jesus pinpoints a primary purpose of woman and teaches men the obligation to maintain purity toward her as the one who bears children but can be easily abused (Mt 5:27–32). More can be said, however, about the impressive women of the New Testament.

First, there is Mary, who, as mother of Jesus, is better known than any other female character in the Bible and has been the best-known woman in the world since those days of the manger in Bethlehem. After all the centuries after Christ the statement still stands: "Blessed are you among women!" (Lk 1:42). Many came to occupy high places among womankind, yet God selected such a humble young peasant woman as Mary to be the mother of the Incarnate One. Out of this mystery, it can be argued, womanhood comes into its own as vital to God's plan of salvation. The fact that Christ, the Son of God, was "born of woman" has been cited as of great significance for the Christian faith in the ecumenical creeds of Christendom.

Mary Magdalene is another case in point. Freed from demonic bondage, she became Jesus' disciple, and her personal ministrations, along with those of other women who had been healed, greatly aided Jesus in his ministry as he went from place to place. She may well have been present at Jesus' trial and sentencing and during his bearing of the cross (Lk 23:27). Clearly she was one of the sorrowing group of holy women who stood as close as possible to comfort Jesus in the closing agonies of the crucifixion and received his body (Jn 19:25; Lk 23:55). She was the first one at the garden tomb to witness the most important event in world history and the pivotal truth of Christianity, the resurrection of Jesus Christ (Jn 20:11-18; cf. Mk 16:7-11 in some texts). She was thus commissioned to become the first herald of the resurrection. Hers is an impressive case, especially in revealing how Christ transformed one particular woman. When he first met her, she was an afflicted and tormented soul, but Jesus healed her of her insanity and maladies, and then accepted her as a loyal and sacrificial follower.

There are others to mention briefly. Priscilla and her husband became the honored and much loved friends of Paul, and harmoniously labored together in the service of the church (Acts 18:2, 26; Rom 16:3; 1 Cor 16:19; 2 Tim 4:19). It may well be that Priscilla was crucial in founding the church in Rome (see Acts 28:14-15).

Lydia was another figure of interest because of the public nature of her confession in support of Paul's preaching at Philippi (Acts 16:11-15). Following her baptism, Lydia always kept an "open house" for the saints of God and her home became a center of Christian fellowship. Perhaps the first Christian church of Philippi was formed in her house. When Paul came to write his letter to the Philippians, he included Lydia in his salutation (Phil 1:1-11). She was also on his mind as one of those women who labored with him in the gospel (Phil 4:3). Lydia sold her dyes and served her Savior. She may well have kept up her business so that she might have the money to help God's servants in their ministry.

It is not necessary to go on, for the point has surely been made that women played a vital part in the early church. Perhaps some New Testament passages put serious constraints on women—on wives in relation to husbands, on women's mode of dress (1 Tim 2:9-15)—but no one can deny that the moment of liberation for women was established in the extraordinary work of Jesus and the response to his coming. Whatever problems surround some of his special injunctions, furthermore, Paul's real and permanent views on the matter of womanhood are stated plainly in Galatians (3:28): there is neither "male nor female" in Christ Jesus. Apart from references to Priscilla and Lydia, Paul's letters show his care for various other women who labored for the Gospel—Euodia and Syntyche (Phil 4:2-3), Lois and Eunice (2 Tim 1:5), Phoebe, Mary, and others (Rom 16). When it comes to a rediscovery of a challenge for women, the model for harmony, parity, and breadth of vision is in the New Testament.[6]

## WOMEN IN MELANESIAN TRADITIONAL SOCIETY

Any society tends to organize itself into groups of common interest and common characteristics. The roles and duties assigned to people depend on the categories into which they fall. The biological division of humans into male and female is the basis for the most elementary social stratification everywhere in the world. In every society the division of roles between the sexes results from the fact that women bear and suckle children and are thus tied to the domestic scene for most of their lives.

In Melanesian traditional societies, the economy is one of subsistence production. People work to obtain their food and secure their other needs from their immediate environment; a large share of the agricultural work falls to women. Sometimes agriculture is entirely their responsibility; in other parts of Melanesia men do most of the heavy work of clearing the scrub, felling trees, burning and cutting trunks or branches, before planting. This is true among my people—the Gunagis of the Chimbu Province in the Papua New Guinea highlands. When men burn branches and tree trunks over the soil, they are intending to fertilize it.

In my society men are dominant.[7] Men's activities are those that call for physical strength and agility and that take them away from home—warfare, hunting, fishing, canoe trading. The tasks of government also fall to men. They exercise authority in matters concerned with right and obligations. Households, kinship groups, and executive political units normally have male heads.

The most important ritual roles also belong to males. They communicate with the ancestors, deities, and the various spirits believed to influence human destinies. Because men dominated the tribal religious practices, women were excluded from certain rituals. In most Melanesian societies, admittedly, there are women's rites from which men are excluded and in some cultures women even feature as magicians and healers, therefore playing a crucial role in religious practices. In the Garaina communities of the Morobe province, for example, the number of female traditional healers equals that of the male practitioners. In my society, however, as I shall show, the women are far less involved in ritual life.

Among the Gunagis, as with other traditional Melanesian groups, it is not thought appropriate for men and women to associate outside the house. Even within the house men often eat separately from women, and men are criticized if they spend too much time with their wives. It is also not supposed that men and women who are not spouses could have any interest in associating for anything other than sexual purposes. There is no prolonged courting in many liaisons and no suggestion of wrong-doing if a man has intercourse with a woman who is not married.

All these imbalances and special points taken into account, the division of roles that gave males the advantage for initiatives (along with hard physical labor, admittedly) does not necessarily tell us which of the sexes was more important for the survival of the group. We have to look at these matters more closely from the economic, political, and religious points of view.

Let us look in some detail at the role of women among the Chimbu highlanders. First, economics. There can be little doubt that Chimbu traditional societies were economically sustained by the toil of women. The women worked in the sun for hours in the gardens. After the men had cleared, it was up to the women to plant, tend, weed, and harvest (while males sat talking in the shade). It was and still is up to the females to take their produce for exchange (or sale) at the market. They bear heavy loads in their *bilum* net-bags, the straps of which hang tightly over their heads.

It has always been up to the wives to bring firewood to the family hearth, to prepare the food, to cook it daily (for two meals, one in the morning and one toward dusk), and to cook for large feasts. On top of this, women were the pig-minders, and when lactating were even the piglet-sucklers! In my area the women were food gatherers as well as gardeners. Another of their important roles was to gather the grasses which, when burnt, were part of the crucial salt-making process. Above all, the absolutely vital economic role of women was as childbearer and child rearer. Women ensured the perpetuation of the human species.

What of politics? In this area women have been pushed into the background. They could support their husbands as part of a family and sustain warriors with food in times of trial. But they were barred from speaking in public; they did not go along on such physically oriented exercises as hunting, and were not involved in tribal fighting—not even in decision making about wars. In fact, instead of cheering on the sidelines, most Chimbu women (and the women of my tribe, the Gunagis) were thoroughly opposed to war.

As far as religion is concerned, women have been kept from the most important rituals. At the opening of the great pig-killing ceremonies (*bugla yungga*), for instance, they have never been allowed to witness the playing of the sacred flutes ("the calling of the spirits"), and they cannot be present when the bigman (or another officiant with the appropriate blood ties) invokes the spirit of the previous bigman to bless the proceedings. Women may prepare food for the sacrifices, but it is the men who offer them to the spirits. Wailing, the women bring the pigs they nurtured to be held down, but it is the men who do the killing and butchering.

There is at least one rite among the Chimbu, however, that is exclusively for womenfolk: the initiation rite of passage following a girl's first menstruation. This rite is for the individual female adolescent. She is to be separated from her clan and hamlet for from two to four months. Her knees are bound tightly together and must remain like that for the whole period. The initiate must not be given any food cooked in a vessel or in a *mumu* (a cooking pit in the ground), but only food baked in ashes. She is placed in a special hut, and every hole in it is closed so that she is left in darkness. Beside the hut is a hearth in which cooking for the girl is done. The only role the men have in all those procedures is to bring the wood for the fire. Every day women come and sit in a half circle facing the hearth and the hut and one by one utter their advice to the young girl as to what is expected of her as a woman. The sponsor of the exercise is usually the child's paternal aunt, who is called in from another tribe (into which she has married) to supervise the activities. This aunt will carry the initiate to a special toilet when necessary, for the girl cannot go out of her own accord. The days of talking go on, and eventually the initiated one is brought out, looking sallow for having been out of the sun. This is taken as a sign of a good, disciplined female, one who will live long.

This, then, was the situation of women in my traditional society. Obviously the Chimbu woman did not have the possibilities for liberation as in the biblical tradition, but that is not to deny that she was important to her society.

## CONCLUSION

Whatever the cultural context, women are crucial for society. It is clear, however, that there are greater chances of their emancipation from inequality and male domination in the biblical tradition. Out of the way Christ has given there emerges a recognition of the essential equality of male and female. That this equality is not perceived by males only tells us what is going on in their confined minds, locked in as many of them are to their small, isolated worlds, needing to break out of them. Smallness of outlook can be found even in the life of the church, which can easily lose sight of the broader visions of Jesus and the New Testament. The Lutheran Church still finds it difficult to ordain women. I cannot see any sound reason for giving in to the difficulties. I myself have been trained theologically at the seminary. I am doing the same work as any pastor, yet under the title of assistant parish worker. That appears unjust and phony. I appeal, not only for my own ordination, but for the ordination of all those young women who have the same calling and have undertaken the same training as male ministers of the liberating Gospel.

# 14

# In Search of a Melanesian Theology

*JOHN KADIBA*
*South Coastal Papua and Northern Australia*

The task of searching for a systematic Melanesian theology has not even begun in Melanesia. We have started to think theologically, at least in a limited way, but we have not begun to develop our own theology in a systematic manner. I think the time is ripe to do this. But how should we go about this task? I present in this limited space a discussion of themes and issues that need to be addressed if the systematization of theological thinking in Melanesia is to be achieved.

## PACIFIC THEOLOGY

The desire to develop a theology that is "home-grown" has been gathering momentum in the South Pacific region of Melanesia, Micronesia, and Polynesia. Colloquia on theological education and theological development in the South Pacific have been going on under the auspices of the Pacific Conference of Churches since 1961. In that year a meeting took place in Malua, Western Samoa, at which the leaders of the Pacific churches discussed upgrading theological education in the region and enabling Pacific Islanders to study theology in their own environment. Since then some significant developments have taken place, especially in the area of theological education in the South Pacific.

The Third Pacific Conference of Churches Assembly (Port Moresby, 1976) recommended that at the next assembly more time be given to the discussion of theological education. As a result of this request, and in preparation for the Fourth Pacific Conference of Churches Assembly, a South Pacific Consultation on Theological Education was held in Papauta (West Samoa) in 1978. One recommendation of the consultation encouraged local, subregional, and regional seminars on Pacific theology. The findings of these seminars were to be published as resource material for theological education. As far as I am aware the latter part of this recommendation has not been fulfilled.

Following the thinking of the Papauta consultation and the Third Pacific Conference of Churches Assembly, the Fourth Assembly of the Pacific Conference of Churches (Tonga, May 1981) discussed Pacific theology. The final statement adopted by the assembly could not begin to show the richness and diversity of opinions expressed in the discussion.

Why such a surge of interest and concern to develop a systematic Pacific theology?

Although Christianity has been in the Pacific for more than a century and a half, it remains for many Pacific people a foreign religion. Dr. Sione Havea, principal of the Pacific Theological School in Fiji, says that

> Christianity must be rooted in our own soil. Theology must be based on historical events. The weakness of foreignness is that it will become a second-hand knowledge and the glad tidings become lukewarm. This foreignness needs to be transformed into a first-hand, native-rooted Good News to the Pacific.[1]

A recommendation to the Fourth PCC Assembly reads in part:

> Theology in the Pacific in the past has been dominated and controlled by Western theological priorities. This has hindered the development of authentic Pacific theologies and created a "theological dependence" on Western theology.[2]

Western theological traditions, languages, and habits that came with the missionaries often are a hindrance to the Gospel in the Pacific. "The Gospel can become native, and so liberate us from imitating the missionaries' cultures and customs. We do not have to be westernized before becoming Christians."[3]

We need to develop a Pacific theology that is based on the concrete experiences and expressions of the Pacific peoples' culture, customs, and beliefs, so that Christianity stands, not just as an imported religion, but as an authentic expression of the people's response to the Gospel in their particular environment.

This Pacific theology will come out of and speak to the political, economic, and social issues of a changing Pacific society. It will emerge from the people's response to God in the changing times and in their "search for survival, unity, identity and welfare."[4]

We need to develop a theology of ecumenism for the Pacific, which will also maintain an ecumenical relationship with the worldwide church.

A Pacific theology would come out of and address itself to a complex and pluralistic Pacific society. A Pacific theology would therefore need to touch the total arena of life and its many situations. It would need to be grounded in traditional culture, which has always believed in a practical religion. It would also need to take into account the national life and the present needs of the changing Pacific.

I am aware that to speak about a Pacific theology is to generalize because the peoples of the Pacific are not all the same, in spite of their "Pacificness." We are made up of different ethnic groups, each with particular cultures and customs. It would be more correct to say "Pacific theologies" instead of "Pacific theology." Even to speak of a Melanesian theology is to generalize. But at this initial and exploratory stage some kind of generalization is necessary.

In the search for a theology that is relevant to local situations, it would be helpful to keep Dr. Sione Havea's words in mind:

> Theology is only a vehicle that may be used in discovering God in his hiddenness. We do not worship theology, but we use theology like using a torch to help us find directions for knowing, worshipping and adoring our God of Salvation and of revelation.[5]

## FOREIGN THEOLOGIES AND FOREIGN CHRISTIAN TRADITIONS IN MELANESIA

Theologies and Christian traditions in Melanesia remain foreign in character and expression. Melanesians who have had a Christian religious experience have been absorbed into church structures and traditions that are foreign to them. They have expressed their new religious experience in and through religious symbols that are exotic to them. So in religious experience and religious symbolism, Melanesian Christians have been alienated from their traditional ways. Hence, there is a foreignness about their Christianity.

Westerners have come to Melanesia with not just one theology but with many theologies. There exist today theologies labeled liberal, evangelical, and charismatic. These theological labels are creations of Western Christians, not of Melanesian Christians. In Papua New Guinea three Christian bodies are labeled according to their theological stance. The Melanesian Council of Churches (MCC), which is labeled by some as "liberal," forms one body; the Evangelical Alliance (EA) is another distinct body; the third group of Christians comes under the Charismatic umbrella. A Melanesian who has been liberated from the divisive and controversial influence and effect of such theologies and is a Christian out of personal search and conviction, would rather say: "I am not a liberal, not an evangelical, nor a charismatic, but a Melanesian Christian under the grace of God."

Church traditions and doctrines that have been brought from outside have divided clans and even families instead of uniting them. What Dr. Sione Havea says of the Pacific peoples could also apply to Melanesians:

> As Pacific peoples we can weep together at our own funerals, rejoice together in our weddings, drink *yagona* (*kava*) together socially, but when the church bells and *lalis* ring or beat on Sunday, we go in different directions. Do we inherit the fact that "we are divided in church and united in crisis"?[6]

A Melanesian theology will have a part to play in responding to this challenge.

A Melanesian who has received a theological education in the West, when confronted with a case of spirit possession, will either take the Melanesian belief seriously and offer a prayer of exorcism or will be a faithful student of Rudolf Bultmann and say: "Bultmann has demythologized spirits."[7] Such Melanesians will have to relearn theology in the light of the realities of their Melanesian context or they will dwell in the realm of theological speculation.

Western theologies and theologians have contributions to make in their particular cultures and situations. Brunner, Barth, Bonhoeffer, Tillich, Robinson, Cox—all have developed theologies out of crisis situations in the West. But those theologies cannot be reappropriated in the Melanesian situation without a good deal of critical reflection.

Much more closely related to the Melanesian context are the theologies of the Third World: African theology, "water buffalo" theology, black theology, and liberation theology. But again we cannot import these theologies to the Melanesian environment and use them uncritically, since they have been developed in different situations. Certainly we can learn from theologians like Kosuke Koyama, James Cone, and Gustavo Gutiérrez—more than from mainstream Western thinkers.[8]

Some churches in Melanesia, such as the United Church of Papua New Guinea and the Solomon Islands, have been fairly well localized. But these churches now have to face the issue of developing an indigenous Christianity. Localization is merely replacing missionaries with locals. This is not indigenization, although it is a starting point in the process of developing an authentic indigenous Christianity.

## THEOLOGICAL EDUCATION IN MELANESIA

By theological education I refer specifically to training in theological colleges or seminaries for those Melanesians who are preparing for ministry in the church. The theological colleges or seminaries in Melanesia have tended to teach traditional theological subjects and follow methods and approaches inherited from Western theological models. This has made the seminary graduates believe consciously or unconsciously that Western theological models are the only ones to follow. Until recently education in the seminaries has been classroom- and library-oriented, and most books in seminary libraries are imported from outside Melanesia.

At a seminar held at Rarongo Theological College recently, concern was expressed that what is learned in theological colleges is not always translated or applied in ways that are relevant to the people. Some feel that the way in which theological knowledge is expressed and imparted has in some ways been oppressive and suppressive. Therefore many people are passive in their theological reflection and action.

Concern was also expressed at the Rarongo seminar about the apparent gap between the seminaries and the people. The theological colleges must become aware of and take into account the problems and concerns of the people. Theological education should be a two-way process. It should educate the people at the grassroots level. At the same time theological educators should be ready to be educated by folk in the villages and at large. The aim should be mutual dialogue and consultation between the people and the theological institutions, between what Professor Charles Forman termed the "academic theology" of the institutions and the "popular theology" of the people. If there is going to be any development toward a Melanesian theology, it must come from experiencing and from the experiences of the people, not from theological institutions.

Theological institutions should foster the development of a Melanesian theology by introducing courses dealing with issues in the Melanesian context and by guiding the students to think and do theology in their context. William Burrows makes an important point when he says that "in the present talk about a Melanesian theology, very little attention has been given to the problem of forming the minds and hearts of the Melanesian theologians who are the only ones who will be able to create an indigenized and contextualized theology" in the future.[9]

Theological colleges in Melanesia must be flexible and innovative if they are to keep abreast of changing Melanesian situations and to depart from traditional models of theological education brought from outside. Classroom theological education curriculum should include studies in Melanesian themes and should take an interdisciplinary approach, making use of different subject areas—Bible, theology, pastoral matters, religion, philosophy, and the social sciences. An interdisciplinary approach in theme studies would offer an alternative to the traditional compartmentalization of the subject areas.

A Melanesian theology should make use of Western theologies and Third World theologies, the Bible, Melanesian religion and philosophy, and the social sciences (in particular anthropology and sociology). The study of the social sciences in theological institutions is important for two reasons: first, they provide us with knowledge about the concrete life situations of the people, and second, we can learn skills from the methodical approaches used by social scientists.

It is time now that the theological institutions in Melanesia (the Melanesian Association of Theological Schools particularly) take the lead in offering studies in Melanesian theology and in conducting seminars that will help in the quest for its systemization.

## THE MELANESIAN CONTEXT

Speaking generally of the Pacific, Dr. Sione Havea commented:

> When I say "Pacific" it means to me a *focus on people*. People who are human and not puppets. They have tears, blood and sweat. When they

are young they need care, when they are sick they need treatment, and when they are "itchy" they want to be scratched (where it is itchy). They are a people born to be free; they want to make their own decisions and list their top priorities.[10]

A Melanesian theology would focus on the people in their particular context. Theology must come from the concrete experiences of the people and must speak to their needs. What is God doing out there with the people and how is God meeting their particular situation?

Although the people in Melanesia have been undergoing radical changes since the Second World War, much of their culture is still preserved in their particular areas. This is what the people own and it makes them special and different. Between 80 and 90 percent of the people in Melanesia are still rural dwellers. Our theological focus must certainly not neglect that datum!

Much of the people's culture remains unchanged, but changes have taken place particularly in the areas where outside influences have been marked. The people have experienced social changes and conflicts, they have experienced political domination and oppression, and they have been subject to economic manipulation and exploitation. The peoples of the Pacific as a whole have been "invaded" and their existence threatened by the superpowers. Although the technology, economy, politics, and education brought by the superpowers have in some ways been helpful, they have in other ways been detrimental to the cultures, interests, and well-being of the people.

This is the Melanesian context today. Out of this context a theology must emerge and then address itself back to the context from which it came. To develop a theology in this situation, then, particular attention must be paid to the people, to their traditional beliefs, customs, and technology, to their religious experiences of the past and present, and to the changing Melanesian society of today.

## THE TASK OF THEOLOGY

"Theology is God's talk to man and man's talk about God and the World. God-talk always involves talk about the concrete world of culture, history and social change."[11] The task of theology is to proclaim and interpret God's relationship with people living in different ages and cultures and in changing situations. Theology makes God's presence more relevant and meaningful to peoples of various times, contexts, and cultures.

The task of a Melanesian theology is to discover and interpret what God has done and what God is doing for the people and with the people, in their particular cultural, religious, social, economic, and political environment. The Gospel must be related to the total person in Melanesia. As Burrows puts it: "Only when Melanesian thinkers grapple with the meaning of Gospel for the whole [person] will a Melanesian theology emerge."[12]

A Melanesian theology would do these things:

1. *Help the church*: A Melanesian theology that emerges from the concrete situation will help the church in Melanesia in its priestly and prophetic roles. People need to come to worship God, but they also need to go out into the world to speak and live prophetically wherever there is oppression, suppression, exploitation, and injustice. God is not only a God of personal justification but also a God of social justice.

2. *Deal with practical/pastoral issues*: A Melanesian theology will attempt to provide some answers to questions raised in practical/pastoral areas.

The relevance of worship in Melanesia could be more than is expressed by singing hymns and liturgies brought from the West. If people in the Highlands of Papua New Guinea chant, why not worship God through their chanting? Why not use more Melanesian music and art in worship? Worship could become more significant in the Melanesian setting if familiar elements were used.

Elements used in the Eucharist could be more relevant. Kava or yagona is more meaningful in Fiji than fermented juices. Yams and taro are more significant than flour made from wheat. The coconut is common to most areas of Melanesia and could be used for communion wine. In the Highlands of Papua New Guinea, where there is no coconut and where the kaukau or sweet potato is the staple diet, why not use water and kaukau in the Eucharist?

On the question of lay people's participation in administering the sacraments, could not lay men and women conduct communion services and baptize? Leslie Boseto, the first Melanesian Moderator (1972–1980) of the United Church of Papua New Guinea and the Solomon Islands, said to a group of ministers and theological students:

> What the system says at present is that you can't give authority to your laymen to conduct Holy Communion or Baptism. You can't do these things unless you go through the system. But God's work is not always through the system.[13]

On the issue of baptism, Boseto stated: "Baptism, to me, is something lay people can do. We have been receiving tradition. Now we need to be open about this question."[14] The United Church Assembly has called on the whole church to discuss lay participation in the administration of the sacraments.

At times the church does not recognize customary marriages among its adherents and particularly among the church workers. Would a Melanesian theology recognize, accept, and bless these marriages or would it condemn them and pronounce them null and void? If a man with five or more wives becomes a Christian, what happens to his wives? What is the church's attitude to polygamous marriage in the Melanesian context?

A Melanesian theology would have to grapple with such questions as these and provide some guiding principles. But it must deal with these issues in dialogue, in consultation with the people, and in concrete situations where these issues arise.

3. *Develop a christology*: The development of a christology in the Melanesian context is an important task for a Melanesian theology. Joe Gaquare, a Solomon Islander, has this to say about the matter:

> The theological understanding of indigenization is based on the Christian doctrine of incarnation. . . . The reconciling mission of God was achieved by the incarnation of his Son, culture-bound to a certain extent as a Jew. . . . In Christ, God became culture-bound. . . . If one accepts the incarnation as a fundamental Christian belief, the Church which is Christ's body in this world has to incarnate in Melanesian cultures. . . . Therefore the theology of indigenization raises a Christological issue based on the Christian doctrine of incarnation.[15]

Father Louis Beauchemin, at the opening service of the South Pacific Consultation on Theological Education, made a related statement:

> "Doing theology" means that reflection of God's self-revelation in Christ cannot take place in a vacuum, for this revelation occurred at a point in space and time, in history for all successive ages and peoples, and has to be studied as addressed to every geographic area and every culture, and in our case, to every area and culture of the South Pacific Islands.[16]

A workshop on "Melanesian Culture and Christian Faith" (Auki, Solomon Islands, October 1978) raised two important additional questions:

> In what way should we understand Christ to be fulfiller of traditional Melanesian, Micronesian and Polynesian cultures? What "Salvation models" and redemption analogies can be found in traditional beliefs and customs, which can be baptized into Christian faith?[17]

These statements and questions point to the need to develop a christology in the Melanesian setting. Can analogies be drawn from traditional ideas and practices of sacrifice, traditional methods of reconciliation and compensation, and from the beliefs in ancestors and culture heroes? Can Melanesian symbols be used? If Christ had become incarnate in Melanesia, would he have said: "I am the Coconut or Kaukau of Life" instead of "I am the Bread of Life"? Would he have drawn illustrations from the Melanesian environment for his parables?

In the attempt to make Christ relevant to Melanesia or to other Pacific regions, perhaps a word of caution is needed. We must avoid compartmentalizing "Christ and claiming him specifically for one region or culture."[18] Once we talk about a "Pacific Christ" or a "Melanesian Christ" we could confine him to our regional boxes. Regionalism often brings yet another disunity running against Christ's teaching. In our search for a Melanesian christology, we would be on safe ground if we talk of "Christ in Melanesia" rather than a "Melanesian Christ."

## CONCLUSION

A Melanesian theology must address itself to the total life situation in Melanesia, taking into account the past, the present, and the future. Its agenda must come from the concrete experiences of the people. "A true Melanesian theology's first concern must be to discern the presence of God in the concrete situation and help the community understand both the demand and the salvation held out in this day."[19]

The time is ripe for a systematic Melanesian theology to develop. But it will be a slow and a long process so long as the foreign theologies and foreign Christian traditions are maintained in and through the theological institutions and churches. The churches must be open and sensitive to God's work among God's people, seeking to look through Melanesian eyes and not be bound by present traditions and foreign theologies. Seminars, consultations, and a great deal of research are still needed. One of the big handicaps that the would-be Melanesian theologians face is lack of funds for research in this area. (Research and writing on this subject up to now have mainly been done by non-Melanesians.)

Final words of caution to the would-be Melanesian theologians are needed. They must grapple with the issues and realities of the wider Melanesian context and with the minds and hearts of other Melanesian theologians before creating genuinely "indigenized and contextualized theology." Any attempt to develop a Melanesian theology out of purely nationalistic motives, or in denominational isolationism, will not produce an authentic result. One last crucial caveat. A systematic Melanesian theology does not have to be systematic in the Western way, following Western categories, or making absolute statements of faith. It would be more truly contextual if it set forth guiding principles, systematically laid down to help Melanesians to do and to think theology in the thought forms and symbols relevant to them.[20]

# 15

# Thinking Theology Aloud in Fiji

*SEVATI TUWERE*
*Fiji*

Any of several points could offer entry into contemporary theological reflection. One could begin with a sociopolitical analysis of a given situation—using a Marxist critique, for example. This approach has been adopted by the liberation theologians, particularly in Latin America. One could start with a historical account of the place under consideration, documenting salient features of the past, which the people there talk about and still remember. These are the events that still influence and shape their lives as a community. This second point of entry is particularly significant for the Pacific islands. Perhaps one could relate the Gospel to a particular culture, to try yet another possible point of entry. My approach is rather eclectic, however, gathering up social-scientific, historical, and theological themes into the one amalgam.

My case study focuses on Fiji. By "contemporary" I mean that which is more than just "indigenous." Indigenizaton carries strong overtones of the past and its continuing influences and thus tends to neglect the present realities of radical social transformation. The term ''contemporary" falls much more in line with the need to contextualize theology, an activity generally accepted in the ecumenical circles of Third World countries. Certainly I intend to take up all that is implied in indigenization in this paper, but it is necessary to press further to take account of other issues, especially the political, economic, and social dimensions of modernization.

I do not seek here to theologize systematically, but rather to set out from a convinced pragmatic basis, insisting that we do not simply theologize. We also act on the pressing question: "What can be done in Fiji now?" We require a theology that urgently invites us to reflection, yet which leads us to appropriate action. Theology should produce a reflection-action dynamic. To take up one side of the exercise at the expense of the other will lead theology to become an unnecessary "consumer item"—something that makes a lot of smoke but has no fire.

We live in a multiracial and multireligious society in Fiji. Our primary concern is to come to grips with the human being in the midst of societal complexity. In the light of the Gospel, the human person is an incomplete experiment. We will always be on the journey toward our completion, our greater destiny. We find completion by continually relating ourselves to our Creator, to our neighbor, and to the world around us. The Fijian understanding of the human person, interestingly, complements this view, especially through the basic Fijian category of relationships.

The Fijian outlook on human relationships is derived from the Fijian interpretation of property. Traditional property includes land (*vanua*), whale's tooth (*tabua*), mats, kava, tapa cloth (*masi*), clubs (*i wau*), canoes, etc. All these are called *a i yau* in Fijian. The term comes from an obsolete Fijian verb that means "to go from place to place." Whale's tooth (*tabua*), for example, must go from place to place, for it is against custom to hoard them. A *tabua* must always be en route between communities. It is used and displayed in many and varied ways: to welcome visitors, to reconcile two parties, to create or legitimize new relationships between two communities (especially through a marriage), to introduce any group or individual to another, and to urge people to remember an agreement being made or a promise to be fulfilled. I call this model *yau voli*. In many ways it corresponds with Martin Buber's "I-thou" relationships and with the main arguments in George Herbert Mead's *Self in Society* and in H. Richard Niebuhr's *Responsible Self*. The reciprocity, the movement of valuables or property between people, provides the paradigm necessary for a theology that would handle the dynamic interactions of Fijian society.

I am trying to address the church in this paper, although this means that I also address myself. It is in a way an attempt at a self-critical analysis. All sound Christian theologies not only point outward; they must also point inward; that is to say, allow for self-criticism. My basic reference point here is the cross of Christ, for I see in the cross the paradox of God criticizing God. "My God, my God, why hast thou forsaken me?" (Mk 15:34). In this utterance, God abandons God. In Luther's interpretation, God rejects God. A Pacific theology, or any theology that calls itself Christian for that matter, can only be justified when this basic and fundamental self-critical analysis is planted within its very center. Without this, we may only be playing around with an ideology—a *mythos* not a *logos*.

I have set myself two major tasks: first, to situate human beings as they are in Fiji today, to reckon with the place where they stand, their hopes, their doubts, and their groans. Second, I intend to raise a question: In what way can the Word of God be heard in this situation? How can this situation be theologically described? I believe that we have not really taken the human situation seriously enough in our attempts to express the Gospel in Fiji. Carbon-copy theologies from abroad still hang around our theological curriculum. They are simply rearranged here and there, all too artificially, to suit the current situation. The period of colonization brought with it a type of theology that looked down upon our culture either as evil or as unsuitable to express the Christian faith.

Fiji presents itself in three closely related ways: (1) traditional, (2) pluralistic, and (3) modern.

"Traditional" refers particularly to the indigenous Fijian people, their worldview, their customs, and culture. The observance of custom or tradition is still strong in Fiji, not only in villages, but even in urban areas.

"Pluralistic" refers to the different religions that are practiced in Fiji. This pluralism is accentuated by the fact that Hindus, Muslims, and Sikhs in the country are Indians, but the bulk of the Christian population is Fijian. There is virtually no such thing as a Fijian Hindu or Fijian Muslim. Diwali, the Hindu Festival of Lights, and the prophet Mohammed's birthday are public holidays in Fiji.

Modernization is taking place in Fiji. The rapid expansion of the tourist industry is one of many contributing factors. Access roads have penetrated inland on the two major islands and airports have been built on various outlying islands. Modernization is gathering momentum and is bringing materialism to our society.

## AN EMERGING ANTHROPOLOGY

Contemporary Fijians are faced with these three different but related forces: traditionalism, pluralism, and modernization. Traditional Fiji can no longer ignore modernization, and modernization must take account of traditional Fiji. There is no one-way street to the future. Pluralistic Fiji has also made its mark on the other two forces. The three forces can never again exist independently, side by side, for each contributes to the life of the others and is shaped by the others. Living in Fiji today means living in the gaps, in the "betweenness." Many who live in the villages go out every morning by bus to work in the towns, and they are influenced by the different things they encounter there day after day. Those on outlying islands are touched by the programs on the radio. We have, then, a new situation, and out of it a new anthropology—a new view of humanity—is emerging. This is not coming about without tensions, conflicts, and the questioning of deep things that we once held and believed. Living in the gaps means we do not live in a vacuum. The gap is created by the presence of the three forces interacting upon one another, and we have to take them seriously. We must know and appreciate customs in traditional Fiji, yet we should also appreciate the reality of pluralism and the promise that aspects of modernization are bringing. Only through critical analysis can the powers of these forces be released. In this give-and-take encounter, they can be made to serve us, not confuse or enslave us.

This new anthropology is groaning in travail (Romans 8), waiting to be born and named. The whole process involves costly participation. We believe that God continues the divine work of creation. We believe that God lives in the gaps just as much as God lives and works in a definite place. God chose to work through the life of Israel. Jesus was born of the Virgin Mary.

Now, in the present time, a new anthropology will emerge through the process of social change. It is my hope that this will not come about in spite of humanity's best interest, or because rapid, confusion-bearing change is inevitable. I hope that we ourselves can activate its emergence and that we shall never let change simply happen without our playing a responsible role in it. We have to work with God the Creator in the creation of this anthropology. We have to make decisions. We should also be held responsible for the emergence of the new human being who can meet the challenges of today and of the time ahead. Our responsibility can only be Christian when this is carried out within the framework of the new creation in Christ Jesus. He is the human being for others.

Each of the three forces will always be a created power, and created powers can become rebellious. When they become rebellious and refuse to come under the lordship of Christ, they turn themselves into idols and human beings worship them instead of the Creator. In Fiji, Christian existence does not get its bearings by simply going to the past for its own sake nor by blindly hopping on the bandwagon of modernization and progress. Christian existence does not settle for pluralism as such. The way forward must be found in the "betweenness." Power for living in this gap or betweenness comes from the Creator, who invites us through the life and work of Christ to become co-workers in the new creation.

God calls us to decide which anthropology we want now and in the future. The way forward does not lie in a straight line (linear) or in a circle (cyclical), but should be worked out as an ascending spiral. We must get the best from each of the three forces at work in our society. This, admittedly, is a difficult task. "Best" is a loaded word. What is best for one may be worst for another. But as a people, a nation, we must work out a set of criteria for choosing those things that we can call best. We must form opinions. We must make decisions. We cannot sit on the fence. Christian existence gets its measuring stick from Christ, who is the Lord. In the sight of God, humans will always make wrong decisions. Making decisions reminds us of our humanity. We may make mistakes; yet, relying on God's forgiving love, we should keep trying.

## THE QUEST FOR AN ACCEPTABLE FORM OF SPIRITUALITY

In searching for a spirituality or mode of spiritual life appropriate to Fiji, a crucial principle can be found in the traditional relation between human beings and the cosmos (or total environment). Central to the cosmos is the habitat known in Fijian as the *yavu*. Basically *yavu* means people: it includes the village, the elders, the customs, and our many traditional ceremonies. *Yavu* literally means *foundation*. Our habitat is also known as *vanua* (literally, "land"). Our people who live in towns refer to the people back in the village as those who sit on the *yavu* or *vanua*. They live on the foundation or land given them by their ancestors. Land in this sense gives meaning to existence, offering an identity. According to Fijian belief, relationships within the *yavu* are not to be violated. Elders must be respected. When someone is wrong according to the mores of the *vanua,* he or she must make amendments in the customary way.

The general relationship within the *yavu* must always be good. Sickness or disease or other difficulties are sometimes interpreted as the result of a relationship that is being violated. Many difficulties can be avoided if relationships within the *yavu* are righted. This expression of spirituality has been with our people since long before Christianity. To feel and understand this spirituality, one need only participate in a Fijian ceremony and note the references to the cosmos as a whole—heaven, earth, and under the earth. The person receiving the whale's tooth, for example, in a ceremony of welcome or reconciliation, informs God in heaven and the ancestors under the earth about the event:

> I lift this up to God in heaven to look
> down upon you and give His blessing.
> Let those under the earth be informed
> of what we are doing now.

In a ceremony like this, the Fijian moves back and forth between different dimensions of the cosmos without difficulty. The problem of dualism is not raised. There is only one reality and that is the reality of the *vanua* in which the physical and the spiritual, the past and the future, are intimately related. The Fijian word for past (*muri, liu*) is interchangeable with the word for the future (*liu, muri*). The Fijian concept of time is explained not so much in terms of duration as in terms of function, or what one does with time. The month of August, for example, is known as the month for digging trenches for yams. September is known as *vula i vavakada,* the time when reeds or sticks are put into the ground for the yam vines to twine around as they grow. (The word for God (*Kalou*) comes from two roots—*Ka* means "Is-ness" and *Lou* refers to the yam garden all covered by the intertwining green yam leaves.) *Kalou* therefore means the "Is" that is alive, living, and giving life.

Fijian spirituality is intimately related to the world of nature, especially to one's relationships with and within this world. The spirituality that the church teaches in present-day Fiji is dualistic. One side of it belongs to the *vanua* and the other belongs to Christianity. This creates a false dichotomy between the spiritual and the physical. In the process human beings are divided. Protest against this is voiced in the form of the continuing presence and practice of sorcery and related phenomena. Why does sorcery continue in spite of the church's witness and the impact of modernization? It seems that it meets a need somewhere. Sorcery with all its dangers is nevertheless an interpretation of reality; it is one view of the world. We live in a world where sophistication is some people's primitivity and primitivity is some people's sophistication.

To get rid of unnecessary forms of dualism, which threatens a meaningful interpretation of the faith in the Pacific, there is a need for a basic shift in emphasis. We emphasize salvation at the expense of creation. This interpretation is not in line with biblical teaching. When the Bible talks about salvation, belief in the Creator is always presupposed. Our modern view of salvation, divorced as it were from creation, is perhaps a contributing factor to our continuing exploitation of the environment. Christian spirituality must not only be concerned with the soul; it must also take account of the environment. Here Fijian spirituality can retrieve what has been lost through misuse and misunderstanding (especially by Western importers of modernization).

## TOWARD A NEW COMMUNITY LIFE

A community life that is meaningful and relevant is one that is future-oriented. It must be filled with hope. A community without hope is dead. We need a form of eschatology that is essentially related to the past. The past without the future is dead and the future without the past is empty. Thus a dialectical relationship between the past and the future is required. The Fijian concept of time provides the idiom for the release of such relationships to take effect. The future (*liu*), which can also mean "past", must be given more prominence in our living in the here and now. A current problem results from an all-too-heavy emphasis on the past and on what we have lost, with the future being almost entirely out of sight. A new community life is needed that embraces the dynamic, dialectical relationship between past and future. This is important now because some people, particularly young people, are overly caught up in things modern. Many find themselves rootless and become frustrated by today's changes. We must educate our young people not only with formal education, but also in ways to combine modernity with the skills of our forebears and the wisdom of our elders. The Books of Proverbs and Deuteronomy tell us about the importance of remembering the past:

> My Son, keep my words, and treasure my principles;
> keep my principles and you will live;
> keep my teaching as the apple of your eye [Prov 7:1–2 (JB)].

The Fijian idioms, metaphorical language, and riddles of our forebears are rich with meaning and have potential for strong correlation with biblical teachings. The Christian faith is centered on the one great memory of Jesus, who is also the Christ of God. Yet the past must be celebrated in sight of and in relation to the future. This is what creates community—a community that both remembers and hopes for something.

My understanding of community is akin to what was known in earliest Christian times as the *koinonia* (the community where all was held in common). The village model of community has left an indelible stamp on our nation as a whole and also on the community of the Pacific region. I believe that we have much to share with people of other cultures and lands about community life—a community where children are the children of the whole village, where elders are respected and sojourners cared for.

Some aspects of this community life, however, are wearing thin under the influence of modernization. We should be concerned not so much about the changes—they will always come—but rather about the attitude we have toward change. Indifference is as dangerous as hopelessness—in fact it is an indication of being without hope. A real soul-searching is going on in Fijian villages today because most people desire above all a sound community life. They do not necessarily want an alternative type of community but only one that is adaptable to the changes occurring all around. Many models in indigenous culture already find endorsement in the Christian faith's commission to carry the Gospel.

Fiji is all about the dynamo of reciprocity, of creatively passing things on and receiving in return. We live side by side with Hindus, Muslims, and others. We need a theology that will set us free to work joyfully with these non-Christian religions in our common struggle for nation-building. As we encounter and give shape to others through our contribution we are also being shaped by them. The community of the dawning future should be one in which each member is ready to give shape to others as well as to be shaped by them. This community should steer away from the inflexible absolutes of collectivism and individualism; the right balance is potentially there in both tradition and the Gospel. We need the power to enable us to go from the past to the future and from the future to the past. The power is the Word or Promise of God—the promise that called Abraham of old, sustaining him on the way and being itself his goal, his destination, his *eschaton* (Gen 12:1ff).

# Part V

## Politics, Tradition, and Christianity

# 16

# The Christian Vision of a New Society

*JOHN MOMIS*
*North Solomons, New Guinea Islands*

What sort of future do we want for our children in Papua New Guinea? This is the most significant human question of our generation. In focusing on it I will present a general analysis of our society as it is now, as it was traditionally, and as it will be in the future.

First, however, I want to draw your attention to a much talked about problem, one relevant to the above question: the "Youth Problem." In my view, youth itself is not a problem; the problem consists in our attitudes toward youth and how we see them as part of our communities. Most importantly, the problem has to do with the kinds of values modernization and progress impose on us in Melanesia.

## MELANESIAN SOCIETY

Let me begin by pointing out some facts about our youth population. Our national population is increasing at an annual rate of 3 percent. Before the year 2000, a little over a decade away, it will be well over five million. A growth rate of 3 percent means that over half of our current population is below the age of sixteen years. This part of the population is dependent on the old to produce. This group—the young—already constitutes a large drain on welfare in education and health services. In comparison, whereas 54 percent of our population is under sixteen years of age, 30 percent of Australia's and only 26 percent of Japan's populations are under sixteen. We now have well over 1.5 million youths under the age of sixteen years. Seventeen years from now this figure will increase by over one million, bringing our youth population in the year 2000 to just below three million. It should be clear that this special group will be searching for a place in our society. From all sectors of our nation this most important and valuable asset will also be struggling with and against the forces of change and development. The young will be struggling for a job, against the signs of *nokat wok, gaukara lasi.*[1]

When we achieved our independence in 1975 we formally decided to be part of the international community. This involved an acceptance of foreign cultures and ideas, which would influence our development. In consequence, Western materialistic values are increasingly affecting the minds of our young people. Part of this influence has come in the form of pornographic movies and magazines, the use of drugs, modern dancing and music, gambling, different dress and approaches to marriage, as well as all that the mass media have introduced.

We believe that there is good in all that God has given us, but the abuses we find in the above influences bring suffering and evil to our society. The so-called generation gap is a natural consequence of the way Papua New Guinea is developing under pressure from foreign investments. It is through no fault either of the youth or the elders that this gap has developed. The fact that this gap exists is more a sign and proof of the kind of development that is taking place in Papua New Guinea. Our nation's youth should be strongly encouraged to think deeply about the bad and the good effects of these foreign cultural influences presently overtaking us.

Our education system has been geared to meet the needs of the foreigners and their institutions. Foreign investment, business, the urban sector, and the capitalist economy are actually being served by the education system. This is done at great expense to the community of which young people are a part. There is a direct correlation between education and employment. The small size of the wage-employee sector means that most of the children entering the education system will not get eventual employment (in the modern economy). The firms will skim off the cream and leave the majority to fend for themselves.

Economic performance is becoming the most important criterion for measuring development. This is slowly destroying the fabric of traditional societies. As we modernize we gradually get locked into the international monetary system. The system requires a relatively small number of educated and qualified managers to run the economy and subsidiary systems such as education; the principal cultural values are competitiveness and individualism.

Traditional society was controlled by its religious life, which united the community. As a result of the undermining operations of the above forces over the last forty years, traditional societies are falling apart. The old "center" can no longer hold traditional society together. We see this in the breakdown of the traditional extended family. We see it in the new "worship forms" of materialism. We see it in the destructive interpretation of individualism, which keeps communities from uniting. We find it in the response of young people themselves, who do not feel an integral part of their community, in which they once found security and fulfillment. Their insecurity, matched by the bewilderment of their elders, often finds expression in mutual rejection and in crime.

The forces discussed above are well known and well documented, but we must also touch upon the newer, less well-known forces. The superpowers of the world and their regional allies view the Pacific as a vast empire of new colonies for military and economic reasons. Canada, Australia, Japan, Indonesia, the United States, the Philippines, and Korea are talking about a "Pacific Basin," the minerals, forests and fishing resources of which they combine to exploit. The good-naturedness and small size of the populations of the Pacific nations, moreover, allow the superpowers to think of and to treat the region as a convenient garbage dump for products ranging from nuclear wastes to prohibited and unsafe industrial and chemical products banned in their own countries. The waters and the islands of the Pacific are an ideal space for military installations and maneuvers by Western and Soviet-bloc forces. France continues its nuclear tests in the Pacific. Papua New Guinea can expect to come under increasing pressure from the superpowers, whose interests are served by intensifying the fragmentation of societies whose values are contrary to militarism, greed, colonialism, and profit.

These, then, are the forces that have been shaping the society we now have. But our analysis of society must also consider its institutions, those systems that control outcomes and mould options. Of these systems the most important in Papua New Guinea is the economic system. I shall now briefly discuss this system since all other systems have a direct functional relationship to it. This economic system is founded on the principle that money is power. For many people, development has come to mean the same thing. Without money there can be no development. We are being taught this doctrine in the schools, because schools are seen to lead to jobs. Jobs bring money and money leads to power.

Money is certainly power in the sense that both it and the concepts underlying it undermine all traditional systems and institutions and all aspects of culture that provided the value base for those systems and institutions. The old culture is shattered and in its place we have distinctly new values and attitudes. The economic system is founded on the values of profit, competition, greed, selfishness, prestige, and success. These values breed a way of life that is materialistc, individualistic, and consumeristic, a way of life in which more and more money is spent on personal possessions, which sadly become symbols of power and wealth.

What about our political system? This system was designed to be democratic. Power belonged to the people. The survival of the parliamentary institutions is encouraging. Yet the conduct and corruption of political parties and politicians are already devaluing these institutions in the minds of the public. Thus the economic system has come to pollute the political system.

Our education system also promotes values of competition, efficiency, accuracy, and advancement, all of which are necessary to national survival if taught within an appropriate cultural context. But the context for those values is provided by the economic system. The economic system has no need for the vast majority of the students who adopt its interpretation of these values. In fact, it sets them on the road to becoming rascals and drop-outs.

Our religious institutions have substituted the values of the present economic system for those of the Gospel. The churches preach hard work and obedience to law and order. They preach to the workers and villages but say nothing to the rich, the employers, about the values of justice, love of neighbor, equality, and human dignity. The hierarchical structure of some of the churches, moreover, reinforces the hierarchical model of society.

The values embodied in all these modern institutions I have named are becoming more and more accepted by the people. The people make them their own, and in imposing these values on themselves they adopt the corresponding attitudes. These values and attitudes strengthen the institutions, which in turn bolster the values and attitudes. This becomes the vicious circle of never-ending mutual reinforcement. Happily locked in this circle, however, respected and unchallenged, the new elite rule the losers in the new economic and social order, secure behind the protection of the institutions, values, and attitudes of our changing society.

## THE NEED FOR LIBERATION

This is the society in which our youth find themselves. What hope is there for them? What is society going to do for and with them? These are crucial questions for our generation.

It goes without saying that our young people need liberation from these forces and influences subtly continuing to mould our society. Liberation, though, must begin with the young people themselves. To build a fire we start by lighting the small branches and the splinters. Only when these have caught on fire will the logs be thrown in. Young people must show their creative initiative; at the same time they should be given the assurance of the national leaders' concrete support in their attempts to organize for the new society.

As committed Christians, we have a duty in this liberation exercise. We must be prepared to die with the young people. Dying with the young means involvement in their struggle and identifying with them even in their degradation. Dying with the young people means feeling forsaken in the absence of God. We see this in the suffering servant, Jesus Christ on the cross (Is 52:13–53: 12; Mt 27:4–6). Only through the death and resurrection of Jesus Christ do we become a new community (Rom 6:1–14). Young people can become fully human, regain their human dignity, if we identify ourselves with them, serve and give our life for them as Christ did for all.

The process of liberation must begin with each person. We must know who we are, where we are going and our personal relationship with God. Young people must be trained in the field of evangelism, for the young should evangelize the young. Only by doing this can we hope to begin the long and painful process of adjustment to the Christian vision of the new society.

## THE NEW SOCIETY

By now we know where we are and at least something of where we need to go to solve our problems. In order constructively, effectively, and more completely to perform the liberation exercise, however, we should have a clear vision of a preferable new society. It is time to describe in some comprehensive way the characteristics of this new society. The model of the society that Christians envisage is dealt with in depth and length in the Bible. Jesus Christ himself spent all of his time on earth teaching and living it. It is really a total attitude to life. I will examine what I take to be the chief characteristics of this new society.

## Respect

As Christians, we look toward a society in which each person is respected and accepted as a creature of God. This would be a society built on the personal dignity of each person and would not use people for selfish ends. "Be humble towards one another, always considering others better than yourselves, and look out for one another's interest, not just your own" (Phil 2:3–4). We look forward to a society in which each person respects the image of God in others (as the image put there by God). We hope for a society in which persons are respected for what they are, not for what they have; a society in which persons are able to choose their way of life and use the individual gifts and talents given them by God.

## Acceptance and Forgiveness

We envisage a society in which people are ever ready to forgive and accept each other. We see a society where the potentials of young people are recognized and acknowledged, a society in which all are encouraged to contribute to their country's development and are appreciated for their contributions by the community.

The community must reflect the love of God by accepting those who have been rejected—by the state, the church, or some other source of denigration. We look forward to a society built on a unity that encompasses the rich and varied cultures of Papua New Guinea. Such a society will be one of forgiveness rather than pay-back, peace rather than violence. It will be a society committed to authentic human development.

## Cooperation

As Christians we see a society based on the unity of Jesus Christ (Eph 2:11–16). We have seven hundred languages and communities in our nation. Decentralization has given us an additional nineteen provinces. All these differences are expected to unite under one flag.

We look forward to dialogue between government and church and between leaders in the community. We seek cooperation between government institutions, church institutions, and youth groups. Prestige, status, and the desire for power often hinder the effective provision of services to our people. Cooperation must exist in the exercise of power. A society based on Christian principles is not one in which a few individuals or groups dominate or control, but rather it is one where power truly belongs to the people. This is asserted by the Constitution. The attempt to actualize the assertion is being made through the process of decentralization. Power and decision making should come from the grass-roots level and with the many local components of our country in mind. Unity in diversity would be our goal. We will thus ensure the cooperative use of power and resources by communities for the authentic human development of the whole people.

## Sharing

As Christians we envisage a society in which each person recognizes the needs of his and her neighbors and is willing to share. It would be a society based on sharing and not on competition and greed. We look forward to a society that is not fragmented and shattered. Its people are "of one heart and soul" (Acts 4:32), each person being willing to give himself or herself for the development of all others in society. As Jesus emptied himself for the life of others, we must be prepared to empty ourselves for the well-being of others. We look forward to a life in community, in fellowship, sharing a common vision and purpose, with common values and goals, based on trust in one another.

We look forward to a "spacious land" where no one is an outcast, where no one is a stranger, where no one is marginalized or oppressed, but where there is "space" for all, because each shares in land, money, cash crops and homes; each shares skills, labor, ideas, and knowledge for the common good; each works to build up a land filled with love, peace, and justice; each shares and has equal access to the facilities available in the community. This is the new society.

## The Equitable Distribution of Resources

We envisage a society whose resources are equitably distributed for the benefit of the whole person. These resources are not simply wealth and natural resources of people and services. Our world today is structured for poverty. It is a world in which over 800 million people live in absolute poverty and 1.2 billion in severe poverty. Coupled with poverty is powerlessness. People who are poor are powerless before the elites in their own countries and powerless before the big companies and superpowers of the world.

God is the source of all resources in our world. In the beginning, humanity was entrusted with stewardship over the rest of creation (Gen 1:28–30) and with the right to use the world's resources (Gen 2:16). Humanity received stewardship over all of creation from the Creator. Proper stewardship requires us to ensure that the resources of society are used equitably. Therefore the first priority should be to eliminate poverty and the gap between rich and poor.

## Classless Society

Christians envisage a society in which there are no differences between rich and poor, between landowners and aliens, between employed and unemployed, between employer and employee. We have described a society in which resources are shared, in which all people participate fully in a spirit of cooperation and acceptance. Such a society will be a classless society. It will not be a society in which all are the same, but it will be one in which each person participates as a liberated, whole person. It will be a society without either oppressed or oppressors, with no rich and no poor.

Our traditional societies were not perfect examples but at least they were such that social relationships were simple and inequalities were limited. They to some extent anticipate, then, the vision of a classless society based on justice and love. Such a society is the inevitable consequence of the complete acceptance of Jesus' command before his death: "Love one another as I have loved you" (Jn 15:12).

## Inspiration

We look to a society in which men and women can look to God for guidance and leadership as God works in today's world. The word of God and Christian principles should be the driving force for our community's development. Our Constitution declares:

> We, the people, do now establish the sovereign nation and declare ourselves under the guiding hand of God to be the independent state of Papua New Guinea.

God in our midst offers guidance for our human affairs. God's inspiration motivates us to view situations, to initiate development and projects, and to work for society's good. If we identify ourselves with the tradition of God's people, we were given a covenant a long time ago that called for participation, cooperation, acceptance, respect, and understanding between God and humankind. "I will set my dwelling among you, and I will not cast you off. I will live in your midst; I will be your God and you will be my people" (Rev 21:3).

We find inspiration in the model that Jesus presents—a model of service to the point of emptying ourselves entirely. Just as the people of the old covenant were told to remember and to act justly, so we people of the new convenant are told to remember and repeat continually that act of service. Jesus Christ reveals a true form of participation: being prepared to give up things that hinder the process of becoming one.

Our vision of a new society requires a transformation task that calls for a God/human effort. We therefore call for a society in which structures, systems, and services of our country be authentic and fully Christian, and in which we can find God in our fellow men and women and through our everyday activities.

## CONCLUSION

The new society of the Christian vision, I maintain, has the above character-istics. This is the society we are building, the kingdom inaugurated by the life, death, and resurrection of Jesus Christ. These characteristics are in fact similar to the national goals and directive principles contained in the Constitution of Papua New Guinea. The challenge for our nation today is to ensure that the national goals are attained.

God, the all-powerful, in love and wisdom chose us to be respected partners in the great work of creation and redemption. Although God did not have human beings as helpers in the beginning, God deliberately chose us and our institutions to build the kingdom, which has its beginnings here and now. In choosing us God made us co-creators; thus the God of Justice seeks to restore justice and peace to the world. Christ, the anointed one, was ordained in the river Jordan and sent on a world mission to restore freedom to humankind and to the world. Christ's mission, which we as Christians share, encompasses all humankind and the whole of creation, not just individuals. The mission of Christ cannot and must not be restricted only to one or some sectors of the human community. His is a universal mission to restore freedom, peace, and justice to humanity and to the world.

For a long time many Christians only paid attention to their personal relationship with their maker and to their interpersonal relationships with the immediate community. Their responsibility toward national affairs was ne-glected. Such an attitude is un-Christian, of course, because it is selfish. It is based on a misconception. Christians cannot talk only of their own personal salvation but must consider that of every man, woman, and child. My own salvation can only be secured in the context of that of other human beings, which in turn is directly influenced and affected by the political and socioeco-nomic situation in the world. Christians are thus called upon to save human-kind and its institutions.

Therefore an authentic Christian approach to life requires Christians to adopt an integral approach to life; that is, their personal welfare and that of their immediate community can only be adequately taken care of if they are also concerned about the public dimension of human existence. Our Constitu-tion specifically calls upon us to take an active role in the socioeconomic and political processes of our nation. If we want to mould Christians in a Christian community, we have to christianize our laws and institutions. Because the set of structures presently in our country creates a kind of situation and atmosphere not conducive to the Christian values of freedom, justice, and love, we must respond in action. It is naive of the churches and Christian leaders to expect the people to live Christian lives under unjust and dehumanizing laws and struc-tures. It is like expecting fish to survive out of water.

As Christians we are convinced that Christ and the Gospel are the answers to the world's problems. We, the baptized Christians, have been anointed to translate the message of the Gospel to humankind by using human laws and institutions. Something within us challenges us to alleviate the problems of poverty, sickness, ignorance, and oppression. The Spirit of the Lord is moving in our midst calling upon us as Christians to make known to the world Christ the Incarnate Word, the One who, by his death and resurrection, effected total victory over sin and its symptoms in the world. This something in believing persons drives them ever onward to transform their world into a more egalitarian and just society. It requires faith in ourselves but implies ultimate faith in our Maker and Savior.

There can be no doubt as to our responsibility. We must join hands as Christian brothers and sisters and begin building the new society. This responsibility rests on us all and on our leaders. Our Christian vision of a new society cannot be realized unless we all humble ourselves before God, join hands, and seek courage and strength.

# 17

# Thoughts of a Melanesian Christian Socialist

## AN INTERVIEW WITH UTULA SAMANA
## Morobe, Mainland New Guinea

*Question:* You have been described as "PNG's [Papua New Guinea's] most controversial premier" and have been branded "radical." Others regard you as a champion of the underdog. Do you accept any of these labels?

*Utula:* I believe I am a Melanesian Christian socialist. I believe I am a humanist and my principles are based on Christian ethics as well as on the Melanesian principle of caring for one another. For PNG to become a community of brothers and sisters, people should respect one another, work together, and share the resources of the nation.

The role of government is to bring about changes in the law or to come up with laws that protect the interests of citizens and facilitate genuine development where the people are involved. However, the way I see it now, the country is moving toward an era when leaders become rich overnight and use their powers to safeguard their own business interests.

I believe that we are moving away from our original purposes of independence—the original aim, which we said was to gain independence in the name of the people for the benefit of the people. We are definitely moving away from that aim. When I see little people, ordinary people, being belted and suppressed by the police I begin to wonder if our police are not becoming like hunters of wild animals. I begin to wonder whether the government is turning our own citizens into something to be disliked and regarded as a bunch of wild animals that need to be controlled by police dogs and laid on with batons, boots, and belts.[1]

My role as a provincial leader is to entertain whatever concern any sector of the society or community brings to the attention of the authorities.

The police are becoming a force that is definitely not protecting or maintaining the basic security of individuals and families of this nation. The police force is now becoming a community on its own, is heavily used by the national government—by top people with the economic and political power—and has lost its community element. I believe there is a trend now such that polarization of the police and community is becoming greater and greater. When you have this kind of polarization you are most likely to fall into the hands of politically and economically powerful men who use the police to safeguard their own interests and suppress the democratic rights of citizens.

We are constitutionally bound to respect the rights of citizens, including their right to protest. The trend away from this is further supported by the introduction of the Papua New Guinea Public Order Bill.[2] The people should seriously assess where the national government is going. The government is definitely moving toward strengthening the police force, and the Public Order Bill is aimed at suppressing opposition and protest against government. Public protest against the government is part of a democratic process in a democratic system of government, which must allow and entertain protests as input to government policy or revision of any government policy that the people do not like.

The police force is an instrument established by the Constitution to maintain law and order and ensure peace in the community. However, the image of the police now is very, very poor. Many ordinary people feel generally that the police force is out to suppress the people; it is an instrument to harass innocent citizens.

The onus is on the police to prove to themselves and to the public that they are carrying out their constitutional duty to protect the rights of citizens and to provide a sense of security. I would say the police have lost their integrity and are not respected by the people. The police seem to be protecting foreign industries and interests rather than providing security for the common people. At this point in time I do not know whether the police force exists to control crime or to control and preserve the class system in Papua New Guinea.

*Question:* As premier of a province what have you to say about the national goals of Papua New Guinea? Do you think the present government is moving in a desirable direction?

*Utula:* To answer the part of your question about the national goals, I will limit myself to the first three goals. That will be sufficient to make the point. I am an exponent of the "Melanesian Way," which is a philosophy of development. I believe this philosophy is well expounded by our Constitution. The first national goal, stated in the Constitution, is "Integral Human Development." This phrase conceives of development as humanistic; all processes and decisions of government should involve the majority of human beings and place them at the center of planning and development. This leads to the second goal, "Equality and Participation." We need a decentralized form of government. We ought to look again at the present arrangement of the provincial government system and improve upon it, but it has been an important step in the realization of the second goal. Without enabling people's decisions to affect the kind of development we are getting—the choice of technology, the kind of projects, and assessments as to who benefits, in fact all the basic questions of ownership—without doing all this we cannot realize equality.

The third goal is "National Sovereignty and Self-Reliance." The Constitution states that our leaders have to be committed to these national goals and make all decisions in the national interest. This implies that the government should act to control areas of economic activity that could too easily fall into the hands of a manipulating or manipulated small group. There should be strict control of foreign investment, and although I do not believe in a total rejection of it, foreign investment must be on our terms; we must negotiate on an equal footing. There should be interdependence between countries, not just a one-way process.

Regarding the pressures that outside governments and business concerns are putting on Papua New Guinea, we should not unwisely exploit our resources, certainly not in such a way as to create long-term economic and environmental bankruptcy for the country. We also have to protect and strengthen the communal base of our society—the various national subgroups defined in communal terms—and maintain Melanesian egalitarianism or equality. We ought to recognize that the people own the resources, and we should not sacrifice these resources to greedy ends nor should we maintain state structures to the common people's detriment. Specifically concerning self-reliance, villagers should be encouraged to play a vital role in production, at a scale and pace that would be within their means along communal lines.

Over the years, capital derived from agriculture should be directed toward industries that are selectively appropriate, especially those that support agriculture, and at a scale village farmers could afford or could be assisted by government to establish. We need to minimize our wants in our country so that we can say: this is a necessity, beyond this is a luxury. Once the luxury becomes a necessity—in the lives of the political elites—then we reach a danger point, which creates inequality and causes dissension and law-and-order problems.

*Question:* What about your attitude to the present approaches of Michael Somare's government in this connection?

*Utula:* In my view the eight aims of the Constitution have been betrayed. Take the principle of equality, for example. It has been betrayed because the people within the bureaucracy, who controlled policy making, could not sacrifice themselves for equality. It is simply not human. The elite has been perpetuating a system in which it can play the dominant role. The consciousness of these people has been what one would expect of those who have learned the language of the white masters and realized that they, too, can become masters. It is not the national consciousness nor was it the objective of independence to replace colonial masters with black ones. The colonial structure has been retained, for the state power that was taken over was designed by the colonial masters. We have not seriously and consciously considered fundamental issues about constitutional, legal, and institutional arrangements more conducive to Melanesian society.

Consider self-reliance. The Somare government has reduced the concept to *fiscal* self-reliance. We are far too reliant now on foreign investment and expensive foreign-controlled schemes. Regarding rural development: In October 1975, Somare announced that the eight aims were clumsy and impracticable and needed to be deferred in favor of industrialization through foreign investment. The money collected from taxes from this foreign investment would then be put into rural development later. But when? In five years, ten years, a hundred years?

In order to fight worrying economic monopolies supported by the neocolonial state, upon which Somare and his cohorts are riding, we must strengthen the communal base against it. Somare has allowed foreign-controlled enterprises to dominate the markets and exploit natural resources to the detriment of the people. The Food Marketing Corporation, the Livestock Development Corporation, and other related government corporations have failed. The only corporations that are working are those that are foreign controlled. But we do not need foreign investment in agriculture. If "they" come to control all areas of agricultural production they will gain the power even to kill our people in the end.

*Question:* When working for Morobe Province, you staged a one-man protest against the visiting Indonesian foreign minister, Prof. Mochtar Kusumaatmadja. Why?

*Utula:* One of the issues raised during the fight for independence was that we Papua New Guineans were against any form of colonialism. We were against any suppression by any outside power on any people, any sizeable ethnic group in the Pacific, the Asian region, or the world.

This was for Papua New Guinea—and still is for others—a basic tenet of nationalism and independence. As a young independent country, Papua New Guinea should contribute to the struggle for independence of other peoples of the world. In this regard I believe that the West Irian issue has to be taken up seriously.

My demonstration against Mochtar, although a one-man demonstration, was not an expression of my own individual sentiments. I believe it was representative of a lot of ordinary Papua New Guineans and their belief that our black brothers across the border should be given due recognition and rights according to the United Nations concept and principles of self-determination and for the sake of every other group fighting for the right to govern themselves.

# 18

# An Appeal for Melanesian Christian Solidarity

*TRWAR MAX IREEUW*
*West Papua*

I write in exile from my homeland. Based on the alarming and dramatic changes occurring in West Papua (Irian Jaya) over the last twenty years, I begin the search for solidarity with the Melanesian people in that part of the world. Only by tackling the consequences of these changes can we achieve a breakthrough, a bursting out of Papua's political isolation in the absolute sense of the word. Only then can the traditional inhabitants, Melanesian by origin, approach an all-embracing development on all levels.

It is gradually becoming clearer that the West Papuans are going to face a number of fundamental problems during the coming decade. Solutions to these problems could be disastrous for the Melanesian population. It is becoming clearer, also, that we West Papuans cannot wait too long before we take crucial decisions and measures. And we have to take them with a great degree of unanimity. If we acquiesce to the present situation as if it were an inevitable fate and adopt an apathetic stand, what is going to happen to all of us over the next fifty years? Do some West Papuans like their fate? Are they content with it? Or do they look with indifference, even irritation, upon those taking up the current revolt, or those who pine away in Indonesian military prisons, or those who are killed in flight or who die of hunger, or the thousands of landless peoples, dispossessed as they have been by the usurper, after traditional landowners were expropriated for the sake of transmigrants? Why should they take the painful steps necessary for saving the future generations of Melanesians when they will never see the faces of those coming after them?

One thing is certain: If we now, all of a sudden, give up the fight, it will be at the cost of the very existence of those future generations of Melanesians. This is true not only for west New Guinea, for the impact will also be felt on east New Guinea—the whole Melanesian region could become intoxicated by apathy. For we are about to be absorbed and annihilated.

The fundamental question that concerns us is: How can we bring forth the will to survive? That is a profoundly human and religious question, not just one to do with politics or military strategy. Our answer can only be that in western New Guinea our people must fight a war against the occupying Indonesian army out of fear of total ethnocidal destruction, for the sake of survival. In political matters we must oppose the Indonesian policy of forced integration and assimilation at all costs. We must try, just as if it were out of a natural instinct, to extract ourselves from the grip of Javanese centralization, which is directed out of Djakarta. We know how hard it will be to stop the present processes. But we must do it because the rot has already set in. If we do nothing the possibility of an acceleration of existing processes will be much greater. Whether we are in polite opposition or not, whether we let the total "cleaning-up" by the Indonesians go its course, the result will be the same. Only the OPM (*Organisasi Papua Merdeka*, Free Papua Movement) now constitutes the crucial opposition to the destructive intervention of Indonesia.

## HISTORICAL AND PRESENT SITUATIONS

*The History*

The first contact of our islands with the West, that is, with the precolonial powers, dates back to the beginning of the sixteenth century. Before that time, we were one people as inhabitants of New Guinea. The foreigners came (the Portuguese, the Spanish, the English, the Germans, the Dutch, finally the Japanese and the Australians), and we were divided up. After these foreigners left, one by one, the Indonesians replaced them. They took the place of the Dutch. Now they force on us their assimilation policy and expansionism from the West. The old partition between East and West remains the same, and, whatever way you look at it, these new acts are facts of colonialism.

Our current efforts to get rid of the centralist power of Java were preceded by a long history of attempts at integration and assimilation. Sometimes I wonder how long ago it really was that the centralization tendency in our part of New Guinea first began. I came to the conclusion that we have to go back to 1828. In that year the Netherlands took full control of west New Guinea. By unilateral proclamation the Kingdom of the Netherlands took possession of our part of the island. From that moment on they brought west New Guinea under the rule of the precolonial administration of the Dutch East Indies and annexed it.

Thus we were arbitrarily pulled out of our natural situation and given into the hands of colonial greed. There was no well-thought-out reason for the move; all developments were planned and worked out in far-off Java and Sumatra and on islands other than New Guinea. Why they took possession of us, then, remains a curiously open question. At the time of the Napoleonic wars, in any case, the Netherlands and the other European states began to reorganize their colonial territories, and an agreement was settled upon by which the border of 141° 47' east was established, and thereby the partition between brothers and sisters of the same (Papuan) Melanesian race became a tragic reality.

The Dutch were the colonial power in Indonesia for about 350 years, and the strongly centralist policy from Batavia, now Djakarta, hails from the time of their regime. The centralist policy we Papuans are now facing (in 1984) is, I estimate, 156 years old, although with some interruption from 1942 to 1944 (and perhaps on to 1962). When the Second World War began and imperial Japan occupied the whole northern part of New Guinea, the centralist policy stopped for a while as far as New Guinea was concerned. In 1944 New Guinea was liberated by the Allied armies. The administration of the Allies lasted until 1946, when they handed our country back to the Dutch. From that moment on until October 1962, the Netherlands conducted a decentralization policy with a special emphasis on making our country independent, as if it might eventually end up joined to or integrated with Papua (and) New Guinea to the east.

After the independence of Indonesia in 1949 our part of New Guinea was a source of political conflict between the Netherlands and Indonesia, and the boundary mentioned above was continually brought into the discussion. Indonesia claimed this part of New Guinea as an integral part of its national territory, but we Papuans felt and thought (and still do) a different way. Already in 1950 a champion of the free Papuan state, the late Johan Ariks claimed before the one-to-one Dutch-Indonesian Commission that annexation of our part of the island into the state of Indonesia would be an insult to the population of this easternmost area. He rightly argued, "We are all Melanesians, not Indonesians!"

This postwar period in west New Guinea was a peculiar episode revealing a Dutch policy that tried to combine sympathy with prestige and that was inspired by a strange mixture of idealism and power politics. The Dutch, of course, were finally no match for the Indonesians. It was only during that last period that the Netherlands did a good job in New Guinea for the sake of its people. They did the best they could at that time for the development of the Papuans, and in 1962 they were disappointed about the powerlessness of their own country to hold on to the region. They left its inhabitants with mixed feelings. At the international level, and especially militarily, the Dutch could not achieve a single thing, and alas, both they and the Papuans were set aside and had to give way to Indonesia.

Ever since 1962, Indonesia, a shrewd nation in manipulating world opinion and a champion in exploiting the needs of the industrialized countries, has conducted an expansionist policy in collaboration with foreign nations, one that leaves a bitter aftertaste in the mouths of West Papuans throughout the world. In 1973 Indonesia renewed the agreement with Australia over their respective neocolonial borders, according to which the line between east and west New Guinea was fixed at 141° east. Within these borders Indonesia developed its philosophy of the state, maintaining the theory, believe it or not, that this imaginary borderline was to be considered a natural barrier. Indonesia has followed a policy of "accomplished facts." They imagine that over a period of a hundred years all Papuans will have been made Indonesian and the republic will be, from that moment onwards, an accomplished fact.

We Papuans claim simply that no justifiable border exists between the east and the west. Based on the facts of the ethnological, geographical, and cultural sciences, we must deny the existence of any such imaginary borderline. Because of this and in line with principles of international justice (which Indonesia crushed in 1969 by usurping our right to appeal to international law) we have risen in revolt. We are aware of our fundamental rights and we are now preparing ourselves for extended war with Indonesia, until these rights are acknowledged. One could almost say that we are forced against our will and our better judgment to accept a revolt as part of our destiny.

## The Present Situation

From 1963 onwards the Papuans of western New Guinea have called incessantly for recognition of their rights. Human lives are still being offered to materialize the ideals of our people. In the meanwhile, the Suharto regime is becoming so intertwined with the interests of the American, Japanese, and Western European nations that a reasonable independence of our country in political and moral matters is nearly impossible. By 1969 the incapacity even of such an international organization as the United Nations had become all too obvious, in spite of an international agreement about our right to self-determination. Indonesia interpreted the UN agreement on west New Guinea (West Irian) according to its own ideas and manipulated the people of the island with a thousand-and-one tales.

Indonesia made a gentlemen's agreement with the Western multinational enterprises according to the adage "one good turn deserves another." These multinationals have, after the disappearance of the nationalistic figure of Sukarno, spread all over the country like termites. They support and activate Indonesia in its role as security agent, allowing the police forces to act severely against the rebellious West Papuans, whenever Indonesian efforts there seem to be in danger.

So our resources are exploited by the multinationals. Besides this there is the military clique under the direction of Suharto. Changing his military uniform for civil dress, he devised the plan of transplanting millions of Javanese and Balinese people to our country because of the overpopulation of their islands. From their "feudal lords" in Europe, America, Japan, Australia, and New Zealand (the IGGI [Inter-Governmental Group on Indonesia]), the civilian-dressed generals of Indonesia have obtained millions of dollars to support this project. The West Papuans have been driven out to strategic villages, and in the coastal areas and townships the measures of assimilation and integration have been felt intensely. Whoever adopts an opinion different from the Indonesian one runs the risk of being accused of communism and of being done away with in some shrewd fashion. From 1963 to 1984, nearly two hundred thousand Papuans have been killed in gruesome ways, for the sake of Indonesian expansion-drift or in the interests of multinational enterprises. Papuans are not safe anymore in their own country. Fleeing to freedom and safety means becoming a refugee in a foreign country. In the early part of 1984, about twelve thousand fugitives crossed the border into Papua New Guinea, searching for refuge where they could live as Papuans. It is a great pity that the government of Papua New Guinea does not know how to reply to this type of Indonesian policy and take a strong stand.

If we do not resist, and just let this process continue, then in fifty years we West Papuans will only exist in reserves, to be watched by the tourists from the West, as is the case with the native Americans in the United States. This process of Indonesianization, moreover, will surely not stop at the 141° east boundary. It will eventually move to the eastern part of the island, and thus the end of the whole Papuan race is threatened. We seem doomed to disappear in this way: first, because we have plenty of space; and second because our country is rich in natural resources. Not unimportantly, however, the Indonesians are led by their own feelings of superiority, as if they have a perfect right to overrule our country and people without any consideration for human persons. I wonder, though, whether they could accomplish this without foreign help.

Thus it is plain that a distinct worrying era is dawning for the Papuans. Is it time to play this political power game with its high stakes and to press to the uttermost by military means for the sake of our country and the survival of our Papuan race? Now that our people are forced to retreat into the jungle, they are starting to organize their opposition against the Indonesians. Over a vast territory our OPM guerrillas hold out in spite of the killing terror of the Indonesians, for the movement knows that virtually the whole population supports it. Is it worthwhile to give your life for your own country, to fight like the members of the OPM (*Organisasi Papua Merdeka*)? I believe, despite the moral and religious problems it poses, we have little choice but to fight. We Papuans are often underestimated, but in this case it is not a question of "How big is the dog?" but "How big is the fight in the dog?"—how capable is it of grimly fighting on?

Since the Act of Free Choice (the act of non-free choice!), the methods of the Indonesians have been quite refined, the standard of living is a trifle higher in west Papua than before 1969, and the terror of the police and the army is more subtle. But one fundamental fact has not changed: the limits of freedom are still determined by the Indonesian intervention army. Under the yoke of the Indonesian army and the police the Melanesians of western New Guinea are being forceably integrated and assimilated.

A disappointed fellow Papuan wrote to me in the middle of 1976, summing up the problems well:

Our mind has totally become dull. . . . Without the Indonesian pressure our country would have gone through a completely different development. However, now there is no problem more urgent than the bundling of all our forces and efforts into the country itself by ourselves, but also abroad by you people, in order to build up a militant front to realize our national sovereignty at all costs. The Indonesian presence in our country diminishes, first of all, our own Melanesian vitality, and yet it should be replaced by our own system, like the Papua New Guinea one. Over there Australia showed its respect for Melanesian identity and dignity, whereas we in West Papua are being humiliated and overruled by Indonesia. The Indonesians imposed on us an Indonesian image, and our name "Papua" is forbidden. We are all forced to vanish into a Great Indonesia. As you will have understood, the intention is to bereave us from our own identity. It is a disguised form of genocide, invented by people from the Indo-Mongol race, that performs this immoral suppression of human aspirations.

The plebiscite, once agreed upon in an international agreement, was in fact reduced to an ordinary questioning of the opportunists and some illiterate tribal elders, who were just before due time bribed with portable transistor radios. It was certainly not the choice of our people to live under this barbaric rule and dominion. That they have succeeded up to now in keeping us under control is only due to the concentration of military forces and power. The total number of their forces is nearly a quarter of our whole population. In addition to this, they are internationally supported, because the West sees in Suharto the hero who saved democracy in Indonesia. In essence, however, he is conservative, if not reactionary. In principle there is nothing in our country which is going to change along the lines of gradual development, unless the unitarian state system, with its philosophy of "Bhineka Tunggal Ika" (unity in pluriformity), is going to change the pre-colonial system. They cannot even be more tolerant towards the peoples from different origins within the Indonesian archipelago, let alone to leave us free to pursue our own development. They still do not understand that a policy of relaxation is the only condition for any process of democratization, whereas terror and violence just destroy human relations. On the other hand, by their violent behaviour the goal of a free Papuan state is only coming closer and closer. For "Long live O.P.M.—*Organisasi Papua Merdeka* (freedom)!"

## THE INDONESIAN PHILOSOPHY OF THE STATE VS. THE MELANESIAN PHILOSOPHY OF SOLIDARITY

*The Indonesian Philosophy of the State*

The present rulers of Indonesia came to power by a political overthrow of the previous government. They "staged themselves up" in order to find favor with the Western countries and to get them to pay the costs Indonesia formerly received on credit from the Soviets and the Eastern bloc for the so-called liberation of West Irian. In essence, the Indonesians continued the same state form and the same state organs as had existed during the Sukarno era—a "unitarian" (monolithic) state form, highly centralized, similar to the one used during the later Dutch colonial period. In addition, they used fashionable slogans from an archaic constitution, which is of little practical use to either the state's infrastructural organizations or to the citizens. They preach a vague philosophy, the so-called *panta-sila*, which consists of very nice sweet dreams that will never come true.

We reject this Indonesian unitarian (one-dimensional) state form, since it is, quite definitely, only a heritage of the old colonial situation. To keep it is insulting to the dignity of the peoples who once lived under that rule. It is beneath our human dignity, then, to be Indonesian citizens. To be part of Indonesia does not open up any possibility for the creation and development of our own social and cultural identity. We reject the Indonesian philosophy of the state, and we strive after an ideal that is more according to our own pluriform characteristics and that is based on equality and mutual recognition of sovereignty between two quite separate countries. From our own philosophy we expect to achieve more positive developments both for traditional Indonesia and for ourselves.

Our philosophy starts from the idea that Indonesia's situation calls for a multistate system, that is, a union of separate states, in which the means and methods of fulfilling cultural aspirations and the meeting of local needs can be constantly reorganized and readapted. A multistate system, obviously, is based on a variety of cultures. It is open to diverse, parallel-experiments, as well as to sound competition and a selective exchange of ideas. Because this ideal simply cannot be realized within the current, impracticable government system, with only half-formulated principles, we oppose the Indonesian continuation of the precolonial situation. We have in West Papua, in fact, a supranational integration at gunpoint, and in the long run it will make not only Indonesia itself but the whole melting-pot of cultures in the region all losers.

If Indonesia were to be transformed into a region with a multistate system, then each member of the system might expect certain advantages.

Each nation would be more capable of finding a balance between the positive and the negative effects of foreign influences, of protecting identity against a growing alienation, and of preventing its national creative faculties from disappearing. In the short term we might see some setbacks in the areas of national production, civil liberties, and the acquisition of technological know-how. But in the long run we would achieve progress and development without the loss of the national culture, respecting our traditions and being "more Christian."

If there is positive progress in the development of the separate states, then a multistate system could come into existence that would be so well balanced that each member of the community of states would be strong enough and sufficiently self-confident as to find new ways and solutions through its own efforts.

This is the view and the philosophy of the Free Papuan Movement. We are a crucial factor in the free game of innovation. History shows that states have been doomed to decline because they ignored forces like us and tried to oppress them. West Papuan national fervor will not leave present-day Indonesia unaffected. Indonesia faces the prospect of decay unless it permits and activates our desire for innovations.

## Melanesian Solidarity for Social Development

When we shall have freed the country from Indonesian suppression, chosen our own national government, and set up its organization, only then can we reflect upon the direction of development and set activities in motion over the whole range of Melanesian life. Only then shall we be able to reflect upon our past and to translate our own patterns from yesterday toward tomorrow. One thing is sure: We cannot take over the heritage of neocolonial rule. The neocolonial policy, which bases its economy on the export of resources, has made our culture passive. We would therefore not be able to take steps ourselves toward industrialization. We cannot dream of achieving the ideas and ideals of many other societies, nor can we try to imitate them. We are first to put our own special business thoroughly in order and only afterwards work in an associative and selective way, mobilizing our people and deepening their understanding of the aim of genuine happiness of a particular Melanesian society.

We will for example want to work out our own *Wantok*-philosophy,[1] which could be developed into a Melanesian way of life, and which could perhaps be an alternative to capitalism and communism. The Melanesian way of life, stated simply, claims three forces to be present in society: individualism, cooperation, and equality. A fixed and finished image of society will not be (and is not now) important to us, but the recognition and concrete expression of forces, values, and functions that are already present is. These could constitute a basis for further development. The questions that must be asked are these: which ideas are going to be developed later? Which rights are going to be worked out and fulfilled? Which needs are going to arise?

These issues will all eventually be presented as invented and conceived by and for our own Melanesian people and adjusted to our own situations. None of the solutions will be forceably imposed. Only a structured context will be offered so that the people, as free and independent beings, with their blend of traditional and Christian values, can fill it in themselves. Our society must have a visible sociopolitical organization in which the Melanesian view of life is accepted. Thus our desire for happiness and well-being will become a reality. Indonesia cannot give us this. Hence our struggle.

Based on these facts, I plead for a courageous and creative method of struggling. That method ought to be systematic, not fragmented into bits and pieces. The many activities being developed on the home front in West Papua give the impression of unsystematic planning. But appearances are deceptive.

All measures for the Papuan cause are like pieces of a single jigsaw puzzle. Nationally and internationally, especially in the Melanesian region (where a number of nations have recently obtained independence and joined international organizations), we can and shall press for many things. We shall tell these nations that our cause is just, and ask them to declare their solidarity with us. I believe that much work needs to be done to lift the prestige and the image of the Melanesian struggle. In the future, and even very shortly, the Melanesian nations will have to establish stable political relations. It has always been my conviction that it is of great importance for each of the Melanesian islands to be part of a larger unity. Melanesian integration will be much stronger, moreover, when West Papua will have freed itself from Indonesia. Then the political and economic importance of the whole region will be even greater than if each one goes on acting as a separate unit.

The Melanesian movement for solidarity must be carried out!

## HUMAN AND CHRISTIAN REFLECTIONS

*Why Do All This?*

The political obligation that binds together the people of West Papua has to do with emotions and chauvinism. The political and diplomatic problem of West Papua is not a simple, easy thing for Indonesia to handle as long as there are still West Papuans left who wander freely through the world. And as long as there is still Melanesian blood flowing through our veins, we shall not stop denouncing the Indonesian crimes against our people. As long as West Papuan blood is still being shed, we shall remain faithful to our political ideal. The essence of our goals is as follows:

to teach Indonesia how better to respect human rights;

to make Indonesia sensitive to justice, freedom, and solidarity;

to guarantee our Papuan and Melanesian identity.

We feel as one in this struggle. Pure metal can only be produced through the most stringent process of refinement. In order to gain our freedom we feel it is our fate to be cleansed. Therefore we do not feel unhappy if we are cast into struggle and pain. As long as we are aware that precisely in this way we can be cleansed, then we keep and exert a measure of self-criticism. A certain degree of hesitation may come into our actions, but we trust that it ensures that we act according to our conscience, realizing what is good and what is evil. At some stage or another each of us human beings has to meet this criterion of self-criticism.

We are also aware that a great many people follow an uncomplicated way of life without many internal conflicts. But if these people want to climb higher, that is, achieve a better destiny, struggles arise as to how to attain the good things and reject the evil. At that moment they will often feel guilty. Many people overcome their guilt by bringing it up to God. Speaking openly and confessing one's guilt to another who is as weak and guilty as oneself is a delicate thing. We always wonder: Who of the Melanesian leaders is trustworthy? Which of the Melanesian churches? But beyond this measure of uncertainty stands God.

I know that I can safely lay open my heart to God the Supreme Being during my prayers. Since the time of our ancestors we have consulted the natural deities according to our customs, and requested help from their power and knowledge in matters of warfare, fishing, sickness, and initiation, in order to receive perseverance, prosperity, and salvation. Similarly, the present generation find it easy to accept the Christian vision and to apply it as a guide in our conflict situations. When I was a young Melanesian, struggling for survival and fleeing for freedom, I had the deep personal experience that God the Almighty is very near anyone who is oppressed and hunted, that God will never leave anything or anybody in creation. I became aware that our Lord God never loses contact with any of us and will never depart from us if our cause seeks truth and justice. Truth and justice, represented by Jesus Christ, are precious. Without this conviction I would probably not have the will to go on combating injustice and claiming respect for human dignity. Although we human beings may sometimes feel totally alone and lost in the struggle, far from any help and anybody's interest, and although we may suffer and sometimes feel like crying, especially when we are treated dishonestly, even by our own people, God is there. And God's purpose for human beings is our ultimate rationale for struggle.

## The Churches of the Lord Jesus Christ

I am of the opinion that the churches in Indonesia and Oceania which have been preaching justice all this time show up weakly in serious matters of principle. They hold key positions in those societies that allow them the freedom to condemn injustice and to choose the side of the oppressed and humiliated. But with West Papua matters shape up differently. In order to save the dignity of the Melanesians in Irian Jaya or West Papua, surely the churches ought to have enough courage to support at least the *goals* of the OPM, which is in opposition to the Indonesian government. Instead, they only reflect on the need to protect themselves against the blows the Indonesian or their own governments might inflict on them, should they make a show of much support. I think especially of the foreign mission societies that have come to West Papua and whose churches have the best intentions towards the Papuans. Should not they now draw the genuine consequences of their own principles?

As followers of Jesus Christ, they ought to have the courage to declare themselves bound to support the struggle for independence of the West Papuans for two reasons: first, because the Indonesian government has brought serious trouble and problems into the country; secondly, because the Papuans have the basic right to give expression to their own values, and so their desires and goals are to be respected.

> Even a Buffalo bellows under the weight of the Yoke,
> And even the Caged Cockatoo bemoans its chains,
> Let alone a Papuan child, so close to nature,
> From the moment of his birth he is surely not bound
>    for submissive servitude.

The moral: If all beings with feelings show from the first moment that they are aware of the evil of subjugation and thus strive after freedom, and if even the animals, which are in any case created to serve the humans, cannot adjust to servitude without showing some measure of opposite instincts, what an unfortunate fate it would be if human beings, who are born to be free, should lose the memory of their original state of freedom and should even lose the desire to regain it! The national anthem of West Papua puts it this way:

> O, my land Papua,
>    thou, my native land,
>    I love thee
>    until the end of my life.

> Thank thee, O Lord,
>    Thou hast given my land,
>    May I be intent
>    On accomplishing thy design.

### PRINCIPLES TO REMEMBER

1. Separation from the centralistic authorities in Djakarta. That is the goal of the struggle of the OPM, and it has to be made clear to Indonesia.

2. The right to have an independent and sovereign state is not the only thing for which we are fighting, but it is a milestone to be attained.

3. In the beginning Papuans might have demanded independence within the context of a democratic Indonesian state. But because Indonesia itself is not capable of making its multiracial society function through a reasonable government, a rupture has occurred between Indonesians as the oppressors and Papuans as the oppressed. Any domination by any person or authority, and especially from the centralist government in Djakarta, is to us degrading, making us seem like a marginal province of Java.

4. The struggle has come forth out of discontent with the Indonesian philosophy of the state (the very notion of an Indonesian Republic), as well as out of the feeling that we as Melanesians are simply not safe and are threatened by total extermination.

5. We reject the unitarian system of the Republic of Indonesia and the Javanese integration assimilation policy as invidious ethnic survivalism and an expression of cultural imperialism. Our common history with Indonesia, the way in which we were brought together through a colonial power's interfer-

ence, is not to be an obstacle to the pursuit of our own national aspirations and independence.

6. Indonesia renounces its own principles, which are formulated in the preamble of its Constitution. After championing the ideals of freedom and justice for all peoples during its independence war, now it does not follow its own basic principles—unless it should actually leave us our freedom and justice and respect our right to self-government.

7. As co-founder and as one co-responsible for the organization of the so-called nonbound countries, with all their ideals and principles, Indonesia degrades its own dignity by suppressing us.

8. The struggle of the West Papuans is directed toward the realization of the possibilities of the politicocultural and socioeconomic development of the Papuans as Melanesians.

9. An effective organizational structure and an action programme geared toward direct social development should be carried out through the OPM, as well as a skillfully thought-out, modern guerrilla strategy dedicated to the long-term realization of the Papuan ideal: *Papua Merdeka* (Free Papua).

10. The struggle of the people of West Papua is to be considered the deed of a people that wants to survive and that does not want to be subjected on its own soil, on the territory its ancestors have been given by God the Almighty. That is why we have declared war on the foreign intruders in the name of our ancestors and for the sake of Melanesian solidarity and unity. The existence of any other nationality in the Melanesian region we flatly deny.

11. We are well aware that our unfortunate position as a people is connected with the situation of other nationalities in revolution within Indonesia. Coordinated fighting against the common enemy in Djakarta may offer the best solution. In that case, our military collaboration and political friendship will prosper the more with these groups if Indonesia continues to refuse to recognize our rights.

12. Only under such conditions as stated above can we be truly free and in control of our own country.

## SUMMARY

We champion peaceful coexistence between ourselves and the Indonesians as Mongol-Asians, based on the mutual recognition of Papuan-Melanesian and Indo-Asiatic nationalism. Indonesia, however, must break with its colonial past and heritage. Historically, the Dutch East Indies once imposed unity in pluriformity. The people of whole areas once lived under Dutch colonial rule, and although they had a certain common fate, they had no true feelings of solidarity. After sovereignty and rule over all of the former East Indies (except New Guinea) was handed over to Sukarno and Hatta, Javanese nationalism and expansion-drift came to the surface.

It soon became clear to the rest of the region where this was all leading. Strengthened by the feeling that "to belong to a majority" was right, and impelled by their resentment about past constraints, the Javanese mounted "the throne of the ruler" and now in turn have colonialized the rest of the former Dutch East Indies. In fulfilling this goal they are supported by many countries, including Australia, the United States, the Netherlands, Japan, and some Pacific nations. Matters would be different if foreign support were not forthcoming and if Indonesia had to finance this military expansion-drift from its own resources. It is and remains, from the West Papuan viewpoint, an unequal fight because the giant Indonesia is being supplied with help and materials, whereas the dwarf OPM is left all alone. If both sides were given equal help, then the fight would be decided to our advantage. That is the moment for which we desperately wait!

Like many oppressed peoples threatened by the loss of their very right to exist, the people of West Papua have been fighting for their independence for a long time. Since the discovery of natural resources in West Papua, most of the Western countries and Japan (within the IGGI consortium) have provided Indonesia with financial support and modern weaponry in order to get a firm grip on the area. The OPM thus finds itself facing overwhelmingly superior forces, but the desire for freedom will overcome the evil of genocide and potential annihilation. The brutal Indonesian oppression and suppression of the people of West Papua has reduced the Melanesian population in that part of New Guinea by nearly 200,000. This oppression has been made possible by international support. West Papuans are being massacred because they do not receive international solidarity and help.

In order to combat this injustice to our people, the National Liberation Organization of West Papua has been fighting a liberation war in western New Guinea for over twenty years. At this very moment an atmosphere of violent intervention is hanging over West Papua, Irian Jaya. When, O God, will it end?[2]

# 19

# Christians in Politics

*WALTER LINI*
*Vanuatu*


In my book *Beyond Pandemonium* I stated that politics and the church are opposite sides of the same coin.[1] Thus, to the question "Should ministers of religion also be active, participating politicians?" my answer is yes! Another related question could be asked: "Should dedicated, committed politicians also be active, participating Christians, or even ministers of religion?" My answer would be most certainly yes! I affirm this both as an Anglican priest and as the prime minister of my country, Vanuatu.

The church is mainly concerned with the spreading of the teachings of our Lord Jesus Christ; to further this expansion every Christian person is expected to try to live up to those teachings and to follow as faithfully as humanly possible the example of Jesus Christ. Politics concerns the art of making the right decision for the benefit of the individual and the community or nation. The politician must have the integrity to stick to his or her decisions, even when they are applied to the shifting sands of international affairs. Now if the politician is a Christian or the priest a politician, there need not be any divergence or conflict of interest, as all Christians, priests, or politicians can and should attempt to live their lives according to the teachings of Jesus.

There are those, however, who see the role of the church merely as the custodian of moral standards, governed by inflexible rules and set apart from the world of politics by the arbitrary division of church and state. There are also those who see politics as the exclusive province of government and consider the church quite out of order should it participate in politics or in any other affair of the state.

That body of opinion, I maintain, would be wrong for such a country as Vanuatu. It would isolate ministers of religion, the General Synod, the General Assembly of the Council of Bishops and all other organs and institutions of the churches from the mainstream of political life in the community. The people arguing this forget that the laity makes up the majority and the greatest strength of the church. This means that all those Christian men and women whom we call the laity who are variously involved with government—whether as presidents, prime ministers, army commanders, government ministers, politicians, public servants, even now the traditional chiefs of Vanuatu—they are all Christians with Christian belief and consciences. They are all members of the church and thus involve the church in politics at every level of national and international life.

In Vanuatu the prime minister is an ordained Anglican priest; it is also true that the last Parliament had six pastors and priests as members. Four out of seven cabinet ministers were ministers of religion! In the new Parliament the government ministers and five other members are also ministers of religion. I am often asked to explain how this came about; I shall briefly outline some of the reasons.

Vanuatu is a nation strong in its Christian beliefs. Our national motto is *"Long God Yumi Stanap"* ("In God We Stand"). Our government and community leaders believe that God is the ultimate power directing the destiny of the republic. If there were any traditional views to the contrary these have faded away because of the degree to which Christians have been accepted in this country. We believe that members of Parliament, be they ministers of religion or laypersons, are all God's instruments and that God ensures that Vanuatu will continue to develop as a truly Christian country.

In this process the government must lead the way. The church is the conscience of the government and people of Vanuatu. It is well that this is so, as this ensures that justice is not merely preached but also practiced and that by our example our country will be respected by other Christian countries of the world in the same way that we respect them. Here in Vanuatu we believe that for politics to be just, fair, and democratic, the church must be involved at every level, guaranteeing the people a true choice and the certainty of good government, truly representative of the wishes of the people, ensuring the enactment of laws that will be truly in line with the teachings of Jesus Christ.

During the last four years we have seen the way in which the hand of God has directed our destiny in a number of ways. Our churches are full and our people are dedicated and inspired. They have accepted the responsibilities of leadership at every level in our society. Our faith in God has given us the confidence and wisdom that enabled us to hold the government together and to successfully encourage unity, peace, and harmony among our various political factions both inside and outside Parliament.

Some of our achievements over the past four years have been nearly miraculous. One example is the ending of the rebellion under Jimmy Stevens. In four short years this new nation has been able to institute and implement its first national development plan, establish a national airline (Air Vanuatu), establish a shipping registry, unify all services, and, above all, to make sure of a stable and dignified way by which to conduct our affairs during the general election. These are all miracles that took place because we see the church and politics as essentially compatible elements of our society and not as divisive and opposite forces. Here in Vanuatu politics and the church are inseparable.

We have been able to unify our people, generate good will, confidence, and trust between people, islands, political parties, and different denominations. As both priest and prime minister I have been able to help other priests, political leaders, and traditional chiefs to come together in peace and harmony. Our achievements and progress would not have been possible if the church and politics were not as one. It is my belief that precisely because we see no division between church and politics, we have been able to achieve much and progress greatly.

Traditionally, in any case, there was no arbitrary division in Vanuatu; chiefs and priests were both political and religious figures, and the extent to which Christianity has been welcomed has made possible this joint fulfillment of the traditional approach and of Christian nationhood.

# 20

# Can I Remain a Christian in New Caledonia?

*PIERRE QAEZE*
*Loyalty Islands, New Caledonia*

The multi-interpretation of Christian doctrine has caused division within the Catholic Church, the Protestant churches—such as the Anglicans and Methodists—and many recently emerged sects. New Caledonia is no exception to this worldwide phenomenon of denominational division. I myself was baptized into the Protestant fold (*l'Église Évangelique*). It did not matter to the white pastor whether I appreciated the beliefs of his church or not; it was my parents' decision that counted most at the time, and their decision was in turn influenced by the idea of conforming to the habits of their society. Did they really understand the significance of their decision? I still wonder!

In growing up I have learned how wretchedly exploitative is the society into which I have been thrust. I was forced to respect so-called New Caledonia. In my early school days, I can well remember, I used to draw planes, boats, and cars, each always named New Caledonia, and each carried the French flag. Now, after having learned what colonialism is all about, I feel that New Caledonia is a bastard name that should be erased completely, together with the French colonialism that brought it. My comprehension of exploitation has led me to reject almost everything I was forced into as a child. That includes Christianity, which seems to be part of the colonialism I now oppose by revolutionary action. Can I remain a Christian in New Caledonia?

To answer this question, I will first introduce the main churches of New Caledonia and outline their respective activities. Second, I will discuss the churches' approach to the present political and social realities of these islands. Third, I will offer a brief comparison between Christianity and my people's tradition (with the question I have posed in mind): and this will lead to my conclusion.

## CHRISTIANS AND CHURCHES

I feel obliged to make a clear distinction between any Christian as an individual and "Christian" as pertaining to an organization, so as not to hurt any innocent, genuine, upright Christian person. Here, then, I am concentrating on churches as institutions. In New Caledonia the three major churches are the Roman Catholic Church, the Protestant Church and the Free Church (*l'Église Libre*). All of them have been active in New Caledonia in attempting to achieve their own objectives. Recently, we have seen the emergence of new religious sects, whose members claim to have discovered the real interpretation of Christian doctrine. I shall discuss all these groups in turn and with a critical eye.

The Roman Catholic Church first came into New Caledonia on the northern end of the main island in 1843. It has been reported that the Roman Catholic Church first planted the French flag in New Caledonia. It has always worked side by side with the French colonial regime. It has provided health services, educated the people to determine their own affairs, opposed any fight for independence. It has denounced and in a sense abetted France's genocidal policy of introducing alcohol to New Caledonia's people, many of whom drink to death.

The racially discriminatory attitude in this church is obvious, for its leadership and affairs are dominated by Europeans. Certainly as a people we have benefited from the Roman Catholic Church. I do not deny that, but from an overall perspective, these benefits appear like side effects and we are left wondering about the church's real intentions. The facts reveal contradictory behavior within the church vis-à-vis the Melanesian people of New Caledonia.

Traditionally opposed to the Catholic Church is the Protestant Church. The Protestant Church first arrived on the Loyalty Islands in 1840 with the London Missionary Society (LMS). This church has always struggled alongside the people. Its affairs are now being run by the islanders themselves. This church has always countered France's attempt to destroy the people's way of life. It has actively contributed to the development of New Caledonians in the provision of health care and especially through education. It has contributed enormously to the political conscientization of the people. It has raised its voice against the "person-killing" that has come through the introduction of alcohol. Protestant church leaders were initiators of antialcoholism rallies. This church, still more significantly, honors and advocates the culture of the people and believes that custom (*coutoume*), that is, the local people's way of life, which has developed over the last hundred years following mission influences on tradition, is the concretization of Christian doctrine.

*L'Église Libre* (the Free Church) is another Protestant church. This church was led by the French minister Charlemagne who defected from the Protestant Church with a splinter group. Some people allege that Charlemagne had a political aim and thought of achieving it through religion. *L'Église Libre*, however, does not differ much from the Protestant Church, although at the time of Charlemagne's defection there were many conflicts between people in the village and among members of the clan. *L'Église Libre* is slowly disappearing, leaving behind many important schools and colleges. The fear of a shameful return to the original church keeps the few remaining followers together and binds them strongly.

The appearance of various sects competing for a say on New Caledonia is a new phenomenon. We have the Seventh Day Adventists, the "One Way" fundamentalists, the Assembly of God Pentecostalists, and a few others (including Bahai). I have decided to lump them together because they all consist mainly of young people who have rejected the cut-and-thrust of politics. Their logic often goes like this: Politics is a vicious game; it is against Christian teachings to play vicious games; therefore, true Christians should not play politics. As a result they have taken a neutral stand on independence, not realizing that to adopt neutrality is to accept the prevailing injustices. They have opted for nonviolence, only thinking about the physical side of violence. I once challenged one of the sectarian leaders, arguing that groups like this have been violent in the sense that the *kanaks* are inevitably hurt by a neutral stand toward independence and by the suggestion that they have no right to possess what is rightfully theirs. This leader had nothing to say in reply.

I must add here that, as far as partisans of the independence movement are concerned, these sects are dangerous in that they tend to silence the masses and reduce them to passivism. It may also be said that sectarian divisiveness only reinforces the old French policy of "divide and rule."

## THE CHURCHES' APPROACHES TO POLITICAL
## AND SOCIAL REALITIES

New Caledonia is unstable—socially, politically, and economically—due to the current struggle for independence. To attempt to prove the morality of colonialism would be a puerile exercise; the questions of justifying the moral uprightness or crookedness of colonialism is pointless. The important questions now revolve around the churches' approaches to colonialism in New Caledonia, given that France's colonialism has not gone away and will probably linger even after formal political autonomy is granted. Thus a pertinent question must be: What do the churches understand by morality?

Some of them have avoided confronting the evils of the current situation. Many leaders and members of the Catholic Church adopt a Machiavellian sense of morality. For them, it seems, human beings are basically irrational and egoistic by nature and their actions are primarily determined by self-interest. Unfortunately this leads the Catholics to tacit support of the status quo because they tend to accept the current unbearable situation as inevitable. Their own self-interest, that is, their own survival as an institution, has become such a priority that they have virtually lost any moral basis for action and existence.

In contrast, the Protestant Church openly fights for popular interests and for the total abolition of social injustices, although its leaders just as often fall back on the concern for their institutional self-preservation.

As for the newly introduced sects, it is difficult to place their approach precisely. They present themselves as the "innocent people," appearing to be apart from the problem. Their leaders are aware of where they are taking the people, which is to a strictly religious stance, but the followers seem ignorant of the consequences. Since they all bury their heads in the sand over the independence issue, in any case, the attribute "innocent" really is false.

Throughout this discussion I have more or less considered Christian matters to be church matters, with little concern for individuals. It must be admitted, however, that there are individual Catholics who are dedicated to the liberation of their country from colonial oppression. There are also individual Protestants who prefer to continue being dependent on France. Individual sectarian partisans, on their part, have to be judged in accordance with the relative seriousness they have toward political involvement, but most try hard to be apolitical.

## THE FRENCH DIVIDE AND RULE

Let us consider the way the French colonial administration has developed its policy in relation to popular pressures within "New Caledonia" and then consider the positions of the churches.

The administration contains social upheaval in the islands basically by encouraging division—by playing off one group against another. This political strategy is hardly new; it was already being put into practice as early as 1878. Some may say that what happened then happened too long ago to be relevant. Yet one crucial event of that year is well remembered in *kanak* history. In that year a local chief by the name of Atai led a rebellion against the French colonial administration. He was almost successful and could have come out victorious. The French, however, used bribery to divide Atai's people, providing alcohol, tobacco, bush knives, and so on to the neighboring chiefs in return for their help in smashing Atai's village. The weak chiefs accepted the offer and killed Atai. He was slain by his own brothers because they could not resist the great desire to own "the cargo."

This 1878 event is a vital yet tragic precedent for the *kanak* people. *Kanaks* today have no excuse for falling into the same trap.[1] Admittedly the French have simply made it too difficult over the years of their occupancy for the *kanaks* to secure self-determination. White and Asian (largely Vietnamese) immigration has meant that the indigenous peoples no longer find themselves in the majority on their own islands.

The *kanak* people are showing signs of not being able to stave off the dangerous virus of divisiveness, so useful for France's strategy. The churches are not able to act in unison to deflect its dangers, and certainly the religions at both ends of the denominational spectrum are suspicious of each other.

The same lack of unity applies to the political parties, even those in which the *kanak* people have a vested interest. French-supported political groups certainly block the road to independence, but so does the dividing of *kanak* political interests, which is both a favored ploy of the colonial government and the disease easily caught by the local peoples. Even recently, one leader of the *Front National de Libération Kanak Socialiste,* the most progressive pro-independence party, has gone his own way, succumbing to external pressures and choosing to act in his own rather than the Front's interest.[2]

## TRADITION AND CHRISTIANITY: INTEGRATION OR CONFLICT?

Let me briefly present my understanding of the relationship between Christian doctrine and the way of life of my people. The exponents of Christian doctrine desire to see the people living peacefully, in an atmosphere of brotherhood and sisterhood, always sharing joys and sufferings, and respecting each other. But what is the reality? When I reflect on what is happening in towns like Noumea, I do not see the effect of the Gospel. Yet it is there that the study of the Bible is most seriously undertaken, there where most people—European—are literate and more likely to think they are children of enlightenment. Paradoxically, it is in the villages that people live in brotherhood and sisterhood, help each other, share and respect each other—there we find more actions than words. This observation forces me to state with confidence that, whereas the verbalization or mouthing of Christian doctrine in New Caledonia is mere talk about the good life (especially to townspeople and expatriates), the tradition in the villages has passed that stage, for it does not tell us what to do but simply encourages us to continue in the way we live.

The tradition I write about here is really neotradition and has been greatly influenced by Christianity. After all, cannibalism and other inhuman practices have been rejected. However, we have not totally rejected our former traditions. Rather we have borrowed some of the positive aspects of Christian teaching. Incorporating them into our life, we have still managed to keep most of our old customs. This can be seen especially in the Loyalty Islands, where traditional values, although challenged by colonial institutions, have so far been resilient. On the main island of New Caledonia this is much less the case, and that is where the chief problems of the country lie.

One might deduce that I have a special answer to the question who or what is a Christian in New Caledonia? Christians are those who believe in the Christian teaching, but to be such they cannot limit themselves to the world of ideas and principles. They must live up to their words and actually do what they preach. If what they preach has any moral basis at all, then they should be prepared to counter colonialism and therefore participate in the struggle for the independence of New Caledonia. Christians in New Caledonia should never be at rest. They should be actively involved in politics, struggling for the cessation of imperialism. Christians should not divorce themselves from reality. One can only judge their faith through their actions in the face of a given moral issue. Only through their degree of commitment can we gauge how serious Christians are as members of a worldwide faith and of a religion that should be dedicated to human liberation.

## CONCLUSION

I return, then, to my initial question: Can I remain a Christian in New Caledonia? Given that New Caledonia as it currently persists connotes a colonial fact and that colonialism is notoriously unjustified, I cannot but affirm that the genuine Christian in New Caledonia is one who is always in a process of revolting against imperialism(s). To be doing that, mind you, Christians will have to be politically motivated, and it may be that the struggle for independence will conscientize them away from identifying themselves as Christian. The logic of the present situation is such that "Christian" has become a term tainted with colonialism. A process of conscientization could lead persons to appreciate their own tradition and their own values and renounce their Christian identification.[3] For myself, I see the end result of this long process of formation as the return to one's own religion; that is, to tradition, which has already incorporated into itself Christian influences. To remain a Christian in New Caledonia without this qualification is simply to remain indifferent and passive to the living moral issues.

Obviously I am not advocating the *preservation* of either Christianity or tradition in New Caledonia. Except for instances when these two are genuinely lived out, these positions taken on their own are positions of pretense. No one can live them and be genuine in the present context. Christianity generally has the wrong associations for the moment and it is futile to imagine that tradition can be relived (with all the horrors we want to leave behind anyway).

Within *kanak* life the integration of "the Christian" and "the traditional" is already underway and has produced a third, "neotraditional," way. You may ask, but does not that mean the people in this position are living the Christian way? (especially since they do use language an outsider might recognize as Christian). To this question I do not hesitate to reply, No, they are living their own way. Their genuineness consists in living the kind of life they live—a life of sharing, caring, and active reciprocity in the villages—not in adopting stances (of pretense).

As for myself, the villagers count me as one among them, although I have gone so far as to be such a Melanesian pragmatist that I do not see why God or Jesus, especially as doctrinal, abstract concepts, have to come into this village practice. Jesus can come into the picture as far as practical ethics is concerned, yes. I could also appeal to others, such as Socrates, if I were illustrating how to handle day-to-day affairs. But for me what counts is how one lives one's life practically and how one works actively for the liberation of the oppressed.

# 21

# A Theology for Justice and Peace in the Pacific

*SULIANA SIWATIBAU*
*Fiji*

We live in a world of rapid technological change, a world in which the amazing achievements of humankind dominate our way of life and thinking. Pacific Islanders, admittedly, have somehow retained their traditional views on the sacredness of nature and the universe and on the vulnerability of the individual human being within these natural systems. But Pacific societies, because they are so small, are being swept irresistably along by the overpowering force of change. Three broad areas of development occurring Pacific-wide are probably the most powerful agents influencing the way in which our societies are evolving today:

1. Recognizable socioeconomic changes are transforming our communal societies into individualistic ones; participation in these changes entails the rapid exploitation of our natural resources, the desecration of our environment, and absorption into the expanding capitalist network.
2. Our cultures are evolving into new forms with the introduction of new beliefs, new ideas, and new value systems.
3. We observe the growing militarization of our region, with accompanying subtle political dominations by those who wield both economic and military power.

## SOCIOECONOMIC CHANGE

We in the Pacific are still largely organized in communities whose smallest viable socioeconomic unit is the village. Bernard Narokobi of Papua New Guinea wrote for most Pacific inhabitants when he described the Melanesian village:

A Melanesian village is a vital and dynamic institution. It is not the shapeless impersonal juristic layout of buildings a modern suburban city

*192*

is. A village is a cultural unit, an organ of civilization, technology, and enterprise. All its members apply their talents at their own pace, without promises, or inducements of higher pay, overseas travel or promotion. People work because it is right to work, and eat because it is pleasurable to eat. The only promotion our people expect is to be recognized for their generosity and helpfulness and to be appreciated. The only inducement they will accept is a promise to be buried with honour and dignity—when they pass through time.[1]

This passage may have idealized the village situation but I think it captures the essence of our communal life, especially since the coming of Christianity in the middle of the last century.

Today, however, we live in a Pacific where respect for individuals is being replaced by aggressiveness, where generosity and sharing are being replaced by acquisitiveness, by the accumulation of money and material wealth. Our people's aspirations are raised, often beyond their means, through powerful advertisements and commercial manipulation. Our nations aspire to continuing economic growth when their resources and possibilities are limited.

A study by two Pacific economists showed that smaller island nations of the Pacific have little hope of sustaining any appreciable economic growth given their current increases in population.[2] Yet both politicians and voters find it hard, under the circumstances, not to ask for more. Our growth is limited, we note, largely because our capabilities to trade are limited. Where we do trade, we are vulnerable to manipulation by large international concerns, such as transnational corporations, or to exploitation by the self-interests of other nations. Exploitation also occurs within our own shores. Our growing elite can easily forget their people and think only of their own interests and greed.

In our desire to accumulate more money and material wealth we risk forgetting God's charge to us to be stewards of the earth. Our forebears knew their environment intimately and respected it well. Our children now often chop down trees indiscriminately, stone animals and birds compulsively, and even kill them wantonly. They reflect the values of a secularizing society that has lost its ancient religious association with nature and has directed its worship toward human technological achievements. The loss of our belief in the sacredness of nature, in other words, has been replaced by new beliefs in the sacredness of human creations.

## NEW VIEWS AND VALUES

For us in the Pacific, new value systems were first ushered in with Christianity. Today Christianity has become an integral part of our way of life and plays a respected role in each village organization. We have gradually abandoned many old ways and adopted many new ways of great value. Both Christianity and our old religions teach us to respect nature. Christianity teaches that God created us human beings in an intimate, integral relationship with nature, and our old value systems admonish us to maintain a right and revered relationship with nature. Our old technologies enabled us to exploit nature's bounty only to the extent that was necessary; usually the optimum reached still maintained balanced relationships in the environment. But the days of such balance are now numbered. Let us examine some of the recent developments.

The use of modern technology makes the consequences of human actions more serious in both space and time. Technology is likely to affect wider areas of the earth and more of the future generations. Compare the modern bulldozer, for example, with the traditional digging stick or knife and spade. One person driving a bulldozer can dramatically transform a hillside in a few hours, doing what would take hundreds of persons working with traditional tools a period of many weeks or even months. The capacity for carrying out such work so quickly, while apparently beneficial, is unfortunately more likely to result in soil erosion and pollution of rivers and streams. But the very idea of getting things done speedily is attractive, and fosters the now-values of a rapid, welcome progress. We live, however, in a limited world. It is limited in its capacity to bear exploitation. We human beings are also limited. While we are made in God's image, we are limited in our cleverness. It is entirely possible for us seriously to hurt the world we live in. We cannot hurt our world without hurting ourselves.

Choices involving the use of advanced technology therefore bring awesome responsibility, which must not be taken exclusively by a small group of "experts." Such responsibility must be broadly shared. When faith in God the Creator and in the kingdom of God is replaced by faith in human ability to solve all problems by technical means, humanity falls into the sin of idolatry. Perhaps here we can see the deeply spiritual aspect of doing something as irresponsible as dumping radioactive waste into the ocean. Stewardship has a different frame of reference if it is based on faith in human ability rather than on accountability to God. Reflection on Christianity, then, will lead us to question the wisdom of recently received shallow values that bring imbalance to our fragile world.[3]

Pacific societies today have much that is derived from Christian teachings. The Christian God has become accepted as the one true God, believed to be worshipped even by the ancient gods. Christian values of love, justice, and caring relationships have become accepted as cherished values basic to our dealings with each other and with our community at large. Pacific Islanders find it difficult to succeed as individualistic capitalists, for the values espoused by business success—aggressiveness, acquisitiveness, and individualism—conflict with their traditional values of communal sharing and their adopted Christian values of love and caring.

Their traditional institutions largely ensured the easy expression of neighborly sharing and a fair distribution of wealth, but institutions of modern economies create an environment that discourages sharing, forces all transactions to be valued only in terms of money, and measures success in terms of material wealth. It might be argued that since Christianity and capitalism have both been carried to the Pacific from the West, then both are Western inputs complementing each other! The Gospel may have been brought by Westerners but it is not Western in itself, not even in origin. And in the West it is being used as a tool of criticism against capitalism and the worst in modern values.

> Be under obligation to no one—the only obligation you have is to love one another. Whoever does this has obeyed the Law. The commandments, "Do not commit adultery; do not commit murder; do not steal; do not desire what belongs to someone else"—all these and any others besides are summed up in one command, "Love your neighbor as yourself." If you love someone, you will never do him wrong [Rom 13:8–10].

Who is my neighbor, our neighbor? Christianity teaches that we are all God's children, all equally loved by God. This leaves no doubt that the "neighbor" is every member of the human community. The teaching to love your neighbor as yourself is to govern relations not only between individuals but also between communities and between nations. Along with and integrally related to traditional Pacific conceptions about sharing, cooperation, and care of the cosmos, this teaching challenges the new, intrusive sets of values that legitimize self-interest.

## DOMINATION AND MILITARIZATION

Today, sadly, relations between nations and peoples are often governed by suspicion, fear, and greed. The rich and powerful exploit the poor and weak, and self-interest governs dealings between nations, despite many laudable attempts to bring about a more just distribution of wealth. The Bible judges such situations:

> Some of you are not satisfied with eating the best grass; you even trample down what you don't eat! You drink the water and muddy what you don't drink. My other sheep have to eat the grass you trample down and drink the water you muddy [Ezek 34:18–19].

Pacific peoples have to learn to deal not only with powerful socioeconomic influences but also with the overwhelming military considerations of nations that have interests in the Pacific. Certain Pacific nations have been persuaded that their security lies in arms, nuclear power, and military strength. But Pacific peoples ought to be asking themselves upon what powers are we depending for our security? The biblical prophets challenged those who placed their implicit trust in the great arsenals of earthly might.

> Those who go to Egypt for help are doomed! They are relying on Egypt's vast military strength—horses, chariots and soldiers. But they do not rely

on the Lord, the Holy God of Israel, or ask him for help. He knows what he is doing! He sends disaster. He carries out his threats to punish evil men and those who protect them. The Egyptians are not gods—they are only human. Their horses are not supernatural. When the Lord acts, the strong nation will crumble, and the weak nation it helped will fall. Both of them will be destroyed [Is 31:1-3].

As nations place their trust more and more in arms and as small countries place their trust in large countries that have the arms, people shift their faith and trust in God to a new, palpably idolatrous faith. Are Pacific countries not guilty or in danger of being guilty of this?

St. Paul tells us that we are engaged in warfare with "wicked spiritual forces," not just earthly, physical ones.

For we are not fighting against human beings but against the wicked spiritual forces in the heavenly world, the rulers, authorities, and cosmic powers of this dark age [Eph 6:12].

The forces behind the arms race surely make this point pertinent. To call the arms race "demonic" is strangely but powerfully true.[4] In both a global and a local sense the powers of institutions, technologies, habits, and assumptions have taken control over us and have brought us to the edge of destruction. Even the politicians, generals, bureaucrats, and corporate executives of the most powerful countries are not in control, but are under the control of powers beyond themselves. These powers (our institutions, our technologies, our money and property, our habits, and even our crusades) possess us like demons because we give them our faith and loyalty. When St. Paul speaks about Christ "disarming" the powers (Ephesians 6) he means that their lie is exposed. They are shown for what they are. The illusion of their power is uncovered, and we stand free of their rewards and punishments. We are decidedly not meant to be possessed by them or be under their control.

In the face of the horrendous arms race, Christians are called to be advocates of peace. Peacemaking is a costly role. Peacemakers are often charged with being hopelessly out of touch with reality. Since true peace is intimately tied to justice, peacemakers must resist injustice, a costly thing to do. Peacemakers are asked to share in Christ's suffering for the world; this role may be accepted in the confidence that "in everything God works for good with those who love him, who are called according to his purpose" (Rom 8:28).

The way should be clear. There is no theology, no doctrine, in the history of the church or in major religions that could ever justify nuclear war. By any traditional standard of church teaching on violence and war, nuclear war would be outlawed. There is hardly any genuine theological debate on this issue, and many churches have been guilty of a terrible silence and accommodation. The truth about nuclear weapons must be proclaimed boldly! Christians must take up their historic task of bringing peace and justice to humankind. If they have lost their role as peacemakers, it is because they have forgotten who they are and because they themselves have fallen victim to the lies and the fears perpetuated by the "powers," the "false gods."

One thing is sure: the nuclear question will not be overcome by an appeal to fear. Its own basis is fear, and more fear will not finally prevail against it. Nuclear violence will be overcome by hope. This does not mean a false optimism, which overlooks true danger. Christian hope must understand danger. But it also knows that the victory of Christ is stronger than the nuclear powers. Christ's life planted within us and among us is stronger than the forces around us. Christian hope manifests itself in tireless activity for peace and justice. It feeds on the conviction that God's love has the capacity to overcome all prejudices and unite all peoples. So we may celebrate hope (Phil 2:5–11)—a hope given not only to Christians, but to the whole world (Jn 10:16; Eph 3:14–19)—and get on with the struggle to help realize and put into practice the better order of things that God wants for the world. This struggle is not one of physical force. We must take the way of nonviolence, confronting and absorbing violence, and wielding power redemptively.[5]

# Notes

## 1. GEOGRAPHICAL, HISTORICAL, AND INTELLECTUAL PERSPECTIVE

1. For background to the archaeology and comparative ethnography, see esp. J. P. White, *A Prehistory of Australia, New Guinea and Sahul* (Sydney, 1982); G. Blainey, *The Triumph of the Nomads* (Melbourne, 1975); J. Golson, "Agriculture in New Guinea: The Long View," in D. Denoon and C. Snowden, eds., *A Time to Plant and a Time to Uproot: A History of Agriculture in Papua New Guinea* (Port Moresby, 1981), pp. 33ff.; cf. A. P. Elkin, *The Australian Aborigines* (Sydney, 1974); A. Chowning, *An Introduction to the Peoples and Cultures of Melanesia* (Menlo Park, 1977).

2. The allusions here are to G. de Foigny, "Terra Australis Incognita," in G. Negley and J. M. Patrick, eds., *The Quest for Utopia* (Garden City, 1962), pp. 392ff.; and G. Souter, *New Guinea: The Last Unknown* (Sydney, 1963), esp. chap. 1.

3. For background, see G. W. Trompf, *Payback: The Logic of Retribution in Melanesian Religions* (forthcoming), chap. 1.

4. For one important overview (up to the post-World War II period), see C. H. Grattan, *The Southwest Pacific. A Modern History*, 2 vols. (Ann Arbor, Michigan, 1963).

5. *The Melanesian Way* (Port Moresby, 1983), p. 8.

6. For important books covering the topics touched on in this paragraph, see C. H. Rowley, *The Destruction of Aboriginal Society* (Harmondsworth, 1972); P. Corris, *Passage, Port and Plantation: A History of Solomon Island Labour Migration* (Melbourne, 1973); F. Steinbauer, *Melanesian Cargo Cults*, trans. M. Wohlwill (Brisbane, 1979).

7. During the fifteenth and sixteenth centuries, note the black king motif in paintings of the Netherlands, Germany, and Switzerland depicting the adoration of the magi; e.g., Jan van Dorniker (North Netherlander, Catherijn Convent Museum, Utrecht) [no. ABM 861], Hieronymus Bosch (Prado, Madrid), Albrecht Dürer (Ufizzi, Florence), Laurenz von Heidegg [LM 8770], Zürcher Nelkenmeister (Kunsthaus, Zürich). The same subject is treated by the Italians Giovanni di Paolo, Stefano Sassetta, Fra Angelico, Fra Lippo Lippi, Sandro Botticelli, Benozzo Gozzoli, Domenico Ghirlandaio, and Leonardo da Vinci (see J. Hale, *Italian Renaissance Painting* [Oxford, 1977], plates 11–15), yet note the black Balthasar in Andrea Mantegna's rendering.

8. For an overview, see N. Q. King, *Christian and Muslim in Africa* (New York, 1971), chap. 1.

9. See J. Glazik, "The Springtime of the Missions in the Early Modern Period," in H. Jedin, ed., *History of the Church*, vol. 5, trans. A. Biggs and R. W. Becker (London, 1980), esp. chaps. 5, 45.

10. See T. Ohm, *Wichtige Daten der Missionsgeschichte: Veröffentlichen des Insti-*

*tuts für Missionswissenschaft der Westfälischen Wilhelms-Universität 4* (Münster, 1955), p. 87 (on Enrico); J. E. J. Capitein, *De Slaverny, als neittryding tegen de Christelyke Vryheid* (Leiden and Amsterdam, 1942). Cf. R. P. Zijp, "Predikaten in Guinea, 1600–1800," in H. L. M. Defoer, ed., *De Heiden moest eraan geloven* (Utrecht, 1983), p. 34 (on Capitein); B. G. M. Sundkler, *Bantu Prophets in South Africa* (London, 1961), esp. chap. 2 (on the Ethiopian tradition, *et passim* on the independent church movement); S. E. Ahlstrom, *A Religious History of the American People* (New Haven, 1972), esp. chaps. 42, 62; M. L. King, Jr., *Stride toward Freedom* (New York, 1958).

11. See J. H. Cone, *Black Theology and Black Power* (New York, 1969); G. Setiloane, "About Black Theology," in A. Tolen, et al., *A New Look at Christianity in Africa*, WSCF Books 2/2 (Geneva, 1972), pp. 66ff., and the literature cited there.

12. For background, see W. W. Fowler, "The *Carmen Saeculae* of Horace and Its Performance, June 3rd, 17 BC," in his *Roman Essays and Interpretations* (Oxford, 1920), pp. 111ff. (black men sacrificed); M. Wheeler, *Rome Beyond Imperial Frontiers* (Harmondsworth, 1955), p. 14.

13. See K. S. Latourette, *A History of Christian Missions in China* (London, 1929), chaps. 3 and 4 (Nestorians in China); H. D. J. Boissevain, *De Zending in Oost en West. Verleden en heden* (The Hague, 1943), pp. 11–13 (Xavier and earlier missionary efforts on Ambon); C. C. Macknight, "Macassans and Aborigines," *Oceania* 42 (1969): 283ff. (Macassan settlements).

14. See S. Latukefu, "Oral History and Pacific Islands Missionaries: The Case of the Methodist Mission in Papua New Guinea and the Solomon Islands," in D. Denoon and R. Lacey, eds., *Oral Tradition in Melanesia* (Port Moresby, 1981), pp. 175–77 (Fijians); G. O. Reitz, "The Contribution of the Evangelical Lutheran Church of New Guinea Development in Papua New Guinea (selections)," in G. Trompf, C. E. Loeliger, and J. Kadiba, eds., *Religion in Melanesia* (Port Moresby, 1980), p. 184 (Lutheran Evangelists).

15. See F. Steinbauer, *Melanesian Cargo Cults*; T. Schwartz, *The Paliau Movement in the Admiralty Islands 1946–1954, Anthropological Papers of the American Museum of Natural History* 49 (New York, 1968), esp. pp. 252–61; Trompf, "Independent Churches in Melanesia," *Oceania* 54/1 (1983): 51ff.; D. Christian, "Two Aboriginal Independent Churches in Sydney" (unpublished paper, University of Sydney, Sydney, 1981); cf. Sundkler, *Bantu Prophets*, esp. chap. 4.

16. Reproduced in H. Laracy, ed., *Pacific Protest: The Maasina Rule Movement 1944–1952* (Suva, 1983), p. 169.

17. For Kath Walker's writing, see esp. *My People: A Kath Walker Collection* (Brisbane, 1970). On Leo Hannett, see "The Drop-Out," in U. Beier, ed., *Niugini Lives,* Pacific Writer Series (Brisbane, 1974), pp. 59ff., cf. J. Griffin, H. Nelson, and S. Firth, *Papua New Guinea: A Political History* (Melbourne, 1979), p. 152. See also W. Flannery, "The Melanesian Institute for Pastoral and Socio-Economic Service," in S. Latukefu, ed., *Christian Missions and Development in Papua New Guinea and the Solomon Islands* (Port Moresby, forthcoming), chap. 19; C. E. Loeliger, "Brief Historical Account of Religious Studies at UPNG" (mimeographed paper submitted to the Melanesian Council of Churches, written at UPNG, Port Moresby, 1982).

18. See also Matiabe, "The Emergence of a Separatist Movement in the Southern Highlands Province of Papua New Guinea" (honors sub-thesis, UPNG, Port Moresby,

1980); "Revival Movements 'Beyond the Ranges,' Southern Highlands," in W. Flannery, ed., *Religious Movements in Melanesia: Case Studies and Reports* (Goroka, 1983), pp. 147ff.

19. See also Pokawin, "Cargo Cults and Development," reprinted most recently in W. Ferea, ed., *Cargo Cults and Development in Papua New Guinea* (Port Moresby, 1985), chap. 27; "Developments in the Paliau Movement," in *Religious Movements in Melanesia (1), Point Series 2* (Goroka, 1983), pp. 104ff.

20. *The Melanesian Way* is in its second edition (Port Moresby, 1983); see also Narokobi's "Who shall take up Peli's Challenge?" *Point* 1 (1974): 93ff.; "What Is Religious Experience for a Melanesian?" *Point* 1 (1977): 7ff.; *Foundations for Nationhood* (Port Moresby, 1975); and a series of Law Reform Commission Reports.

21. Produced by Charles Chauvel.

22. See Jojoga Opeba, "The *Peroveta* of Buna," in Trompf, ed., *Prophets of Melanesia* (Port Moresby, 1981), pp. 127ff.; "Taro or Cargo?" (Honors sub-thesis, UPNG, Port Moresby, 1977). A doctoral dissertation is forthcoming.

23. See "Silas Eto of New Georgia," in Trompf, ed., *Prophets of Melanesia*, pp. 65ff.; "The Emergence of the Christian Fellowship Church" (Master's thesis, UPNG, Port Moresby, 1975); "Spirits and Powers in Melanesia," in N. Habel, ed., *Powers, Plumes and Piglets: Phenomena of Melanesian Religion* (Adelaide, 1979), pp. 97ff.

24. See Trompf, "A Pacific Theology: Finding the Common Ground," *Mission Review,* 19 (April/June 1982): 8.

25. See also Thomas, *Mumbulla Spiritual Contact* (Canberra, 1981). For relevant background articles on the Aborigines, see the contributions by H. C. Combs, B. G. Dexter, L. R. Hiatt, N. Peterson, and D. A. Vachon, in E. Leacock and R. Lee, eds., *Politics and History in Band Societies* (Cambridge, 1982), pp. 427–90.

26. See Momis, "Values for Involvement," *Catalyst* 5/3 (1975): 1ff.; "The Priest and the Polis," *Catalyst* 8/1 (1978): 7ff.

27. Utula Samana's writings and speeches are currently being edited by the Guanaian scholar Kwasi Nyamekye, UPNG.

28. He has told his story in a mimeographed work entitled *Ria Raar Boek* (Delft, n.d., 29pp.).

29. *Beyond Pandemonium* (Wellington, 1980); cf. *Pacific Islands Monthly* (June, 1983), frontispiece.

30. See Suliana Siwatibau and D. B. Williams, *A Call to a New Exodus: An Anti-Nuclear Primer for Pacific People* (Suva, 1982).

## 2. GENERAL PERSPECTIVE

1. See E. Fischer, *Marx in His Own Words* (London, 1968), pp. 153–54.

2. Huston Smith, *The Religions of Man* (New York, 1965), p. 10.

3. See R. M. Glasse, "The Huli of the Southern Highlands," in P. Lawrence and M. T. Meggitt, eds., *Gods, Ghosts and Men in Melanesia* (Melbourne, 1965), p. 37; cf. B. Gayalu, "The Gebeanda: A Sacred Cave Ritual: Traditional Religion among the Huli of the Southern Highlands," in N. Habel, ed., *Powers, Plumes and Piglets* (Adelaide, 1979), pp. 19–24.

4. S. Neill, *Christian Faith Today* (London, 1956), p. 42.

5. See *Justice for Aboriginal Australians*, Report of the World Council of Churches Visit to the Aborigines, June 15 to July 3, 1981, A.C.C. (Sydney, 1981).

## 3. INTERACTION BETWEEN INDIGENOUS
## AND CHRISTIAN TRADITIONS

1. I admit Pacific Island missionaries (from Fiji, Samoa, Rarotonga, etc.) were sent to PNG, but they were trained by the whites in the South Pacific nonetheless, and although various other missionaries are non-European, the Christian missions have the indelible stamp of white influence and products upon them.

2. *Wantok* means speaker(s) of the same language. During colonization and up to this time, speakers of the same (or cognate) languages have entered into reciprocal relations, and even though they may have been enemies at the village level (i.e., in different tribes, which were at war with each other), they accept their need for mutual support when living away from the home area. People from whole regions or provinces can consider themselves *wantok*(s) when in a large urban area (such as Port Moresby or Lae).

## 4. CHRISTIANITY AND MELANESIAN COSMOS

1. The names are of gods among the Wautogig villagers of the Arapesh or Buki people. The Living Iruhin is the Supreme God of the Buki.

2. Talio (Taleo, Tumleo) refers to the northwest monsoon, and Rai to the southeast trade wind.

3. *Haus tambaran*: house holding the objects of the gods, spirits, and ancestors, and used for ritual purposes.

## 5. CHURCH AND CULTURE

1. This paper was published in *Nelen Yubu*, a journal of missiology from the Northern Territory. The editor wishes to thank Rose Kunoth-Monks and Rev. Martin Wilson, M.S.C., the editor of *Nelen Yubu*, for allowing the article to be reprinted here.

2. See T. G. K. Strehlow, "Central Australian Religion: Personal Monototemism in a Polytotemic Community," *Special Studies in Religion* 2 (Adelaide, 1978), pp. 14ff.

## 6. FROM PAGAN TO CHRISTIAN PRIESTHOOD

1. Some writers refer to this god incorrectly as Malu.

2. For the missionary impact on the Torres Strait see N. Goodall, *A History of the London Missionary Society 1895–1945* (London, 1954), pp. 420ff.; cf. G. Peel, *Isles of the Torres Straits* (Sydney, 1947), chaps. 10–12.

## 7. MELANESIAN CULT MOVEMENTS

1. See F. E. Williams, *Orokaiva Society* (London, 1930), p. 3; "The Vailala Madness in Retrospect," in E. Evans-Pritchard, et al., eds., *Essays Presented to C. G. Seligman* (London, 1934), pp. 372–78; W. E. H. Stanner, *The South Seas in Transition* (London, 1953), p. 71.

2. For a general discussion and description of the Orokaiva, see Williams, *Orokaiva Society*, pp. 1, 54–56; R. G. Crocombe, "A Modern Orokaiva Feast," *Orokaiva Papers: New Guinea Research Bulletin* 13 (1966): 13; E. W. Waddell and P. Krinks, "The Organization of Production and Distribution among the Orokaiva," *Orokaiva Papers* 24 (1968); D. I. E .S., *Districts of Papua New Guinea* (Port Moresby, 1969), p.

91; E. Schwimmer, *Exchange in the Social Structure of Orokaiva* (Sydney, 1973); cf. *Papua Annual Reports,* 1914–15, p. 48; 1918–19, pp. 96–97.

3. See P. Worsley, *The Trumpet Shall Sound* (London, 1970), p. 61; cf. C. Abel, *Savage Life in New Guinea* (London, 1902), pp. 104–28.

4. On Baigona's inception and development, see Williams, *Orokaiva Magic* (London, 1969 [reprint]), pp. 3–9; cf. *Pap. Ann. Rep.,* 1911–12, p. 129; 1912–13, p. 154; Worsley, *The Trumpet Shall Sound*, pp. 64–69.

5. See J. D. Waiko, "Cargo Cults; the Papuan New Guinea Way," in *Niugini Reader*, ed. H. Barnes (Melbourne, 1970), pp. 44–77.

6. See *Pap. Ann. Rep.,* 1911–12, p. 129.

7. Ibid.

8. Ibid., cf. Williams, *Orokaiva Magic,* p. 8.

9. *Pap. Ann. Rep.*, 1911–12, p. 129.

10. Ibid. See also Williams, *Orokaiva Magic*, pp. 7–9; Worsley, *The Trumpet*, pp. 64–69.

11. Oelrichs was able to identify only two of the numerous herbs used. These were *woajei (euphorbia drummondi)* and *damana (euphorbia rulifera)*; cf. 1911–12, *Pap. Ann. Rep.*, 1911–12, p. 129; and Worsley, *The Trumpet*, p. 65.

12. See *Pap. Ann. Rep.*, 1912–13, p. 154. In fact, one of King's South Sea Island missionaries, Frank, was happy to be operated on by Eroro, the Baigana doctor. When King found them in the middle of the process, he told them to go on, basically in the hope of ridiculing the whole thing (see C. J. King, *Copland King and His Papuan Friends* [London, 1934], p. 23; Fr. Cassidy, submission to the Sacred Synod [Dogura, 1956]; Dogura Papers Box 2, p. 7 [NG Collection, UPNG]).

13. See Worsley, *The Trumpet*, p. 68.

14. *Pap. Ann. Rep.*, 1914–15, p. 50.

15. Worsley, *The Trumpet*, p. 68.

16. *Pap. Ann. Rep.,* 1911–12, p. 129.

17. Ibid., p. 129.

18. Ibid.; cf. Waiko, "Cargo Cults," p. 45.

19. *Pap. Ann. Rep.*, 1911–12, p. 14.

20. See Worsley, *The Trumpet*, p. 68.

21. Ibid. A.R.M. = Assistant Resident Magistrate.

22. Ibid., p. 16; cf. Williams, *Magic*, p. 8.

23. Rev. Copland King, in King, *Copland King*, p. 32.

24. Ibid., p. 31.

25. *Pap. Ann. Rep.*, 1911–12, p. 14.

26. See Worsley, *The Trumpet*, p. 69; Williams, *Magic*, p. 337.

27. Williams, *Magic*, p. 3.

28. Ibid.

29. Ibid., pp. 23ff.

30. Ibid., p. 23. For the direction of spread and influence in general, see *Pap. Ann. Rep.*, 1914–15, p. 58; Williams, *Magic*, pp. 16–77; Worsley, *The Trumpet*, pp. 74, 81.

31. Though Buninia is often regarded as the original prophet (Williams, *Magic*, pp. 12ff.), there are rival claimants as to the story of origin; see Waiko, "Cargo Cults," p. 46.

32. See *Pap. Ann. Rep.*, 1914–15, p. 58; Worsley, *The Trumpet*, p. 70.

33. Worsley, *The Trumpet*, p. 81. For photographs of Yaviripa and Bia, another leader, see Williams, *Magic*, pp. 72, 200.

34. See Waiko, "Cargo Cults," p. 46; Williams, *Magic*, pp. 70–71.

35. See Williams, *Magic*, pp. 60–64; Worsley, *The Trumpet*, p. 82.

36. For details, see Williams, *Magic*, p. 73; Worsley, *The Trumpet*, pp. 82–83.

37. See Williams, *Magic*, pp. 72–73; Worsley, *The Trumpet*, pp. 82–83; C. T. Wurth, "Buna Journal, 1919–1920," p. 4 (*Buna Journals,* 1907–1921, Box 6531, PNG National Archives).

38. See Edmond Donoba in Jojoga, "Taro or Cargo? A Study of Taro Cults among the Orokaiva of the Northern Province" (B.A. honors dissertation, UPNG, Port Moresby, 1977). Whilst Edmond Donoba proclaims personal inspiration, Yavavi, one of the disciples of Buninia and Bia was said to have spread the movement to Buna (Worsley, p. 81).

39. See Worsley, p. 81.

40. See Williams, *Magic*, p. 66. At one stage Williams counted about seventeen species of taro and was of the opinion that there may have been as many cults as the number of species available.

41. For discussions on sects and variant cults, see Williams, pp. 66ff.; Worsley, pp. 77ff.

42. For a description of Riroga and Eriri ritual dances see Williams, p. 20; see esp. the photograph after p. 120.

43. See F. E. Williams, *Orokaiva Society*, pp. 230–259; *Magic*, pp. 11, 37.

44. Edmond, in Jojoga.

45. See Worsley, p. 81.

46. Ibid., p. 77.

47. Ibid., pp. 76, 84.

48. See *Pap. Ann. Rep.*, p. 58.

49. Ibid.

50. Waiko, p. 45.

51. Williams, *Magic*, p. 7.

52. See Stanner, p. 71.

53. Williams, *Magic*, pp. 86–89.

54. Ibid., pp. 88ff. See also A. P. Chinnery in Worsley, p. 70. Chinnery, who described a particular *kasamba* dance performed by Buninia's group, concluded that the songs composed were full of foreign words.

55. Williams, *Magic*, p. 94. See also Chinnery, *Pap. Ann. Rep.*, 1914–15, p. 58. Here, in reference to *Jipari*, Chinnery stated that certain features of the performances were painful to watch, since although some participants appeared quiet, others shrieked wildly and rolled their eyes in a horrible way.

56. Williams, *Magic*, p. 83.

57. Ibid., pp. 91–92. Indeed treatment by medication, e.g., using bromide of potassium, was a practice adopted earlier (1905–1906) by some officials, even against the advice of doctors; medication was administered to some Binandere men for fits, etc. In one case a man had to be shot when he stabbed a constable sent to secure him (*Pap. Ann. Rep.*, June 30, 1906).

58. Williams, *Magic*, p. 91.

59. See Williams, in Evans Pritchard, pp. 372–78.

60. Williams, *Magic*, p. 95.

61. Ibid., p. 43; cf. Worsley, p. 72.

62. For debates on challenges to leadership and traditional ceremonies, see Worsley, p. 77; Williams, *Magic*, pp. 32, 97.

63. See for instance, the *Kekesi* cult (ritual) observed earlier; Worsley, p. 70.

64. See *Pap. Ann. Rep.*, 1914–15, p. 58; cf. Worsley, p. 21; Canon Bodger, "Fuzzy Wuzzy Angels of Papua" (n.d.), p. 13.

65. Worsley, p. 80.

66. Ibid.

67. See ibid., pp. 77–80.

68. "Akikia," an important ritual chorus common in the Taro ceremonies, used during the *Jipari* or shaking fit, left many colonial officials confused. In official communications between the Resident Magistrate Kumusi Division and the Government Secretary, for instance, attempts were made to sort out what *kikia* or *akikia* meant and it was resolved that *kikia* meant *kaikai*, "to eat," in pidgin. (For ref. see Box 6572, PNG National Archives.)

69. Worsley, p. 82.

70. Ibid., p. 81.

71. See Jojoga, p. 12.

72. Worsley, pp. 82–83; Williams, *Magic*, p. 73.

73. See Jeremiah in Jojoga, p. 28.

74. My informants at Buan and Sanananda, where the Gaiva sect was prominent, pointed out that there was no Taro sect by the name *kekesi*, said to have been founded by Bia (against Worsley, p. 80). They claimed that they were only aware of the *Kesisi* rite, which was an important ritual in their Gaiva sect. It seems that Williams misinterpreted the word although he had described the ritual perfectly elsewhere (cf. Worsley, p. 73). *Kesisi* is a special ritual in which taro is ceremoniously chopped or sliced in small pieces, cooked, and distributed among the guests at the feast or *kasamba* by the host group. For further references, see Jojoga, pp. 115–116.

75. See Jojoga, p. 113; *Pap. Ann. Rep.*, 1912–13, p. 154.

76. Among the Orokaiva, seclusion periods before initiation ceremonies often lasted anywhere from six to twelve months. The duration of the period would depend upon the availability of taro and other garden produce. Taro often takes six to twelve months (*duberi-da*) to mature. However, if there were unsuccessful harvests, the period was longer.

77. See, for instance, the Wabag case, according to I. T. Thwaite, Patrol Report (P/R) No. 4, 1952–53 (cf. R. Lacey, "A Glimpse of Enga World View: Some Thoughts from a Wandering Historian," in G. W. Trompf, ed., *Melanesian and Judaeo-Christian Traditions* [Port Moresby, 1975], esp. pp. 47–48).

78. Today, two of the most common dance-dramas of the Orokaiva are the *kasamba* and the *baruga* (or *poroga*). The *kasamba* derived from Taro whereas the *baruga* or *poroga* emerged from Baigona.

79. E.g., Edmond Donoba, in Jojoga, p. 84. See also Siunaba Daniel, in Jojoga, p. 15.

80. *Pap. Ann. Rep.*, 1910–1920, p. 62; 1924–25, p. 44. Cf. Worsley, p. 83. Indeed, if this is any indication of the importance of Taro activity, Edmond and his colleagues were right in saying that the Taro cult was productive rather than counterproductive.

81. See Edmond, in Jojoga, pp. 85, 96.

82. See Waiko, p. 47.

83. For discussion, see R. Firth, *Elements of Social Organization* (London, 1951); I. Hogbin, *Social Change* (Melbourne, 1970).

84. See, e.g., H. Nelson, *Black, White and Gold* (Canberra, 1976); J. Waiko, "A Payback Murder: The Green Blood Bath," in *Journal of the Papua and New Guinea Society* 4(11), 1970: 27–35.

85. For the Siar insurrection, see W. Kigasung, "Early Native Resentment to European Presence in Madang," in *Yagl Ambu* 4(4), 1977: 248ff.; cf. Lacey, "The Siar Insurrection, 1904," in *Oral History* 1(4), 1974: 20ff.

86. The cults of the 1930s included the Asisi cult among the Orokaiva. Its prophecies were millenarian, hostile, and cargoist. See Worsley, p. 20; cf. *Pap. Ann. Rep.*, 1937–38, p. 35; *Pacific Island Monthly* (Jan. 1946): 52.

87. See Paliau Maloat, "Long Story of God," in T. Schwartz, *The Paliau Movement in the Admiralty Islands 1946–54, Anthropology Papers of the American Museum of Natural History* 49, 2 (New York, 1962), pp. 352–57. For some views on Paliau's movement and influence see Worsley, pp. 193–204.

88. The fact that his last attempt to show me anything (before his death in 1978) was in 1974, shows how conservative and protective custodians of special knowledge are among the Orokaiva. Strict rules were followed in disseminating information—using symbols and signs.

89. For a discussion of the religious nature of Melanesians, particularly the Orokaiva, and their relation to Christianity, see I. Stewart, "The Life Style of the Anglican Mission," in *Journal of the Polynesian Society* 4(2), 1970: 79–85; D. Henslowe, *Papuan Post* (Sydney, 1949 [?]), pp. 36–37.

## 8. THE DEMOLITION OF CHURCH BUILDINGS

1. Oral Testimony (hereafter OT): Jacob Keti, Hardy Mavutu, Opeti Joe, Maleli Unusu and John Tione, Kenani, Nusa Simbo (March 18, 1981); Gideon Kaegais, Nusa Roviana, New Georgia (April 1, 1981).

2. See Esau Tuza, "Spirits and Powers in Melanesia," in N. Habel, ed., *Powers, Plumes and Piglets: Phenomena of Melanesian Religion* (Adelaide, 1979), pp. 97–108.

3. OT: Sualalu, Nusa Roviana (April 4, 1981).

4. I use the word "head" instead of "skull," for the latter seems to isolate personal characteristics of people and makes discussion center on magic.

5. OT: Moses Qalopui, Navala, Reuben Rukana, Papara, Choiseul (June 28, 1977); Vurokana, Kenani, Choiseul (June 29, 1977); Milton Talasasa, Munda and Zini Hite, Kindu (July 13, 1977); Rini Vailo, Sanaporo, Bella Lavella (March 6,1981); Simeone Panakera, Pienuna, Canonga (March 13, 1981); Peter Izu, Narovo, Simbo (March 17, 1981); Siope Job, (Natikiniva), Tiqe, Marovo (May 6, 1981).

6. OT: Reuben Rukana (as above). See also J. F. Goldie, "The People of New Georgia: Their Manners and Customs, and Religious Beliefs," in *The Royal Society of Queensland Proceedings* (July 23, 1908): 23–30.

7. OT: Ribi Nodoro, Banganöe, Choiseul (June 29, 1977).

8. G. G. Carter, *Tie Varane: People of Courage from Solomon Islands* (Rabaul/ Auckland, 1981).

9. See Esau Tuza, "Seeking Contexts within Which New Relationships Can Be Explored between the Overseas Churches and the Christian Fellowship Church," Mimeographed paper presented at the Joint Board (Methodist/Presbyterian) for Overseas Mission Study Day, Auckland, July 25, 1981, pp. 1–20.

10. Words in brackets are mine.

11. Codrington quoted in Esau Tuza, "The Emergence of the Christian Fellowship Church," Master's thesis, University of Papua New Guinea (Port Moresby, 1975), p. 16.

12. OT: Reuben Rukana and Milton Talasasa (as above).

13. See Douglas Oliver, *A Solomon Island Society* (Boston, 1967).

14. See Harold M. Ross, "Leadership Styles and Strategies in a Traditional Melanesian Society," in *Rank and Status in Melanesia,* De la Societé de l'Homme 39 (Paris, 1978), pp. 11–12.

15. See Harold W. Sheffler, *Choiseul Island Social Structure* (Berkeley, 1965), pp. 185–86.

16. OT: Rukana (as above).

17. See Tuza, "Spirits," p. 100.

18. OT: Timothy Paugu, Narovo, Simbo (March 17, 1981).

19. OT: Talasasa (as above).

20. See R. C. Nicholson, *The Son of a Savage* (London, 1924).

21. Hiqava preserves the right pronunciations of Ingava. See Carter, p. 6.

22. Gumi succeeded Hiqava, although Gemu is the elder of the two. See Carter, p. 6. See also Edge-Partington, p. 23 (see n. 24 below).

23. *Tamate* should have been spelled *tomate* (spirits).

24. T. W. Edge-Partington, "Ingava, Chief of Rubiana, Solomon Islands: Died 1906," *Man* 7 (1906): 22–23.

25. Goldie, p. 29.

26. Tuza, "Emergence," p. 25.

27. Ibid., pp. 14–15.

28. Woodford in K. B. Jackson, "Tie Vaka, Tie Hokara: Black Man, White Man. A study of the New Georgia Group to 1925." Doctoral dissertation ANU (Canberra, 1978), p. 96.

29. A. R. Tippett, quoted in Tuza, p. 9.

30. Jackson, p. 96.

31. Corris, in Tuza, "Emergence," p. 14.

32. Luxton, in Tuza, "Emergence." Other chiefs who may be considered in this respect are Kwaisulia, and Mahoola, both returned laborers from Queensland. See Peter Corris, *Passage, Port and Plantation: A History of Solomon Islands Labour Migration, 1870–1914* (Melbourne, 1973), p. 61; Gorai of Bougainville, in A. R. Tippett, *Solomon Islands Christianity: A Study of Growth and Obstruction* (London, 1967), p. 144; Magharatulo of Vella Lavella (Bilua), in John McLachlan McKinnon, "Bilua Changes: Culture Contact and Its Consequences. A Study of the Bilua of Vella Lavella in the British Solomon Islands" (Doctoral dissertation, Victoria University, Wellington, 1972), pp. 95–101.

33. See Tuza, "Spirits," pp. 105–107.

34. Ibid., p. 106.

35. See A. M. Hocart, "Mana, Again: Natural and Supernatural," *Man* 22 (1922): 139–41; H. I. Hogbin, "Mana," *Oceania* 6 (1936): 241–74; A. Capell, "Mana: A Linguistic Study," *Oceania* 9 (1) (1938): 89–96; Raymond Firth, "The Analysis of Mana: An Empirical Approach," *Journal of the Polynesian Society* 49 (1940): 483–510.

36. OT: Talasasa, as above.

37. OT: Ibid.; cf. Tuza, "Spirits," p. 107.

38. OT: Kaegasi, as above. The Lotu = Church.

39. OT: Micha Mada and Najikana, Sepa, Choiseul (Jan. 26, 1981).

40. Carter, pp. 15–22.

41. Ibid., pp. 126–131.

42. OT: Timothy Poko, Petats, Buka (June 16, 1981).

43. Esau Tuza, "A Loving Educationist: A Short Account of Abel Pitakömöki of Choiseul, Solomon Islands" (mimeographed paper, 1979). See also Carter, pp. 29–32.

44. Tuza, "Loving."

45. OT: Isaac Taqasabo, Boe, Choiseul (June 1977).

46. In Tuza, "Loving," p. 9.

47. Ibid., p. 1.

48. Europeans' graves too can be considered in this respect.

49. Elijah Dalisaru died on April 9, 1980. Interview was carried out with people at Kaqoloqa (February 7, 1981). See also Tuza, "Seeking Contexts."

50. Tuza, "Emergence," p. 19.

51. Ibid.

52. OT: Titus Taqolo, Tasure, Choiseul (1952); cf. Tuza, "Emergence," p. 89.

53. OT: Rukana, as above.

54. Tippett, pp. 190–200; cf. Tuza, "Seeking," p. 10 and n.45.

55. For these two prayers, see Tuza, "Emergence," p. 89.

56. Leadley, Diary 1937, quoted in Tuza, "Emergence," pp. 90–91.

57. Church buildings at Paradise, CFC headquarters, Sasavele, Madou, and Tamaneke are also very large buildings.

58. The Rev. J. F. Goldie was the pioneer missionary and the chairperson of the Solomon Islands district from 1902 to 1951. See Tuza, "Emergence," pp. 35–82.

59. See Frances Hine Harwood, "The Christian Fellowship Church: A Revitalization Movement in Melanesia" (Ph.D. diss., Chicago University, Chicago, 1971), p. 274. BSIP-British Solomon Island Protectorate.

60. OT: Holy Mama, Paradise, New Georgia (July 1977).

61. Even at 76 years of age, Mama still draws. His drawing of the branch of the vine at Tamaneke is impressive.

62. Harwood, p. 281.

63. Tuza, "Seeking," p. 12.

64. See Tuza, "Emergence," pp. 129–88.

65. See Carter, pp. 32–38.

66. Ibid., p. 34.

67. The experience of *sabusabukae* used to be confined to *hiama* (priests) or healers. See C. M. Woodford, *A Naturalist among the Head-hunters* (London, 1890), pp. 150ff.

68. Rove, in Tuza, "Emergence," p. 201.

69. Naule, in Tuza, "Emergence," p. 201.

70. Harwood, "Christian," p. 133.

71. Tuza, "Emergence," pp. 194ff.

72. See John Barr, "A Survey of Ecstatic Phenomenon and 'Holy Spirit Movements' in Melanesia," *Oceania* (forthcoming). See also Wendy Flannery, "All Prophets: Revival Movements in the Catholic and Lutheran Churches in the Highlands," *Catalyst* 10(4) (1980): 229–57.

73. Tuza, "Emergence," pp. 200ff.; Carter, p. 34.

74. "New Way" was the name given to the CFC in 1961. See F. C. Leadley, "Report on the New Way of Worship," in file marked "Etoism," Methodist mission archives, Auckland.

75. Tuza, "Emergence," p. 136.

76. See Nathan Kera, "John Wesley's Lotu: Evangelistic Missions on Choiseul," *Open Door* (Sept. 1941): 6–7.

77. People can cry when Holy Mama enters the church. I have a recording of a Sunday service at Madou, Vonavona (July 28, 1977).

78. Tuza, "Emergence," p. 135.

79. Leadley, in Tuza, "Emergence," pp. 178–82.

80. "B" refers to my own collection series.

81. Part of Holy Mama's sermon preached at Madou (July 28, 1977).

82. OT: Holy Mama (May 7, 1981).

83. In that year Methodist leaders condemned CFC's religious ecstatic experience as caused by the "evil spirit." This led to the schism.

84. I could not verify the 1928 date for, officially, either 1932 or 1934 have been years when the Holy Spirit was said to have come down at Kolobagea.

85. "Holy Mama," CFC document, 1972.

86. March 10, 1981.

87. May 7–9, 1981.

88. This is supposedly a hymn but I have not identified it in my collections.

89. OT: Holy Mama (July 27, 1977).

90. OT: Holy Mama (May 8, 1981). See also Emily Muirika, Rehana Mamu, file on "Tina Iliri" (becoming changes or watching visions).

91. See Tuza, "Emergence," p. 216.

92. See H. W. Scheffler, *Choiseul Island Social Structure,* pp. 204ff.

93. Tuza, "Spirits," p. 102.

94. OT: Holy Mama (May 8, 1981).

95. This part precedes entry to church buildings. See Appendix to chapter 8.

96. Letter from Sakiri to Goldie, in C. T. J. Luxton, *Isles of Solomons: A Tale of Missionary Adventure* (Wellington, 1955), p. 184.

97. Goldie in R. G. Williams, *The United Church of Papua New Guinea and the Solomon Islands* (Rabaul, 1972), p. 260.

98. Whether this belongs to Holy Mama or is borrowed from elsewhere is not yet certain.

99. See Tuza, "Seeking," pp. 9–10.

100. OT: Sam Kuku, Patutiva (May 10, 1981).

101. See Tuza, "Seeking," p. 11.

102. OT: Silas Lezituni, New Tiberius, Vella Lavella (March 10, 1981).

103. Tuza, "Seeking," p. 11.

104. Garry Trompf, "Independent Churches in Melanesia," *Oceania* 54/1 (1983): 51–54; cf. cover of *Pacific Islands Monthly* 49 (7) (1978).

105. Vincent van Nuffel, *The Mystery of the Temple* (Port Moresby, 1976), pp. 119–20.

106. See H. W. Turner, "Primal Religions and Their Study" and "New Religious Movements in Primal Societies," in V. C. Hayes, ed., *Australian Essays in World Religions* (Adelaide, 1977), pp. 27–48; cf. Turner, "Old and New Religions in Melanesia," *Point* 2 (1978): 5–29.

107. See Barr, "Survey of Ecstatic Phenomenon."

108. See Tippett, pp. 248–64.

## 9. THE LAND IS SACRED

1. A *nulla-nulla* is typically a smoothed club used in hand-to-hand fighting.

2. These lakes lie south of Bega on the southern New South Wales coast.

3. On the linguistics and archaeology of the area, see P. White, articles by

P. J. Hughes, R. J. Lampert, J. M. Flood, and P. Hiscock, in S. Bowdler, ed., *Coastal Archaeology in Eastern Australia* (Canberra, 1982), pp. 16–45.

4. See J. P. White, "Prehistory," in P. Stanbury, ed., *The Moving Frontier* (Sydney, 1977), p. 21.

5. Lake George and Euchumbene are the only large lakes near Canberra.

6. Jack Mumbulla, a famous Aboriginal, died in 1918. Born around 1909, Guboo was nine or ten when Jack Mumbulla died, and because there were no more traditional initiations after Mumbulla's death, Guboo and all those after him have not received the local initiation rites. Despite this loss of the old ways, however, Guboo was subsequently chosen for his leadership qualities as elder of the Yuin tribe, and has conducted various (neotraditional) initiations.

## 10. ABORIGINAL AND CHRISTIAN HEALING

1. For location see W. H. and L. F. Oates, *A Revised Linguistic Survey of Australia, Australian Aboriginal Studies* 33 (Canberra, 1970), pp. 50–51, 54.

2. Following this interview, Mick Fazeldean conducted a healing session with one of the conference participants. During the proceedings he appeared to take something, some material, out of his "patient's" body.

3. See chapter 8 (Esau Tuza's article).

## 11. SPIRITS

This article appeared in a slightly different form as "Spirits in Melanesia and the Spirit in Christianity," in W. Flannery, ed., *Religious Movements in Melanesia Today* 3, Point Series 4 (Goroka, 1984), pp. 92ff.

1. The author comes from Panaeati Island of Misima District, Milne Bay Province.

2. Michael Green, *I Believe in the Holy Spirit* (Grand Rapids, 1975), p. 18.

3. C. A. Anderson Scott, *Christianity according to St. Paul* (Cambridge, 1966), p. 135.

4. Green, p. 18.

5. See J. B. Pritchard, ed., *Ancient Near Eastern Texts* (Princeton, 1969), pp. 369–71 (hymn of Aton).

6. See Green, pp. 28–29 for further reading.

7. Note esp. W. Flannery, ed., *Religious Movements in Melanesia Today* 2, Point Series 3 (Goroka, 1983); and J. Barr's forthcoming Master's thesis on Holy Spirit Movements in Melanesia (University of Sydney); foreshadowed by the foreword and first chapter of the above volume, and by his "Survey of Ecstatic Phenomena and 'Holy Spirit Movements' in Melanesia," *Oceania* 54/2 (1983): 109ff.

8. The author is a member of the United Church.

9. Green, p. 51.

10. For further reading in areas of culture outside the ones familiar to me, see E. Tuza, "Spirits and Powers in Melanesia," in N. Habel, ed., *Powers, Plumes and Piglets* (Adelaide, 1979), pp. 97ff.

## 12. SEARCHING FOR A MELANESIAN WAY OF WORSHIP

1. For an author who stresses the great variety of Melanesian cultures, see A. Chowning, *An Introduction to the Peoples and Cultures of Melanesia* (Menlo Park, 1977).

2. See esp. B. Demarist, *General Revelation: Historical Views and Contemporary Issues* (Grand Rapids, 1982).

3. E.g., J. Gaquare, "Indigenization as Incarnation: The Concept of a Melanesian Christ," *Point* 1 (1977): 147–48.

4. See ibid., p. 147; cf. A. R. Tippett, *Verdict Theology in Missionary Theory* (Pasadena, n.d.), p. 158.

5. See A. Matiabe, "Revival Movements 'Beyond the Ranges,' Southern Highlands," in W. Flannery, ed., *Religious Movements in Melanesia: A Collection of Case Studies and Reports* (Goroka, 1983), pp. 147ff.; A. Griffiths, *Fire in the Islands!* (Wheaton, Ill., 1971).

6. See e.g., B. Sundkler, *Bantu Prophets of South Africa* (London, 1961), esp. pp. 354ff.

## 13. A PLEA FOR FEMALE MINISTRIES

1. Martin Luther, *Table Talk*, trans. and ed. T. G. Tuppert (Philadelphia, 1967), p. 171.

2. See, e.g., G. W. Trompf, "On Attitudes toward Women in Paul and Paulinist Literature: 1 Corinthians 11:3–16 and Its Context," *Catholic Biblical Quarterly* 42/2 (1980): 196ff. and the literature cited there.

3. J. Calvin, *Sermons on Ephesians* (1577), trans. A. Golding (London, 1973), p. 567.

4. Luther, *Lectures on Genesis*, ed. J. Pelikan, in *Works*, vol. 1 (St. Louis, Mo., 1958), p. 206.

5. Ibid., p. 118.

6. For further reading on women in the Bible, see J . R. Batten, *Women Alive* (London, 1955); T. Brown, *Nameless Women of the Bible* (New York, 1921); J. W. Chadwick, *Women of the Bible* (New York, 1960); W. M. Mackintosh, *Bible Types of Modern Women* (New York, 1920).

7. See P. Brown, *The Chimbu* (Cambridge, Mass., 1972), pp. 63ff.

## 14. IN SEARCH OF A MELANESIAN THEOLOGY

1. Sione A. Havea, "The Pacificness of Theology," *Mission Review: A Quarterly Journal on World Mission for Australians* (Dec. 1977): 3–4.

2. A recommendation to the PCC Fourth Assembly (May 2–15, 1981).

3. Sione A. Havea, p. 4.

4. A working paper, PCC Fourth Assembly.

5. Sione A. Havea, p. 3.

6. Sione A. Havea, "The Pacific and Theology in World Perspective," South Pacific Consultation on Theological Education, Papauta (Jan. 11–17, 1978).

7. See as background Bultmann, in H. W. Bartsch, ed., *Kerygma and Myth*, trans. R. H. Fuller (London, 1957–62), vol. 1, pp. 1–44; vol. 2, pp. 181–94.

8. See, e.g., K. Koyama, *Waterbuffalo Theology* (Maryknoll, 1974); J. Cone, *A Black Theology of Liberation* (Maryknoll, 1986); G. Gutiérrez, *A Theology of Liberation*, trans. C. Inda and J. Eagleson (Maryknoll, N.Y., 1973).

9. William R. Burrows, "Theologising in the Melanesian Context Today," *Point* 1 (1977): 242.

10. Havea, "The Pacific and Theology," See also his "Moving towards a Pacific Theology," *Mission Review* 19 (April/June, 1983): 4–5.

11. Burrows, p. 242.

12. Ibid.

13. From a tape made during the United Church Evangelism Workshop held at the Christian Education and Communication Centre, Malmaluan (1979).

14. Ibid.

15. Joe Gaquare, "Indigenization as Incarnation: The Concept of a Melanesian Christ," *Point* 1 (1977): 147ff.

16. Fr. Louis Beauchemin, Opening Address, South Pacific Consultation on Theological Education Report, Papauta (1978), p. 55.

17. "Melanesian Culture and Christian Faith," Solomon Islands Workshop (October 1978), report prepared by Cliff Wright, pp. 8–9.

18. Havea, "The Pacificness of Theology," p. 3.

19. Burrows, p. 252.

20. See also G. W. Trompf, "On the Need for a Melanesian Theology: Some Introductory Remarks," in Trompf, ed., *Melanesian and Judaeo-Christian Religious Traditions*, UPNG Extension Studies Booklets (Port Moresby, 1976), vol. 4, pt. D/1, pp. 128ff.

## 16. THE CHRISTIAN VISION OF A NEW SOCIETY

This paper was written as a speech at the Provincial Youth Convention, New Ireland, Papua New Guinea (1983).

1. "No work available," in the Tok pisin and Hiri Motu *linguae francae.*

## 17. THOUGHTS OF A MELANESIAN CHRISTIAN SOCIALIST

The first part of this interview was conducted by and published in *The Papua New Guinea Times*, then a biweekly newspaper (Dec. 2, 1983, p. 28).

1. Soon after making this statement Utula Samana was arrested for physically protecting a young man from what he took to be police harassment. He spent one highly publicized day in jail and was subsequently acquitted. See *PNG Post Courier*, Dec. 8, 1983, p. 1; Dec. 9, 1983, p. 1.

2. The Public Order Bill (first proposed in 1970) portends to increase police powers of search, arrest, and summary imprisonment.

## 18. AN APPEAL FOR MELANESIAN CHRISTIAN SOLIDARITY

This article was translated from the Dutch by Koos Smith with Garry Trompf. See also *Arena* 73 (1985): 95–103.

1. *Wantok* is from Papua New Guinea, lit., "one-talk," or a person who shares one's language or cultural background, and with whom one enters into reciprocal relations. See chap. 3, n. 2.

2. For further reading about the West Papuan cause, see N. Sharp, *The Rule of the Sword: The Story of West Irian* (Melbourne, 1977); E. Utrecht, *Papoeas in Opstand* (Rotterdam, 1978); TAPOL (UK), *West Papua: The Obliteration of a People* (London, 1983); Research Institute of Oppressed Peoples, *The Tragedy of the Papuans and the International Political Order* (RIOP Report 1), Amsterdam, 1985.

## 19. CHRISTIANS IN POLITICS

1. Wellington, 1980, p. 19.

## 20. CAN I REMAIN A CHRISTIAN?

1. On Atai and the rebellion, see Linda Latham, *La Révolte de 1878: étude critique des causes de la rébellion de 1878 en Nouvelle-Calédonie*, trans. E. Terzian, *Publication de le Société des Études Historiques de le Nouvelle-Calédonie* 17 (Noumea, 1978), chap. 2 (on the revolt) and chap. 4 (aftermath).

2. For the best account of political parties in New Caledonia, see H. Hill, "Political Parties in New Caledonia," in R. J. May, ed., *Political Parties in Melanesia*, Political and Social Change Monograph (Canberra, 1984 [forthcoming]).

3. On the concept and practice of conscientization, see esp. P. Freire, *The Pedagogy of the Oppressed*, trans. M. B. Ramos (Harmondsworth, 1970), pp. 71ff.

## 21. A THEOLOGY FOR JUSTICE AND PEACE

1. B. Narokobi, *The Melanesian Way* (Port Moresby, 1983), p. 13.

2. T. I. Fairburn and C. Tisdell, *Economic Growth among Small Pacific Countries: Can It Be Sustained?* United Nations for Regional Development Paper (Nagoya, 1983).

3. Most of the above three paragraphs have been taken from S. Siwatibau and D. Williams, *A Call to a New Exodus: An Anti-Nuclear Primer for Pacific People* (Suva, 1982), p. 70.

4. Statement of the Disarmament Conference of the World Council of Churches Commission on International Affairs (April, 1978).

5. Most of the above five paragraphs rely on Siwatibau and Williams, pp. 72–73, 84–85.